THEY WERE SO YOUNG

I didn't do anything brave
or even exciting. But I did
what I was asked to do —

And I am very proud to be
in this book with these brave men.

They Were So Young

MONTREALERS REMEMBER
WORLD WAR II

Patricia Burns

FOREWORD BY
Desmond Morton

Véhicule Press

Published with the generous assistance of The Canada Council for the Arts, the
Book Publishing Industry Development Program of the Department of
Canadian Heritage, and the Société de développement des entreprises
culturelles du Québec (SODEC).

A DOSSIER QUÉBEC BOOK

Cover design: JW Stewart
Set in Adobe Minion by Simon Garamond
Printing: AGMV-Marquis Inc.

CANADIAN CATALOGUING IN PUBLICATION DATA

Burns, Patricia, 1939-
They were so young : Montrealers remember World War II
(Dossier Québec series)
ISBN 1-55065-167-6
1. World War, 1939-1945–Quebec (Province)–Montreal.
2. World War, 1939-1945– Personal narratives, Canadian.
I. Title. II. Series

FC2947.25.B87 2002   940.53'71428'0922   C2002-904978-4

Véhicule Press
www.vehiculepress.com

Distributed in Canada by LPG Distribution
800-591-6250

Distributed in the U.S. by Independent Publishers Group
800-888-4471
www.ipgbookcom

Printed and bound in Canada on alkaline paper.

With great respect and gratitude
to those who served.

Contents

Acknowledgements

I HAD MANY QUALMS about compiling these personal memories of the worst war in the bloodstained history of the world. So much has already been written about World War II and so much time has passed since these events that I sometimes felt I should leave well enough alone. However, I began to realize that we cannot know too much about what happened to Canadians more than half a century ago and that the veterans and their families have important stories to share. I had to overcome my reluctance to asking veterans, especially those who had seen front-line service with all it entails, to relive those traumatic times. Many suffered a recurrence of nightmares after telling their stories. Whenever I expressed these fears to friends, their answer was always to go ahead, that these stories are a part of our history that must not be forgotten. One veteran agreed to tell his story by saying, "Although I am a bit shaky here and there, the memory of my beloved war comrades commands me to help you." It was also a very emotional experience for me both in listening to these stories and doing the necessary background reading. I can only say that there were times when I laughed and more when I cried.

I could not have even thought of collecting these stories without the kindness of so many people. Their help ranged from providing names to giving much-needed moral support. One of the first persons to hear about my wish to interview veterans was Andrew Melville and it was his unstinting help and generous comments about my abilities that gave me the courage to go ahead. He provided a comprehensive list of notable Montreal veterans, without which I would not have known where to start. Thank you so much, Andrew, for your invaluable help. Pierre Vennat of *La Presse*, not only agreed to be interviewed but also shared his vast knowledge of the French-Canadian military contribution with me.

I would also like to thank my family: my daughter Erin Olizar Fowler and my son-in-law Captain Rory Fowler of the Princess Patricia's Canadian Light Infantry who gave me much needed practical advice and moral support; my sister and my friend, Mickey (Kathleen) Naisby, who organized our visit to Normandy and whose support in everything I do is nothing less than munificent; Bill, Don, Bev, Jimmy, Erika, JoAnn, Brenda, Connie and Roy who are always there for me; all the Nevilles, especially my Aunty "Mug" (Margaret), who shares my love of books. Thanks also, to my good friends; Marion and her late husband George Georgion, a Royal Navy veteran who answered all my naval questions; Maxine and Lloyd Kouri, whose help ranged from helping me to carry my new computer out of the big box store on a wet November day to providing names of people to interview. Others who helped in countless ways are Diana Della Porta, Lillian Papp, Cathy Tsolakos and Vince Circelli, Mike Boone of *The Gazette*, Lt. Col. (ret'd) Camille Bourdon, Edie Cavanaugh, Mo Chapman, Vicki and Ken Cole, Donna Whittaker, Norma Chyka, Capt. (ret'd) Jim Conway, Betty Coughlin, Reverend Stephen Crisp (Anglican chaplain at the St. Anne's Military Hospital), Bernie Farrell, Belva and Richard Burman, John Lehnert, Marie-Andrée Robinson, all the good people at the Kahnawake Legion (Branch 219), Ann Fortune, Catherine Richards, Marion Fryer, Merle Harris, Alan Hustak, Sue and Vic Kuwabara, John McDonaugh, Logue McDonald, Madame Justice Pierrette Sévigny j.c.s. and Richard McConomy, Michael Morin, Ken O'Donnell, Normand N. Silver (vice-president of the White Ensign Club), Jane Skelton and Dorothy Williams.

My biggest thanks go to all those who agreed to be interviewed. I know how emotionally wrenching it was for some of them to relive those years and I feel deeply honoured that they were willing to share their stories with me. It was an experience I shall never forget. Thanks also to the wonderful wives (and husbands) of these veterans who welcomed me into their homes, sometimes more than twice! A special thanks, also, to Nicole Pomerleau Forbes and Madame Malouin for their kindness which surpassed the normal demands of hospitality.

I would also like to express my most heartfelt gratitude to Dr. Desmond Morton who kindly agreed to write the foreword to this book.

A final note of thanks must go to the wonderful publishing team at Véhicule Press—Simon Dardick, Nancy Marrelli, Vicki Marcok and Bruce Henry. It was a huge pleasure to work with them and I consider myself very fortunate that Simon not only thought my project worthwhile but also supported it every step of the way.

Foreword

WHY SHOULD VETERANS interest us now? It is half a century since Canadians fought and died in Korea, and even longer since the Second World War. The last survivor of the First World War, 1914-19, doubtless a centenarian who lied about his age, will soon be gone. We owe our elders respect and gratitude but, frankly, our interest is selective and must be earned.

Like most Canadians, I have lived all my life far from war or even danger. Our reputation as the "peaceable kingdom" is honourably earned and attracts people who seek to share our tranquillity. Our peace had to be earned, of course, and about two million Canadian men and women served in Canada's twentieth century wars. One of them was my father, who left in 1941, survived D-Day and the battles of Normandy, and came home to his nine-year old son in the summer of 1946. He and his friends talked seldom about the war but much about the human bonds that had helped them survive. One cold night in 1950, driving back to Winnipeg from Shilo, after meeting soldiers leaving for the Korean War, he told me so much more than I could understand or remember. How I wish that I could have recorded those memories, as Patricia Burns has used her skills and technology to make this book possible.

Veterans are not special people. For me, some of their interest starts with their ordinariness. They were people like us when war began in 1939 or 1950 or whenever it was that they walked into a recruiting station. Some felt a practical appeal. Times were tough. Unemployment affected one Canadian worker in six in 1939, as in1914, and it was at a postwar high in 1950. But there were other motives, too. Overwhelmingly, Canadians were volunteers, and however little any of them knew about the navy, army or air force, no Canadian after April, 1915, had any romantic illusions about war. In five days, the enemy had killed, wounded or gassed 6,000 Canadian soldiers, half the fighting strength of Canada's contingent in France. Canadians went on dying or returning too maimed for any further service, to share experiences of death and agony, horror and incompetence, such as you will read here.

Ordinary people encountered the extraordinary and returned to share the rest of their lives with other Canadians. Many could not imagine what veterans had experienced or why some of them felt compelled to share their memories. Such people will doubtless avoid this book as they have doubtless tried to avoid all the challenging aspects of human life. Others must prepare to share reality with men and women caught in circumstances they could never anticipate and who struggle here to help us understand what happened.

History, as we encounter it in school and often on a library bookshelf, is often a coldly boring collection of dates and events, victories and failures, and self-serving explanations. What is missing are people, like the ones whose stories Patricia Burns has collected in this book. Read Charly Forbes and you may know why crossing the Walcheren Causeway was one of the bravest deeds Canadian soldiers ever did, and you will also learn that it was in vain. Read David Hart and learn just how horrible Dieppe was—and why it may have been necessary if our side was to learn enough to win the war. And on a personal note, I have heard Georges Malouin's experience before, from army and air force veterans. Remember: against many prejudices in his own Quebec community, he had volunteered his life to defend Canada against Hitler. His encounters with vicious, ignorant bigotry happened among Canadians. Why did it take us until 1972 even to accept the principle of bilingual Canadian Forces? And remember, as Pierre Vennat recalls his mother, and Joanne Schoeller remembers her brothers, that not all the wartime heroism happened overseas. Nor, when you remember war brides like Mary Armstrong Mérrette, was it all Canadian.

Desmond Morton
Georgeville, Québec
August 2002

Introduction

MY SISTER MICKEY and I stand at the entrance to the Bretteville-sur-Laize Canadian Military Cemetery. It is July 11, 1998. We know exactly where to go—through the Doric columns of the long portico, past the Stone of Remembrance, turn right after the next eight rows of graves, stop at the bench and there it is. Officially the reference is XXVI. H.1. I read:

> D.122961 Trooper, G. HARTMAN 17th Duke of York's Royal Canadian Hussars, 10th July 1944, Age 20, The only son of E. and W. Hartman, Montreal, Quebec, Canada. In loving memory R.I.P.

Mickey and I stand quietly and our taxi driver, Gérard, joins us in our silence. I say a quick prayer. All I can think of is how happy I am finally to be able to visit my cousin's grave—the cousin I never knew. The Bretteville cemetery is an exquisitely beautiful place. Crabapple, Norway maples and *Thuya occidentalis* trees are strategically placed and the graves, which stand in perfectly even, single rows, have well-tended flowers adorning each one. Manicured grass completes the picture. The birds are trilling loudly on this July day as if to say, "Don't worry. We'll sing for the boys and keep them company forever." I want to stay for hours but Gérard has already spent the better part of the afternoon driving us along the beaches of Normandy and I feel pressured to hurry. There are 2,793 Canadian soldiers and seventy-nine RCAF airmen buried here and, as I walk from grave to grave, I see names of young men from every province. One epitaph breaks my heart, "Adieu mon enfant." I hurry along the rows. My God, here lies a man of fifty-two! Can it really be? The next shock is seeing "R.F. Taylor, The Calgary Highlanders, Age 16." Was his name Robert? Did his mother call him Bobby? Did his father scrape together enough money to buy him a bicycle for his twelfth birthday? Most of the boys are in their twenties but then I see "D.G. McKenzie, 1st Hussars, Age 16." Doug? Don? How many mourned him at home? He might have left a two-year-old sister who would only know her big brother from photographs. There is another sixteen-year old from Quebec buried here but I can't find his grave. Gérard Doré of Val-Jalbert whose family only knew of his departure from

Canada when they received his first letter from Britain. How old were these children when they enlisted and what were they expecting to experience? Not this, certainly.

I am feeling overwhelmed and rush back to my cousin's grave. I think of all the things I heard and read about him. He enlisted on November 8, 1941, nineteen days before his seventeenth birthday. Lying through his teeth, he assured them that his next birthday would be his eighteenth. He had finished two years of high school and was working as an office clerk when he and his friend decided to join up. He left his home at 2494 Quesnel Street and, after training in Huntingdon and at Camp Borden, embarked for England in the spring of 1942. He had time to find a girlfriend and got into his normal share of trouble. On July 22, 1942, he was given seven days C.B. (Confined to Barracks) for being Absent Without Leave. In Glasgow, he had his picture taken in uniform—a proud young fellow with the timid smile of a cathedral chorister. Just an average kid, I suppose. He was killed at Caen and I imagine that my aunt coped as best she could with her terrible loss. He was her only child and her life. She always referred to him as, "my Gerald." She would never welcome a British war bride into the family or be a grandmother. It is time to leave the cemetery. On the way out, Mickey and I prepare to sign the Visitors' Book. Of all the words in the English language, I can only find these: So sad. So very sad.

The man who led Canada through the war years, Prime Minister Mackenzie King, seemed as bland as the rice pudding that appeared regularly on Canadian dinner tables. In spite of his lack of charisma, he was able to guide a divided and totally unprepared country through six years of war and postwar reconstruction until his retirement in 1948. He oversaw Canada's immense contribution to the war that included more than one million men and women in the armed forces. The RCAF contributed one squadron to the Battle of Britain and forty-eight squadrons served in other theatres of war. The British Commonwealth Air Training Plan was based in Canada and trained thousands of airmen from Commonwealth countries. At the end of the war our air force was the fourth largest in the world. Our navy grew from one that might have done Andorra proud to the third largest in the world and, together with the unsung heroes of the merchant navy, kept the vital lifeline open to Britain. The men of the merchant navy were civilians with no military status. Fewer than 50 percent of them survived the sinking of their ships and theirs was called "a suicide job." The army fought bravely at Hong Kong, Dieppe, Sicily, Ortona, the Gothic Line, Normandy, Falaise, the Scheldt and the Rhineland. Canadian industries produced trucks, tanks, ships, aircraft and munitions. Canada went from being, in 1939, a country with just over a million people out of a total population of 11.5 million on "relief" to a booming, prosperous nation that had become a respected world power. The cost was high, however. The dead numbered 44,927 (including 73 women); the wounded, 53,145 (including 19 women) and 8,271 became prisoners-of-war (Royal Canadian Legion figures).

The government of Quebec's Premier Maurice Duplessis was against conscription and "England's War." Spirited anti-war rallies were held all over the province. Adding to the excitement at some of these rallies were the brawls that broke out between anglophone servicemen on leave and francophone civilians. Adrian Arcand, the virulent anti-Semitic leader of the Parti de l'Unité Nationale and Mayor Camillien Houde were both arrested and interned for the duration of the war. Many French Canadians, however, were well informed about what was going on in Europe and 200 men a day were applying to Montreal's two French-speaking regiments, Les Fusiliers Mont-Royal and Le Régiment de Maisonneuve (one of the first in Canada to fill its ranks when war broke out). The defeat of Duplessis in the provincial election of October 1939 was called the first victory of the war. It had been won by Mackenzie King's promise that there would be no conscription for overseas service, a promise he was able to keep until late in the war. It wasn't easy for a French-speaking recruit. In the navy and air force, English was the language used. Even the No. 425 (Alouette) Squadron in the air force used some English. It was really only in their own regiments that they felt at home. More than half of the 55,000 francophone volunteers who served in the army were in anglophone units. By 1944, Canada's need of replacement soldiers meant that 16,000 conscripts (called Zombies) were to be sent overseas, causing more riots in the streets of Montreal. Some Zombies (crying and trying to escape) were herded onto the ships in Halifax by military police with rifles and bullwhips. This could not have been a pretty scene. Resistance to the war was also to be found in certain ethnic groups out West, but the general feeling that French Canadians didn't want to fight seemed to overshadow, in many minds, the incredible contribution and consistent bravery of those who did.

The response to the war was less complicated for those of British background. Many had recent ties to Britain and were happy to help in her time of great need. Montrealers of all ethnic groups enlisted, however. One Arab Canadian, Abraham Moufrage, joined the Black Watch in spite of his parents' apprehensions. When he lost a leg in Normandy, he was afraid that his family would not accept his handicap. Their answer was swift and unequivocal; "We want you back home even if you have no arms or legs." The sting of rejection was felt by many who spoke French or looked different. David Tsubota of Montreal was the only Nisei to serve in the RCN but he was discharged, probably on racial grounds, after only three months. He then joined the Black Watch, fought at Dieppe and spent two and a half years as a POW. Although the black community of Montreal "did its bit" during the war by volunteering and fund-raising, blacks were rarely allowed to join the elite ranks of the service and recruits in the army were very often given menial jobs.

To understand the thousands of young Montrealers who volunteered for service during the war, don't look at the veterans in their navy and grey Legion uniforms. Look, instead, at the young boy bagging your groceries at the supermarket; the teenager on a skateboard or riding a bicycle; the thirty-something father leaving the mall with two or three young children in tow; the students streaming out of high schools and universities; the girl working as a lifeguard for the summer. These were the young people who overwhelmed Montreal recruiting centers in September 1939 to volunteer to help defeat an evil and powerful enemy bent on world domination. One stalwart, James Robertson of West Brome, walked 110 kilometres to Montreal to sign up. By September 15,700 men a day were being checked by the fifteen medical boards that were set up in the city. Their parents waved them off, dutifully or tearfully, and the sacrifice was tremendous. Many fathers saying good-bye to sons had all too vivid memories of the horrors of the First World War. Many families had three or four members in the services. One Montreal family, the Bennetts, had five sons and one daughter in uniform.

These young Canadians volunteered for many reasons. Many joined up for adventure and because their friends were enlisting. They could not, perhaps, articulate their political feelings but most had heard enough to know that Hitler, Mussolini and Tojo had to be defeated at any cost. If the war seemed far away to some, the presence of U-boats in the Gulf of St. Lawrence brought reality home. Many had been jobless; the army paid $1.30 a day plus $60 a month dependents' allowance and $12 per month for each child. Many under-age boys lied about their age to enlist. In one notable case, Montreal Alderman John Kerry, who was close to fifty-five with poor eyesight, showed papers that proved him to be forty-nine. His application was doomed to rejection as were those of the many gentlemen who dyed their thinning grey hair black in hopes of acceptance.

Women played a large role in the war effort. They volunteered on the home front as they had always done by working in daycare centers and recycling facilities, growing gardens, and knitting. By the fall of 1944, more than one million women worked full time in industry. Many worked part-time or maintained farms. About 50,000 women served in the Canadian military. They had to overcome the general impression that they were of low moral character. Their pay was a third less than the men they worked beside. In spite of these obstacles, they joined the RCAF(WD), the army (CWAC) and the navy (WRCNS) working in many different occupations which allowed men to be released for combat service. For many women, it was a heady time of personal growth and they left the service reluctantly at war's end. More than 4,000 nursing sisters joined the three branches of the service and for those who received wave after wave of horribly wounded men, the war was real and ugly.

Having learned the sad skills of war, any romantic notion about combat soon evaporated when servicemen first saw action. Men in the navy suffered terrible seasickness and never knew when their ship might be torpedoed. The boys in the air force had to try to keep their courage up to face yet another sortie. The daily lists of casualties posted on the wall made them wonder when they would also "buy it." Ground troops went weeks without bathing and were inflicted with all kinds of discomfort and disease and every type of insect the terrain provided. They did not want to imagine what the fly sitting on their bully beef had been feasting on just seconds ago. Add to all this, the unbearable sadness of losing friends who had become like brothers. Many of them worried about a brother fighting in another battle or wondered if they would ever get home to see their latest child. What they all experienced was unbelievable stress and constant mouth-drying, heart-stopping, bowel-loosening fear which was sometimes assuaged by alcohol but never went away. Simply put, combat is torture and it is said that all men break eventually. There is no getting used to it. It is amazing that so many were able to continue for so long without breaking down and who could really blame those who did? For many who came back, all the waters of Lethe could not erase from their minds what they had seen. We owe them a lot.

Air Force

Owen Rowe

Along with about 400 volunteers (black and white, men and women) from the British Caribbean who enlisted in Canada's armed forces, Owen Rowe left his home in Barbados to help with the war effort. He had the rare distinction of serving in both the Canadian army and air force. He has lived in Montreal most of his life and has had an eclectic career which included teaching, journalism, social work and diplomatic service principally with the Montreal-based West Indies Commission and the Barbados High Commission in Ottawa. Mr. Rowe is active in Canadian Legion activities in Montreal, with a special interest in perpetuating the memory of what he terms, "The Caribbean-Canada military connection in World War II."

LET ME FIRST STATE the context in which I made the decision to leave Barbados in 1942 and enlist voluntarily in the Canadian military. In those days, Britain was the mother country and every Empire Day, May 24, we would have a school holiday and sing songs like "Rule Britannia" and "Land of Hope and Glory." When England declared war on Germany, Barbadians said, "Go ahead, England. We are behind you." There was tremendous patriotic fervour for Britain. When the British warship *Hood* went down under German torpedo attack, that devastated me and many others. Also the German U-boats were infiltrating Caribbean sea-lanes to the extent that, in Barbados, a protective net had to be installed at the entrance to Bridgetown Harbour. This notwithstanding, a German torpedo crippled the ship *Cornwallis*. So we knew the war was very, very real indeed. We realized that we were not able to defend ourselves so we said that the thing to do was to go someplace and take military training to bring Hitler to his knees.

Originally I had wanted to go to England to join the air force but they said I was too young. Later I heard that Canada was agreeable to allowing West Indians to come and enlist provided we passed the medical exam. They also stipulated that we should have some sort of technical training. I had been a public school teacher for two years, so I complemented my qualifications by taking a course in mechanics, which I passed. My father, a school headmaster and organist, always told me that he had wanted to fight in the First World War but was too young, and it made him very happy because I would be doing what he was unable to do in 1914.

There were about twenty-eight of us who came up together in 1941. The YMCA in Barbados gave us a send-off with a sumptuous dinner and heaps of praise for our patriotism. We didn't know each other at the time, but developed our friendships later. My father was the only one who vociferously welcomed my going. Many people at the pier that day, although wanting to help in the war effort, thought we were too young. Some of them lamented, "They are just *children!*" The youngest one would have been nineteen. I myself was twenty, but at least three of the men were married and had families. So keen was I on going off to war that I wrote a poem called "A Soldier's Farewell." It actually wrote itself:

Land of my birth,
Oh dearest earth
Beneath whose shining skies I toil;
I must now leave thy sacred soil,
And risk my blood on foreign lands
To save Thee from the harsh demands,
Which tyrants, heartless, would impose,
If none to Freedom's Call arose.

I go—with warm tears in my eyes,
For I shall miss thy smiling skies;
The rapture of thy myriad stars;
Those festive nights—with soft guitars;
My Love, and all that I hold dear;
Which just, in dreams, can now be near.

Land of my birth,
So filled with mirth;
I go—and I may not return,
But Fires of my Love shall burn
For Thee, bright as thy noon-day sun,
Sure as the Vict'ry to be won.

It was on May 13, 1942 that we left on an American ship, the *George Washington,* which travelled without convoy. Very often for safety we chose to remain out on deck and one day we spotted a school of sharks in the ocean. We jokingly said, "If the boat is torpedoed, we will not drown because the sharks will get

Flying Officer Owen Rowe, RCAF
Rockcliffe Air Base, Ottawa, 1945.
One of the 400 volunteers from the British Caribbean
who enlisted in Canada's armed forces.

us first!" After twelve days at sea we reached New York Harbour where we disembarked and took the train to Montreal. We were sworn into the army and then most of us went to Huntingdon for basic training. From there I went to Vimy Barracks in Kingston, and joined the Royal Canadian 6th Division Corps of Signals.

We West Indians are used to very spicy home-cooked food and we didn't at all like the rather bland diet served in the army, but we got used to it. We consoled ourselves that we were getting the nutritious, well-balanced meals that our rigorous training required. When on short leaves from military duty we would head for the homes of West Indians in Montreal for a home-cooked meal and chitchat about life back home. Winters were terrible. We suffered dreadfully from the cold. But I remember how excited I was when I had my first sight of snow. I ran out and scooped it up in my hands and ate it. One of the real painful experiences of winter was going on "route marches." Wearing military kit you would march as far as fifteen miles no matter how cold it was. When we got back to barracks we would often head straight for the stove and do the wrong thing—hold up our hands as near as possible to warm them. The result would be what they call chilblains—the painful swelling of our hands and face.

In early 1943, I was scheduled to go to England. Prior to departure they gave us embarkation leave. I spent the five days in New York, at the home of a fellow soldier, Clyde Griffith. When we came back, we were told that next day we would have to turn in all our bedding and be sent by train to a troop ship on Canada's East Coast for the bumpy voyage to England. That day they had the roll call and somehow my name was not called. I waited and waited and there was no mention of Rowe. My anxious enquiries seemed to get nowhere. Finally an officer in charge conceded that something must have gone wrong, but emphasized that he could not keep back several hundred men to thrash out the problem. The contingent left with all my pals with whom I had trained and shared military discipline, swapped jokes, and forged so many fond memories. I just burst out in tears. That had to be the most painfully poignant memory in my entire military career. A week later they told me that another man, with my name, Rowe, had not reported back from embarkation leave and would be considered a deserter. They set aside his documents to court martial him. Inadvertently, they had removed my documents instead of his.

Well, six months later, I was again to have gone overseas but we were confined to barracks because one of the men had scarlet fever. They took my name off and I wondered whatever was I here for? My next posting was at Camp Nanaimo on Vancouver Island where I worked on a military radio station. Once more I was slated to go overseas—this time to the Pacific. Well, it happened again. They called me to the office and said, "Rowe, we're sorry. You're not going." "Why? What happened?" I asked angrily. They said, "The Americans are pretty well running the show in the Pacific and we are sort of subordinate to them. They have a segregated stand and we don't want you to run into any racial discrimination so we are not letting you go." Surely I was jinxed in this army, so I asked them if I had their permission to apply for a transfer to the Canadian air force. They said they would release me if the air force would take me.

I reported to the RCAF and passed all the relevant tests and was accepted. My training started at No.3 Manning Depot in Edmonton and continued at the No.2 Wireless School in Calgary, and then at the Air Gunnery School in Belleville. I remember spending hours in the "Link Trainer" which simulated real war conditions. For an air gunner it was vitally important instinctively to identify whether an approaching plane was friend or foe and whether you should be trying to shoot it down or otherwise. Accordingly, there was an exhaustive aircraft recognition program in which we viewed the profiles of planes in all conceivable positions. The enemy aircraft would be Messerschmitts, Focke-Wulfs, etc. Allied planes would be Spitfires, Mosquitoes, Liberators, etc. Our training was reinforced until it became second nature. For gunnery practice I would shoot from my plane at a drogue (target) towed by another plane. We also took training in Morse code and in the operation of radio communication equipment so that we could use a radio beam as a navigational aid and communicate with base headquarters. It was all so dangerously adventuresome. Military training also provided opportunities for participation in many athletic events such as boxing and track and field. I recall winning a lightweight boxing championship in Edmonton in 1944. It was also a proud moment for me, in 1945, when I was a member of the victorious track team in Trenton.

Racism? Admittedly there were a few incidents. One time I was in Edmonton with this fellow airman, a French lad called Armand Charles. Proudly wearing our uniforms, we went to a nightclub, paid our way in and sat down. Suddenly a man came up to me and blurted out that I had to leave. I said I didn't understand what he was telling me. He then said, "If you want to understand what I'm telling you, your FRIEND can stay but YOU have to go." Then I got the connection. In the meantime he called a big wrestler to throw me out. So my terribly embarrassed colleague and I left, horrified and in utter disbelief. If only I had reported this incident to the military command, the club would have been made off-limits to airmen or, if I had told some of the other guys at camp, never mind they were all white, in their rage they would have descended upon the nightclub and wrecked the joint. But I was too much of a gentleman and didn't want to make an incident of it.

I must emphasize that it is totally out of proportion to dwell on these racial incidents because in my military career I have generally enjoyed excellent relations with whites. For example, I had a white friend, Ab Krauter, with whom I trained in Edmonton. We have remained friends up to this day. Only last week I received a hello, by e-mail, from him and his wife, Edna. And, of course, the McCoys and I are still good friends after more than fifty years. When I was training in Huntingdon, there was a church minister who asked local people if they would invite soldiers to their homes. We went to the McCoy's and, by God, it was like a home away from home. There were Mother, Edna McCoy, her son Jim and his wife Margaret and her other son, David. They served cookies, pie, and so on but the most important thing is that you could feel the warmth of their love. Love is something you cannot hide. They were so loving that I just gave my heart to them. Many years later, in 1971, when Jim and Margaret were in Barbados they sought out my parents and sent me back beautiful pictures of the get-together at their home. I was very saddened when Jim died in 2001.

My first commissioned rank was pilot officer. I was later promoted to flying officer. You should have seen the congratulations that I got from the guys when I got my wings! My next thought was when do I go overseas? But this hope was quickly dashed. The commanding officer matter-of-factly said: "You guys can all kiss goodbye to the idea of getting overseas because the Americans have come up with the atomic bomb and the war is going to be over in no time." What devastated me was the first time I didn't get overseas. But since then there was no real sting anymore. It was just something I had learned to accept. Although I really hadn't done what my father and I had set our hearts upon my doing, I felt I played an important role on the road to victory. For winning the war had to be a team effort all the way.

As my war story comes to an end, four West Indian World War II compatriots come to mind:

Mascoll Best, a handsome lad and former champion cyclist, left Barbados with me in 1942 and enlisted in the Canadian army. Alas! He was killed in battle at Caen, France and buried over there. I hallow the photograph I have of his grave.

Milton Cato, of St. Vincent, served in the Canadian army overseas, with the rank of sergeant. After the war he studied law in England, and returned home in 1949 to practice that profession and also enter the field of local politics. When St. Vincent attained full independence on October 27, 1979, he had the honour of being the first prime minister of that new nation.

F.N. "Neville" Murray, of Trinidad, joined the RCAF in 1941 and later served with the Lion Squadron of the RCAF Bomber Group in England. He attained the rank of squadron leader and was a veteran of twenty-seven attacks on enemy targets. He was awarded the Distinguished Flying Cross (DFC).

Phil Archer, of Barbados, attained the rank of squadron leader with the RCAF overseas. He was a daring fighter pilot who was awarded the DFC on February 10, 1943, at age twenty-seven. He was killed in action four months later and buried in a military cemetery in Pas de Calais, France.

Finally, let me confess that the experience of World War II matured me. It was the greatest thing that could have happened to this young, serious-minded, wide-eyed lad from Barbados. And my heart is full of love and admiration for all those guys and a few girls also, who left their Caribbean homeland to do their bit to forge victory over a cruel enemy bent upon world subjugation. Not only did they help win the war, but whether they returned home or stayed on to make Canada their country of adoption, they also met the postwar challenge and "won the peace". We are all a small, but proud, part of both West Indian and Canadian history and that's worth documenting.

Enid Gow Page

Enid Gow Page grew up in Notre-Dame-de-Grâce and joined the RCAF (Women's Division) when she turned eighteen. She has kept in touch with many of the women she met in the service and organized a reunion of WDs in Montreal in 1995 which attracted 481 veterans from as far away as New Zealand, England and Australia. The invited guest speaker was the popular Dr. Roberta Bondar, a woman who is as much a pioneer today as the young women who enlisted more than half a century ago.

I WANTED TO HELP in the war. I had lost two very special cousins who came from out West. One had come to live with us for about four months before he joined up so I got to know him quite well. He was an absolutely super guy who was taking geology at McGill. He joined as an observer and graduated in the first class of the British Commonwealth Air Training Plan and was shot down over the North Sea. He was never found and for years I said that he just had amnesia and wasn't really lost but was out there somewhere. I just couldn't face it. I was only sixteen when he died. His brother, Bud, went over to Africa and was killed there. One other brother, who was in the RAF, did come back and their sister Phyllis also joined the air force. Can you imagine having four in one family in the service? (she pauses) I've got tears in my eyes. My heroes at the time were people like Buzz Beurling but my main hero was my cousin Lawrence, a super person and it was all such a terrible waste.

I thought of the army first but I wasn't tall enough. I thought of the navy but I couldn't get a trade that I liked so I went into the air force which should have been the first choice really. They could give me the photography course that I wanted so I enlisted on April 16, 1943, when I turned eighteen. I also wanted to be a weatherman but they said that I couldn't take two courses at once. I didn't say anything to my family, just went all by myself and did it. My parents were proud and pleased and knew that I would do well. They never said that I shouldn't be doing it. Some people at that point didn't really know the girls and felt that they were in the air force to meet boys. One of my father's friends asked him how he could let me do this because he thought I was going to meet awful people. My father said, "We've brought her up the right way and we trust her." The fact that they trusted me made me strong when I needed to be. It's amazing what that does for you and it meant a lot to me that my parents were okay with my decision. You had to have quite a strict medical and that took a while because they thought I had diabetes. I had to have all sorts of tests at the Royal Vic and it took about three or four months before they found out I didn't.

When I finally got past this diabetes thing, I was sent to the Manning Depot in Rockcliffe for basic training. It was a showcase station because, being near Ottawa, we always had to be at our best and ready for VIP visits. We all had to write a will and leave our worldly possessions to whomever we wished. I was so proud of my uniform. It was wonderful. It had a plain skirt and a jacket in air force blue with brass buttons and a hat that we all hated. They were soft at the top like the RAF women's hats. Awful. After about two years we were issued new ones which were firmer and looked much nicer. We also had a pale blue shirt and a black tie, black shoes with laces up the front and lisle stockings. In the summer we had a khaki suit and we also had dresses in air force blue which we could wear only on the base.

In basic training, you get up at the crack of dawn to the sound of a trumpet and have a shower in a room with shower stalls (with no curtains) on one side and sinks on the other side. This room was called the ablutions. Our barracks were H shaped and you could go from one side to the other through the ablutions. I was in a room with eight, maybe ten, women and we had double bunks. Then we'd have to walk from our barracks down to the mess hall and have a pretty ordinary breakfast, you know, bacon, toast, eggs, some days we had pancakes. There was school morning and afternoon. We'd have marching lessons, lots of marching, which I loved. I had been in the Girl Guides so I was a marcher before I got to the air force. We had air force protocol lessons. You had to learn all the ranks and all the bars so you'd know whom to salute. We also learned a little bit of the history of the air force. We were not to tell anyone what we had learned and, when my mother came from Montreal to Ottawa for my graduation, I said that I couldn't tell her how many people were in the class because it was a military secret. But she was right there and could have counted us if she had wanted to. (laughs) One of the first things we had was our TABT (Typhus A and B and Typhoid) shots and they knocked you right out. You were so sore, it was awful. I remember I couldn't get up into my upper berth because of my swollen arm and one of my friends heaved me up and I went right over the top and down the other side!

There must have been about 200 of us in my training squadron; some were cooks, some were car drivers, some were secretaries and whatever and after basic training we went off to different stations across Canada for our courses. Because the photography course was in Rockcliffe I just stayed there the whole time. You started at the very bottom, ACW 1 (Air craft woman 1), then ACW2 which meant that you had a little propeller on your sleeve. I became a corporal after about eight months and worked in a section with four men. I was spoiled rotten by these four guys—a queen among kings! They really treated me royally, although I also became the chief sweeper and cleaner-upper.

I had had some photography experience. I had worked for William Notman and Son as an apprentice after graduating from high school. I got, I think, $6.00 a week, but I learned about $100 a week's worth of knowledge. I didn't do very much, just put the pictures into the frames, but I went into the darkrooms and asked all the questions I could. None of them really knew *why* they were doing what they were doing because they weren't trained but when I joined the air force we had a three-month course and I learned why I was adding hydroquinone to the mix and learned all about optics. More than half the class were men, twenty-one men and eleven girls. Photographers were used in many ways. First of all to take pictures of people who were joining up. We photographed crashes. That's a horrible thing to have to do. We made slides of planes by the hundreds because they had to go to all the stations where the pilots-to-be were learning silhouette identification. Another thing we did toward the end of the war was take pictures of Canada by air for plotting maps. I worked at what they called the "White House" and, after basic training I didn't take many pictures but did mostly developing and printing of the pictures. The ones who went overseas did reconnaissance flights and took pictures before and after a raid to see what had been hit and how much damage had been done. They were very, very important but not many women did that sort of work. You had to be twenty-one to go overseas and I was out by then.

During the course we learned how to take pictures from the air. We had this hand-held camera, an F-24. It was pretty heavy, weighing about twenty-five or thirty pounds, and was attached to the plane by a rope. We had to lean out of the plane with the door off and it was scary. You weren't really hanging out but you had to lean out enough to get away from the frame of the door so you wouldn't get it in the picture. We also had to take line overlaps which means that you take five pictures in a row. When you have them printed they're put onto a long piece of paper and you can look at them through a special viewer and get three-dimensional pictures. That was fun because you were lying in a special place in the nose of an Avro Anson which was glass (Perspex), and kicking your feet to tell the pilot which way to go to get you in line for the picture. One time when I was up, I asked the pilot if I could land in the nose. He said, "I'm not allowed to do that." I said, "What's going to happen?" After some coaxing, he said okay so I was lying in the nose of the plane as we came down and down and, by the time we were about 1,000 feet up I said, "No, I can't do this." If the plane had crashed I'd be the first to hit the ground. (laughs) We were told never to land without that camera, we were supposed to jump out after it because it was very valuable, more valuable than we were, probably! I had no fear of flying then. I don't like flying now. Then, I knew the pilot, I knew the aircraft maintenance people, I had a parachute on and I just felt safe.

At the end of three months, we got better marks than the boys did which surprised us and *them* because we had to learn the circuitry of the electrical part of the camera. I wasn't a feminist then and I'm not now but we were paid, I think it was 90 cents a day, and the boys were paid $1.20 for doing the exact same work and even, at eighteen, I thought it wasn't fair. The other thing was that they got to have a half a day off after their TABT shots and we didn't, which really bothered us. (laughs)

Sometimes we used to go into town for a movie and a good meal. On the site, there was a library and we had movies and dances quite often. They'd usually have a band and there were many more men than women. There was a snack bar where you could have a Coke. At that time I was going with an army fellow in Ottawa that I had known here in Montreal. He was a great dancer and we had good times. Sometimes I would bring him to the dances or I would go to one with him at the YMCA in Ottawa but I always had to be back by 10:30 except on the weekends. I went home quite a few of the weekends, I would say three out of four because I was so close and it was only $2.50 to go on the train. I often didn't have even that much and I'd have to write to Mom to send me the money so I could go home. Once I had special leave to go home because I saw a plane crash. I was standing at the big window in the "White House" and saw this Mosquito taking off. It crashed and three boys were killed right in front of me. A Mosquito is a wooden plane. All its struts and things are wooden and it's covered with cloth so it just collapsed. Awful. There was no one to meet me at the station, of course, because they didn't know I was coming. I took the streetcar home and got to the front door and cried, "MOM, DAD! I SAW A PLANE CRASH TODAY!" It was just awful and my parents were so good. I needed to get home after seeing something like that and they knew just what to do.

We were the junior service and the boys were certainly called the "Brylcreem Boys"; mainly because they went on sorties and went through hell being attacked but they came back to their own beds, whereas the army— they were slogging through mud, never had a bed, didn't have good meals and were fighting all the time. That was horrible. And the navy—can you imagine being in the navy and being torpedoed? It must have been terrible. That's why, if there was any jealousy, it was the air force boys who got it because they didn't have a total, everyday war. They had terrible bombing experiences but came home to their own beds and their own friends.

We had a wonderful parade on D-Day. The whole station came out at Rockcliffe. We prayed for all the people who were taking part. It was an incredible feeling; all those airmen and all those armies and all those navies were out in those little boats and it was happening. You knew there had to be losses but you could sense that the war was ending. People were happier. They weren't sending people overseas as much anymore. People were coming back to do work in Canada. It must have been in the spring of 1944 that they offered us a discharge. I wish I'd never volunteered for it. I wish I had stayed in to the end and even a lot longer. I'm very sorry I did it. It came out in DROs (daily routine orders). Anyone who wanted to go to university could apply to get out in time to start classes in September. We all talked about it at breakfast and two of my friends and I did it. They went through your marks and if they thought you could make it at university they let you go. I tried to enrol in McGill but men had preference so I went to Dorval airport and became a meteorological assistant. It was great, like being in the air force again with all the planes.

I was in Germany in 1978. It was a very unsettling feeling to see the places where the Allies had fought and the bridges that had been bombed. I was sitting beside a girl on a boat on the Rhine and maybe she figured I was pretty sad. She said, "The war's over. You've got to forget." But then when you're over there you're thinking of Lawrence and Bud and Fred and David—all these people.

My time in the air force is something I wouldn't have missed for anything. It was a wonderful experience to learn photography and I met wonderful friends. One of my sons asks me why I go to reunions and remember that terrible time. For us it wasn't a terrible time. The boys that we lost, we would have lost anyway if we'd been home, but being in the air force was being part of it. We were helping and we enlisted so that—now this is interesting—"We Serve That Men May Fly" was our motto, but at eighteen it didn't mean as much to me as it does now. What we did was release other people to go over and be killed. That wasn't on my mind at all in those days. We were releasing them to serve, but they didn't only serve, they died. I could cry. (said very softly)

Sydney Shulemson

Sydney Shulemson was part of the Montreal YMHA fencing team. In 1936, on the advice of the Jewish community, he turned down a chance to compete for Canada in the Olympics in Germany. He spent four and a half years in the air force, three of them in Britain where he became one of the most highly decorated pilots of the RAF Coastal Command. As a flight lieutenant, he led a wing of four squadrons whose duties were to disrupt the German supply lines in northern Europe. In 1943, as a flying officer, he was awarded the DSO (Distinguished Service Order) when he led a successful attack against a heavily defended convoy of ships and also saved another pilot from an attack by a German aircraft. The next year he received the DFC (Distinguished Flying Cross) for his consistently-successful leadership in these dangerous missions. He is the most decorated Jewish Canadian pilot who served with the RCAF in World War II. After the war, he continued his career in printing and business brokerage, retiring at the age of eighty. In July 2001, he was inducted into the Quebec Air and Space Hall of Fame.

WHEN WAR WAS DECLARED on Labour Day weekend in 1939, I was camping in the Laurentians. All we talked about that weekend was the war and so, on Tuesday morning, instead of going to the office, I went to a place which I knew was an air force establishment in Westmount at the corner of Metcalfe and Sherbrooke. I got there for nine o'clock in the morning and, when I arrived, there was no parking nearby and a huge line-up of people from the entrance to the building down Metcalfe almost to de Maisonneuve. I parked my car and joined the line. Everybody I knew was there waiting to be interviewed. Finally, around noon hour I got to the front of the building and looked in. There was a large, empty room and, at the back, was a trestle table with an air force corporal sitting behind it. I walked up when he motioned me to come. He said, "Name", and wrote down my name. "Address", he wrote down my address. Then he looked up at me and said, "Can you cook?" I said, "Cook! I want to be a pilot." He said, "OUT, OUT! We need cooks."

That was my first attempt to get into the air force. I waited and continued with my work. After the period of the so-called "Phoney War" where very little activity was being reported, the war began to look as though it was heating up. I learned that there was a recruiting office in the old Gatehouse Building— now the site of a tall building on René Lévesque near Beaver Hall Hill. This was a very nice looking office on the first floor up. There were girls typing and there was an officer at the counter who greeted me, asking what he could do for me. I told him I wanted to join the air force as a pilot and he said, "Very good. We have to arrange for an interview." He started flipping through pages of a book, which made me wonder. I expected to be interviewed right away but he scheduled an interview three months from then. I said, "Three months! The war may be over by then!" He said it wouldn't be, but I told him I wasn't waiting three months to find out whether I could join or not.

I had been in what was called the non-permanent active militia (the 2nd Montreal Regiment Artillery) for a long time and I continued my association with them. In August 1941, I found out that there was another recruiting office above the post office on Bishop Street at the corner of St. Catherine. The recruiting officer there was someone I had done business with and I told him that I wanted to join the air force as a pilot and I wanted to join today. I also told him that I needed a little time because I had business to take care of. So I took the medical and was recruited that day. I had orders to report to the Manning Depot in Toronto on the Monday of Labour Day weekend. My family was concerned because, in 1941, I was not a youngster. I was twenty-six years old and I didn't *have* to join. My sister had also left home to take a job with the British Embassy in Washington. There's an interesting sidelight there because she was working for a banker in Chancery and his and my sister's job was tracing payments for materials that Germany was buying overseas and so they were finding the targets that I was later attacking—a very unusual situation. My younger brother joined the air force too, but he never got overseas.

From Manning Depot in Toronto, I was posted to Rockcliffe near Ottawa where I did sentry duty through the winter. I then went to the Hunt Club in Toronto for initial training and then to London, Ontario for elementary flying training. From there I went to Aylmer for service flying training where I graduated as a pilot. I was earmarked from the beginning because I had done well in the ground school as well as in the flying. I got my commission and was posted to Summerside, P.E.I. to qualify as a navigator in Coastal Command. It wasn't called Navigation School; it was called General Reconnaissance School and I earned the same qualifications as an observer. All Coastal Command pilots were also qualified as navigators and the tradition in those days of long-range patrols was to have two pilots, one acting as navigator and alternating as pilot.

I went overseas in 1942 to a place called Acaster Malbis in England, which we used to call "Aqua Velva". I had trained on Harvards but now we flew twin-

(Above) Photography Class 14, Rockcliffe Air Base, Ottawa, 1944.
Enid Gow Page is in the first row, 5th from left.

(Below) Enid Gow Page at work in Rockcliffe.

Sydney Shulemson in a Bristol Beaufighter which he flew
for a whole tour of operations.
"I did not intend to get shot down."
Royal Canadian Air Force photograph by G.G. Truscott.

engined Oxford aircraft. At Operational Training Unit, I trained on various aircraft: Blenheims (including the Blenheim Five which was built in Canada and was called the Bolingbroke), then Bristol Beaufighters. With military aircraft, if they're going to be manoeuvrable, they have to be unstable. The Beaufighter, for instance, had the highest wing loading in the Allied air forces, forty-two pounds per square inch. Wing loading is the opposite of "safety factor" so the Beaufighter was a very difficult aircraft to fly. You had to know what you were doing because its lack of stability under certain circumstances meant you couldn't get away with doing crazy things.

As an airplane buff, I guess my favourite plane was the Typhoon which was a single-seat fighter aircraft used extensively in train busting and in close support to the army. It was also a very good fighter and was used as a long-range fighter. Of all the aircraft I flew, that was the best. When I went through Central Gunnery School of the RAF, I took the course on both Spitfires and Beaufighters, the only person to do so. It was confusing. I'd sit on the runway thinking, "Oh gee, which aircraft am I in?" The Spitfire was much more sensitive to the controls than the Beaufighter. My first trip at Central Gunnery School was in a Spitfire. I was told to do some 60-degree dive-bombing practice and so I attacked the target, released my bomb, pulled up and blacked out immediately because I pulled up too sharply. Fortunately, I was high enough so that I recovered from the blackout and was able to get the plane straightened out but you couldn't treat a Spitfire like it was a Beaufighter.

At the end of my OTU, the whole class was set up as a squadron. We flew our own aircraft out to Burma and were assigned to Ferry Training School. A medical check-up revealed I needed to have a cyst on my back removed and by the time that was over, my group had left and so I was at the OTU as a single. I was assigned to 404 Squadron (a Canadian squadron) as a reinforcement pilot in Coastal Command. They had lost six crews in succession on their first trip and they were a little concerned about sending me out and so, for two or three weeks, I was doing training flights and getting to know the area and so on. Eventually, what they thought would be a safe trip came up. It was to escort a Royal Navy flotilla operating about 200 miles south of the Arctic Circle directly north of the Shetland Islands. This was to create interest among the Germans and make them think that it was an attack on Norway when really it was to divert their attention from a commando attack on the French coast.

The navy had two large forces there that were sent north from Scapa Flow;

one was a cruiser force with escorting destroyers and the other was an aircraft carrier with landing barges and escorting destroyers. I was assigned, along with another member of my squadron, to do a fighter escort of the cruiser force. A cruiser force operating in that area doesn't really need a fighter escort but they had us do it to attract German attention. Of course, we got it. The Germans sent out aircraft to do a reconnaissance of what was happening up there and, instead of it being a nice, safe trip, it turned out to be a very action-packed thing because of all the German aircraft and the interaction with the aircraft from our own aircraft carrier. (laughs) This fellow from Ottawa—I think his name was Kosh—was commander of this Royal Navy flight and he got entangled with one of our chaps. Fortunately, he recognized that what he was attacking was a Beaufighter—not a Junkers 88, which is very similar in outline—and he broke away. Our squadron wound up shooting down four huge flying boats (airplanes that take off and land on water) and the Royal Navy shot down two more so that was my first trip. I shot down one of the flying boats and participated in the shooting down of another and my aircraft was badly damaged by return fire.

Most of my tour on the squadron was not fighter escort to naval forces but anti-shipping strikes along the west coast of Europe: the coast of Norway, off Heligoland, the Dutch coast, the entrance to the Baltic and along the Bay of Biscay on the French coast. The Germans had their supply routes. They had ships coming through the Mediterranean up the French coast and into the Baltic. They had iron ore and tungsten and nickel from the mines of northern Norway coming down the coast of Norway, again into the Baltic and into Germany. Those were our targets. Our convoys were being attacked by U-boats and E-boats (motor torpedo boats), but the Germans had to defend themselves against attack by our aircraft and so their merchant vessels were very heavily armed with anti-aircraft guns. They always travelled in convoys with naval escorts, also very heavily armed with anti-aircraft guns. We were attacking the most heavily defended targets and that's why our casualties were among the highest in the air force.

On the 26 of February 1944, we took off in the morning, detailed to attack a convoy off the Norwegian coast. I was flying a Beaufighter which had a crew of two, pilot and navigator/wireless operator. Between us we had all the courses in the air force. We had four 20mm cannons firing from the front and operated by the pilot. We carried eight rocket projectiles which were on rails under the wings. Our armament was equivalent to a British County Class Cruiser with a crew of about 450 and we were a crew of two. We found the convoy, which was comprised of several merchant vessels and escorting M-Class minesweepers, which were almost like destroyers and were heavily armed. They tried to defend themselves with AA fire and by using what was then a new weapon which I reported to intelligence back home. They fired a rocket which exploded and threw out a sort of bomb carrying cables with bomblets on it so that if you flew into it, any one of these bomblets would destroy your aircraft. We were also using a secret weapon which were rockets designed to put holes in the ship below the water line and thereby sink them. They were very effective and we used them during most of the time that I was on the squadron and, by surviving, I wound up the most experienced rocket pilot in the RAF. While on this mission, I decided to go and photograph a ship I had seriously damaged a few days before on an attack on another convoy. I found it lying, broken in half, on a tiny bit of a beach at the foot of a cliff. After photographing my trophy and coming back to rejoin the squadron, I found a German fighter was attacking one of my men. The German was right behind the Beaufighter and about to fire and, while I was not quite close enough to shoot him down, I fired a burst from my cannons to attract his attention. Sure enough, he turned away from the Beaufighter and then turned on me and we engaged in a long dogfight. Eventually, I got away.

My aircraft was frequently hit. On one attack on a convoy, I wasn't wounded and got my plane back, but it was so badly damaged that it was not repairable. We used to carry a homing pigeon with us and if we were downed at sea, we could send it with a message giving our position in latitude and longitude so that we could perhaps be picked up. On one occasion a cannon shell penetrated our fuselage and killed the pigeon. It also severed the control wires for my trim control. I had foolishly trimmed the aircraft into a dive so I had great trouble pulling it out of the dive. My navigator had to come forward and help me hold the aircraft up all the way home. When we got back to base and found that our pigeon, "Binder", had been killed, we had a ceremony and an official burial for him. The squadron gave him a symbolic DFC and we never carried a pigeon after that.

I had a couple of crashes and I'm suffering the consequences now. My first crash occurred when I was in training on a Harvard when my instructor was showing me forced landings. He came in over the fence of a farm field with the engine idling and, instead of easing the throttle forward to open up the engine into full power, he slammed it forward and the engine just backfired.

We pancaked into the ground and I hit my forehead on the instrument panel. I have a cervical spine problem and constant headaches and have been in pain since then.

Another time I was detailed to do a fighter escort with another aircraft of a Swedish ship carrying ball bearings to Britain. We were to escort the ship through the Baltic into the North Sea. Going from the north of Scotland to the base in southern England from which we were to go into the Baltic, I ran into extremely bad weather with torrential rain. We were flying very low and could hardly see anything and I flew over an airport. I did a quick turn and got my number two to land first and then I went in. It happened to be a naval air station—a dummy deck landing station where pilots were trained to land on aircraft carriers so the runways were very short. On the approach to land, one of my engines cut out, just died, and the aircraft tried to flip. I got it straightened but landed going sideways and ripped the undercarriage off. Of course, when that happened, the gas tanks ruptured and the high-octane petrol flowing onto the hot engines set the aircraft on fire. I don't know how I got out but I did. My navigator got out too and he was unhurt. I was standing on this runway with blood all over my battledress. The station medical officer— who happened to be a New Zealander—put me on his motorbike (that was the scariest part of the whole thing) and took me to the medical building. He treated a cut over my eye and cleaned me up a bit. I didn't know where it hurt the most. I was bruised all over and had a fracture in the elbow. My hips and knees were very sore because when I hit my knees on the instrument panel the shock was transmitted to my hips. In 1946, when I complained of pain in my hips, my doctor diagnosed me with traumatic arthritis. It kept getting progressively worse until it became intolerable and I have two artificial hips now.

I spent the night in this medical facility and the next day I asked for a flip in one of their Swordfish "string bags". We called it a "string bag" because it was a biplane with wiring between the wings holding them together. My squadron sent an aircraft to pick my navigator and me up and within about a week I was flying again. The local Montreal papers liked to print things about local men who'd done something and war news was always a big thing. I used to write to my parents saying things were very dull and nothing was happening and they'd read the newspapers and say, "He's lying." (laughs)

I had the honour to lead a wing that comprised an RAF squadron with about 30 percent Canadian air crews, a Canadian squadron with about 30 percent British air crews, a New Zealand squadron, an Australian squadron and a half squadron of Norwegians. My own navigator was British. The commanding officer, Haakon Wenger, of the Norwegian squadron had been a very good friend to me when I first joined the wing and he was just a member of the squadron. He taught me a lot and helped me a great deal. The Polish boys were very, very good. Once we were escorted by a Polish squadron of Mustang fighters when we went out to attack a convoy off the south coast of Norway. Of course, we went over at a very low level hoping to avoid getting involved with German fighters. I had a tough time getting away from one myself. We used to make landfall close to a point on the coast where there was a fighter base so that we would turn away from the base and they'd have a stern chase. They'd have to take off and catch us. Well, as soon as we got there, the Poles climbed up and yelled in German, "Come on, you goddamned Germans. Come on up and fight." (laughs) That was the last thing we wanted but they weren't going to fly all the way across the North Sea on one engine and not get into a fight.

Flying is dangerous. Military flying is very dangerous and flying in action where you're firing bullets can be even more dangerous. If you don't recognize that, you have to be a fool. You have to have what is called "moral fortitude" and determination to carry through in spite of the opposition. I can tell you a lot about "Lack of Moral Fibre" (LMF). There were cases in which I was personally involved. A member of my squadron, on several occasions, had turned back after leaving to attack a convoy claiming engine failure or engine problems. The second time it happened when I was leading, immediately on my return I asked for his aircraft and took it on a flight test. I proved that there was no engine problem and told our commanding officer what had happened. I told him that this chap didn't belong on the squadron and certainly wouldn't be part of any group that I led because in turning back, he alerted the Germans that we were there. We used to fly across the North Sea and, as leader I used to fly at thirty feet above the water. I was swinging propellers with seven-foot blades so the tip of the blade was only twenty-three feet from the water. The man at the back of the formation could climb up to a maximum of seventy-five feet. We would stay low like that to avoid the German radar screen. Radar operates in straight lines and because of the curvature of the earth we could get more than halfway across the North Sea without being detected. However, if someone pulled up and turned back the Germans would get to know that there was a force moving towards Norway. This chap was declared LMF and sent back. A Canadian squadron always had a Canadian doctor. We had a very good one, Grant Beacock, and his input would be that this chap just couldn't take any more.

I encountered LMF on another occasion. After my tour of operations, I was considered to be an expert on rocket projectiles and any time there was a crash of an aircraft that was equipped with rockets, I'd be invited to sit on the board of inquiry to find the cause. There was a crash at the end of the runway on takeoff. Examining all the evidence, we decided that the pilot had lost his nerve and tried to abort the takeoff and couldn't because he was already going too fast and was too far down the runway. He crashed into a fence and was declared LMF and demoted and declassified. No more flying for him and out of the air force. You couldn't depend on him, you see.

I was brought up by an observant Jewish family, but I am not a religiously observant Jew (although very much a Jew), so the dietary rules were of secondary importance to me. Not that I enjoyed the RAF food. It was terrible. Whatever you got is what you had to eat if you were hungry. There was a period when I was living mostly on fruitcake that my family used to send me. In northern Scotland a typical meal would be lamb covered with a terrible yellow custard and Brussels sprouts.

Did I ever worry about being taken prisoner by the Germans? Of course, I had to give a thought to the possibility of being shot down and taken prisoner but I mastered my trade and just did not intend to get shot down.

We had fun in Britain, of course. Bittersweet fun because in every station there were always casualties and there was the bitterness of losing a buddy. The men are not just friends; they are like brothers. It was tough losing them and we'd lose one almost every trip. At Acaster Malbis we used to bicycle to a pub called, "Shoulder of Mutton." The local people were extremely nice to us. When we arrived they'd immediately give us a place near the fireplace because it was bitter winter and I thought I'd die of the cold—I used to sleep with all the blankets I could find and all the clothes I owned. They would greet us beautifully and treat us as honoured visitors.

I didn't get to many dances because I was stationed in the far corners of the empire. (laughs) Coastal Command is always on the coast and in training I was at Catfoss in Yorkshire near Hull and there wasn't much in Hull. We also didn't have much time off. When I was in a squadron I used to get three weeks of leave every three months which I used to spend in London and there I had a good time. Bombing was part of it and you withstood it. We'd go to dances.

There was tea dancing in the afternoon at Grosvenor House and in the hotels and pubs we'd meet other air force people. I met all kinds of girls and I remember, at one point, after I finished my tour, I was ordered to report to Canadian Air Force Headquarters in London at Lincolns Inn Fields. There were a lot of Canadian young ladies in what we called the WD (Women's Division) and I remember being struck by their strident Canadian accents because I was accustomed to talking to these Scottish and English girls with their softer accents. I thought, "Oh, my gosh, I've been away from Canadian girls for so long that I'm not used to the accent any more!"

I was through being shocked by Germans but what did shock me after the war was the attitude of the western allies to the Jews who had been liberated from the camps as skeletons. A Canadian civil servant responsible for immigration in the King administration said, "No Jews are too many." Canada, the United States, Britain and the rest of the world ignored them and refused them admittance. That's what made Israel possible and it was easy for me to say that, although I was a Canadian, I would do everything it took to help Israel. I have a claim to be a grandfather of the Israeli Air Force because I attended a conference in New York as the Canadian representative before the War of Independence. We were exploring what military help might be available and I told them that if they were going to declare themselves a state, then they had to have an air force. They wanted to know how to do it and I told them that it had only been two years since the end of World War II and there were all kinds of surplus military aircraft around the world and many Jews (800 air force in Montreal alone) who had been in the armed forces.

Part of my duties was accepting the applications of people who wanted to join the Israel defence forces. One of them was George "Buzz" Beurling. He had many Jewish friends and they would approach me and tell me that he wanted to join. In the meanwhile, he was being offered $5,000 a month (and this was in 1947) to join the Egyptian Air Force. I suspected his motives but eventually agreed to meet him in secret. I met with him many, many times and I still had trouble figuring out what his motives were. I told him, "First of all, there's no pay; we have no money. Second of all, no uniform, no rank, no Spitfires." He still wanted to join. I discussed this very extensively with my colleagues in New York and with the Hagana and they said that it was up to me. I decided that he'd be an asset but that we would have to take special care of him because I figured the Arabs would try to assassinate him. I guess I didn't do enough because, in my opinion, he suffered a very suspicious death.

He was doing an air test of a Norseman prior to flying it from Italy to Israel when it caught fire and crashed. A Norseman is a fabric-covered aircraft and if you want to set it on fire, all you have to do is put an oily rag in the exhaust manifold. In my opinion that's what happened.

I was driving around and heard on the radio that he had been killed. I phoned my people to confirm it and they did. Then, surprisingly, I got a phone call from Frederick Beurling, his father, who said that he was told not to believe any report of his son's death unless it was confirmed by me personally. I immediately went to visit the family in their home. Of course, they were very distraught, having lost a distinguished son and I was distraught myself. During the conversation his mother said, "And to think that he is to be buried in the unholy city." I thought, "Rome, the unholy city?" I couldn't understand and asked her what she meant and it turned out that his father was a lay preacher in the Plymouth Brethren which is a Christian sect which reads the Bible literally. He had been brought up in this very religious environment and he could never fight against the Jews because he believed that Jews are God's chosen people. So that was his motivation and I didn't understand it until then. I asked the family if they would be happier if he was buried in Israel. They concurred and I arranged for his reburial in the Christian section of a military cemetery near Jerusalem. I've had many regrets about it since then because I think Beurling is a Canadian hero and should have a memorial in Canada.

Beurling was a very young man obsessed with his career in the air force and he didn't adjust to civilian life as well as he should have. He had the nickname "Screwball" but he was not a screwball. He was a very serious-minded young man who went to infinite lengths to exercise his eyes to improve his eyesight and he trained himself in deflection shooting. As a graduate of Central Gunnery School of the RAF, in theory I knew more about gunnery than he did but he took the time and the effort to train himself to be the best deflection shot in the world. Deflection shooting takes mathematical calculations. For instance, if you're thirty degrees off, you give him 50 percent of his speed. If the aircraft is flying at 200 miles an hour, you aim one hundred miles ahead, not an actual distance but one hundred miles of deflection as measured by your gunsight. He sat in an aircraft for hours on end practicing so that he didn't have to do the mental calculations. He would shoot an aircraft down with four bullets. Nobody else did that. As a deflection shot, he was the greatest in the world but he did have this mindset that having been the best in the world, as a civilian he was nothing. So that was another motivation for him. He wanted to get out there and improve his score.

You can't be involved in a war and not be affected drastically. The war is never far from me. I've had the good fortune of being able to concentrate on the positive aspects of my participation in it. I can spend hours with friends talking about the comical things and the fun things that happened. The other side of it is that everywhere I go I'm interviewed and I relive all of it, so the war is not far from me ever. Fortunately, I survived and my family did not have to go through the trauma of losing a son.

I loved flying. I haven't flown in forty years as a pilot and I still miss it. When an airplane flies overhead, I look up and think, "Gee, I'd like to be flying that one."

Robert O'Connell

In August 1946, after finishing his sophomore year at Loyola College of Montreal, he entered the novitiate of the Holy Cross Fathers in Massachusetts. The war did not, "knock the idea of becoming a priest out of my head" as he thought it would. Reverend Robert O'Connell C.S.C has served as assistant of St. John the Evangelist Parish in Edmonton, Alberta since the spring of 1996.

DURING HIGH SCHOOL I, like so many others, had resolved to join the RCAF. I graduated at seventeen and so had another year to put in. I went to freshman Loyola to bring me up to eighteen. I signed up on Bishop Street on October 29, 1942. I was sent to Manning Depot at Lachine where my brother John was. John had joined in August 1942. Football had been his thing at St. Leo's and with the Junior Pats. It was still the football season so he got in a number of games at the Manning Depot before going into training as an air-gunner at Mont Joli. At Christmas I was sent to St. Hubert on tarmac duty. I had Christmas off but I was on duty at New Year's. I remember vividly because I went to a dance that New Year's Eve and had to rush to get back to St. Hubert to report and stay awake all day.

"Tarmac" was gassing the Harvard aircraft, washing them, shovelling coal, cleaning the hangars and performing all the jobs there were. However, tarmac only lasted four months. My next posting was to No. 4 ITS (Initial Training School) in Saskatoon. This was all ground school. EFTS (Elementary Flying

Training School) followed during July and August on Tiger Moth aircraft in Regina and then SFTS (Service Flying Training School) from September to December 10 at Saskatoon again. I graduated with my wings and a commission. John went overseas in September 1943. The last time I saw him was at the old Bonaventure Station as he wished me goodbye for my trip out West to Saskatoon in April. Then I spoke to him over the phone for his trip overseas. There was a bit of a lump in my throat when I hung up the phone, perhaps a premonition of what was to come.

Then I was posted to GR (General Reconnaissance) in Summerside, P.E.I. It was really a navigator's course for pilots for two months. My next posting was Nassau in the Bahamas. What a gorgeous change from P.E.I. in the winter! I was flying again, this time on B-25 Mitchell bombers. This was at Wilkes Field close to town. Eddy and Wally Simpson were holding forth then and would complain when the aircraft would be directed over their house.

After a month or so I transferred to Oakes Field and got onto the B-24 Liberators. These were 4-engine aircraft used in anti-submarine work, convoy duty and general bombing work by the Americans along with their B-17s. At the end of the course we all volunteered for India. It just happened at the time that Ferry Command was flying a quantity of "Libs" out to India so they attached us temporarily to themselves. As it turned out, the Yanks were flying them to Montreal, then to be picked up by Ferry Command. So up we went to Montreal for a month. It must have been mid-August when we took off from Dorval. We were headed for Gander which was closed in, so we were diverted to Goose Bay for one day. Val Chartier, one of my classmates from Freshman Loyola, was stationed there. I haven't seen him since.

The hop to Prestwick was just overnight. We flew out at 18,000 feet for the first time and used oxygen. Most of our training had been at 5,000 feet, the coastal height. We could leave the base with £1 a day or stay on the base for nothing. Of course, I made a beeline for Yorkshire to the Moose Squadron where John was stationed. It was very sad for me. I learned that John had taken off on May 12, 1944 and the aircraft had not returned. At that time there was no news yet from the Red Cross so I spent my time visiting homes set up for us through the Knights of Columbus. Food, of course, was a problem then. "Upper Wick" in Worcester with the Bennett family was a joy. They had a dairy and fruit farm and we lived like kings.

Although I had kept in better touch with John at this stage, he didn't give much information, no doubt for our parents' sake. When he was shot down it was his sixteenth trip and we didn't even know he was on "ops." The object of the trip was Louvain, Belgium. Two Canadian planes were knocked down that night. May 12 was also Mother's Day and John had sent our mother a bouquet of flowers.

The word finally came and we had to report back to the base at Prestwick. Our flight was direct to Rabat-Salé in Morocco skirting the European war. Then our longest flight was to Cairo across the Sahara. We could see all the broken-up tanks and debris from the desert war. From Cairo we went to Shiba in south Iran and from there to Karachi. Finally we landed in Allahabad—the end of the journey.

We then did a few odd jobs ferrying mines about the country, till we were finally assigned to 200 Squadron in Madras. From here we did some Coastal Command work on the Bay of Bengal. From Madras we practiced with the new "Leigh" light. It was a large light (a million candle power), hung out on the wing. The idea was to pick up a sighting on the radar then home in on it with the lights out. Then, as you approach close, you flick on the light, especially the big one, and scare the bejabbers out of, say a submarine on the surface and then drop your depth charges as you cross over. We went to Cuttack in the north for a few weeks over New Year's and I remember playing football with the Brits. This squadron, by the way, was British but there were a number of "colonial" crews: Australian, New Zealand, and Canadian.

My last posting was to Jessore whence we would make trips into Burma. We would go in one aircraft at a time and drop supplies to the guerrillas. These were friendly tribals, who hated the Japs. It was a bit of a problem finding the drop zone because they'd be tucked away up in the mountains hidden from the enemy. They'd put down some strips on the ground and set off a smoke signal. We did actually pick up a convoy of Jap trucks going along the coastal road as we flew over. There were ack-ack positions about, too, but we had them marked on the map. One crew ignored them or didn't know of them. One of them looked down as they passed over the coast and said, "I wonder what that smoke is down below?" He was answered a few moments later as there was a rattle-rattle against the wings. Of course we all took a little trip down to look at the holes next day.

I only did three trips over Burma as I was sent back to Nassau to take a skipper's course. I was a co-pilot up to then. I would have picked up a new crew eventually. But the European war had ended and after a month in Nassau we colonials were sent home. Soon they dropped the bombs and everybody packed it in. It was an interesting trip on the return: Madras, Bangalor, Bombay, Karachi, Persian Gulf, Cairo, Khartoum, Kano, Accra, Ascension Island, Trinidad, Nassau.

John is buried in the British section of the main cemetery in Brussels along with the two crews. I have visited his grave a number of times. The last time was on the occasion of my taking a course in Louvain. I was visiting a convent and the sister showing us around outside in the garden happened to mention that a bomb had landed right close to the fence. But I said, "Was there not just a single raid on Louvain during the war?" She agreed. So that was John's raid. The bombs had fallen helter-skelter, she said, because the Allied bombers had been surprised and jettisoned their bombs to make a getaway. There was a tunnel under one of the main streets in Louvain joining two important buildings. A large number of people took refuge there but a bomb landed right at one end of the tunnel and forty people were killed from the concussion. The reason neither of the aircraft escaped was due to the efficiency of the German defences by that time, just one month before D-Day. The fighter defences were set up to cruise in a square box on the radar screen. If an enemy entered, the radar guided the defending aircraft to it. The Lancaster had no belly turret like the American B-17s, and a defending fighter could come up beneath the larger bomber in the dark, and just rake its whole length.

I don't know how my parents took John's death. For a brief time he was called "missing" and I was still away training myself. But when my mother said goodbye to me eventually, I could tell how deeply it was affecting her. She had little time to mourn, really. John was killed on May 12, 1944 and she herself died on January 25, 1945.

Louis Geoffrion

He grew up in Westmount in a bilingual family and, in 1939 at the age of nineteen, left his studies at the Montreal Classical Institute to join the air force. Soon posted to Fighter Command, he flew Hurricanes and Spitfires in Africa and Europe. He went overseas as a sergeant pilot in the fall of 1941 and received his commission in the field in Africa in March 1943. When he returned to Montreal after the war, his father was rather discouraged to have a son who used a very plummy RAF accent replete with British expressions like, "bang on, old boy", "bloody awful" and "whizzo". He joined his father's brokerage firm, Geoffrion, Robert and Gélinas and continued in the air force reserves, becoming squadron leader of No. 438. In 1987, he became its honorary colonel. This interview was enlivened by his wonderful gift of mimicry.

I THINK WAR is the most disgusting thing that can be inflicted on anybody but in the war against Hitler, I think we were morally right. In 1938 my father had me working in his office and, one afternoon, Hitler was making a speech. Dad had us all listen to it and, although I couldn't speak German, the voice was angry and full of evil. I can't explain it any more than that. My dad told me that the Jews were being very badly treated and were going to jail. We certainly didn't know about concentration camps at that time. I can also remember when Hitler marched into the Ruhr, Austria, and the Sudetenland. In Montreal there had been a strong voice against signing the registration card and there was a reticence by some politicians who were afraid of what it would do to their vote. I can remember one night a group of us went to the Atwater Market and told the RCMP that if they couldn't do the job, we would. Another time a group of university students walked down and went through this restaurant with a telegraph pole because it had a windmill in front which looked like a swastika. (That sort of ended that restaurant.) And they also raided a tavern that had a Germanic name. I can also remember when they arrested, erroneously, I thought, a lot of good Italians but most of them were later released.

I was going to war. The day that war was declared, I was in the Officers' Mess of 118 Squadron on the corner of de Bullion and St. Joseph Boulevard ready to join up. The CO, Group Captain Marcel Dubuc, (a fantastic guy and a very brave man) who had taken me flying about a year before, asked me what I was doing there. I said I had come to join up. He said, "Go back to school, Louis. The war will be over by Christmas."

I arrived in England in the fall of '41 and did my OTU (Operational Training Unit) in Carlisle, which people used to call the "British Yukon" because it's just before the Scottish border. It was a very cold winter and I remember on Christmas Day it was snowing. There were eighty of us and we all ended up in Africa. I was a fighter pilot and the only guns I fired at OTU were against a drogue, which looks like a long sleeve and is pulled by an aircraft which is maybe 800 feet ahead. We had dye on our .303 bullets. I had green dye on mine and, after practice there wasn't *one speck* of green on the drogue. I went to see our CO and I said, "Sir, I did a very bad job this morning. Do you think I could go back up and try again this afternoon?" He said, "I'm sorry, old boy, but we just haven't got the time so you'll have to learn on the job. "My God," I thought, "this is awful."

I reported to No. 213 (Ceylon) Squadron near Cairo at the end of July 1942. We were five new boys and the CO told us that they were putting us through training. We did more battle formations in those four weeks than at *any* OTU. We were flying Hurricanes which I still maintain was one of the best shooting platforms ever created in Britain—better than anything the Germans had. It was a sturdy, heavy aircraft that could take a lot of punishment. They would bring a Hurricane down to 500 feet and we would fire at its shadow on the sand. As the aircraft moved, of course, the shadow moved so we had some practice with deflection shooting although we didn't have any up-and-down motion. I was never really a good shot but whatever I had, I learned there. Our job was ground strafing. Forty-eight aircraft would go across the desert to an airport like Fuka or Daba that were the closest to El Alamein and machine gun everything that was there.

The bell would ring, "SCRAMBLE". We'd jump into our aircraft and it was only supposed to take us a minute-and-a-half to be in the air. We'd hear, "070 ANGELS 30". On the compass 070 is nearly east and, as fast as we could, we'd climb to 30,000 feet. You're always alone in a Hurricane. You fly the aircraft, operate your own machine gun, navigate and operate the motor. You are watching and getting ready to shoot. You tense up before you go into action, but there's very little fear in the air. It's so fast. You're on nerves. You're shooting and never think of getting hit. Say you're approaching a target at 220 mph—the first thing you do is lock the straps on your seat. Your right hand is on the joystick and on that, there's the bomb release, the firing button and the brakes. Your left hand operates the throttle, the mixture and the pitch. As you go up, you have to change speeds, oxygen, temperatures and mixtures. If that is not well understood by the pilot, he's going to lose out because the enemy is going to understand it and is going to show you exactly how it should be done but, by this time, you're going down in flames.

Group Captain Max Aitken was Lord Beaverbrook's son and later, in 1944, he'd take four squadrons, twenty-four aircraft, and he'd space us 500 feet apart. You multiply it. It's a long line of airplanes. We would all take off and join up in this long line and fly maybe fifty miles in a sweep over the Mediterranean looking for German airplanes and then make a turn and come back. Not a word was said. It was eerie. Max Aitken was a *fantastic* fighter pilot. He was British but his father was as Canadian as they come and was in charge of all war production in England. It was a big job and he was one of the winners of the war.

One morning we scrambled. At that point I was at Misurata, an aerodrome about 800 miles from Cairo and near the Bay of Serti. We were scrambled to 30,000 feet. I had shorts on and my feet and hands were frozen. I pulled up my long socks as high as I could. All I had on my hands were leather gloves. I'm glad we didn't have to shoot because I don't think I would have been able to press the button. When we came down, the medical officer was there and said, "Geoffrion, I'm warning you. If you get any kind of sickness from this exposure like frostbite or pneumonia, I'll have you on a charge of self-inflicted injury." Of course I thought he was being an old fogy but he was right. We were going from 100 degrees F on the ground to −30 degrees F in the air and that morning we did it three times. We didn't have compression and were on pure oxygen, which is very tiring. You're living artificially.

I was on the squadron for nearly two years and part of our time was devoted to escorting ships. Just before the invasion of Sicily, there were ships coming down from Egypt after going through the Suez Canal. We would go over the Mediterranean and pick up a whole herd of ships at longitude and latitude such-and-such and we had a very particular way of approaching a convoy. If the sun was coming from the east, you always approached the convoy from the west so you wouldn't come out of the sun. The navy got shot up enough and they had itchy fingers. They'd shoot first and then ask who you were after you were downed. With our long-range tanks we could stay out maybe four hours—half an hour to get there and the same to get back. This kind of operation only counted for 50 percent of our tour time (200 hours).

One of the things that I can remember more than anything else is the grit of the sand in the bully beef sandwiches that we had for lunch. We'd all line up at the cook's tent and they would put it on our tin plates. I'd walk back to my tent, scrape the sand off the food and then eat it. Sand has a very funny feeling in your mouth. The water always tasted salty because our wells were close to the ocean. The Germans had thrown dead goats or, worse, dead bodies into the good wells which condemned them very quickly. I can remember shaving with beer. We also had water delivered to us which we had to keep to drink and wash. You didn't want to smell. That was the worst thing. You've got to be clean as much as possible. It's a morale thing.

Our lifesaving kits were about the size of a flat-fifty cigarette tin but twice as high. In it there was morphine and a needle. There were also squares of porridge and chocolate of great concentration. One day I ate some concentrated chocolate and I didn't eat after that for two days. Unreal the concentration of energy that was in it; boy, it worked. We had a little razor and pills that we could throw into dirty water to make it drinkable. There was also a toothbrush, a little bit of toothpaste and a small soap.

There must have been thousands of ships when they invaded Sicily and we covered them. The minute the Allies landed in Sicily, the Italian pilots with their aircraft surrendered to us and carried on the fight against the Germans. If they ever got caught, I can't tell you what would happen to them. Those Italians knew it was a fight to the end. They were very brave. There was no surrender for them.

On October 30, 1943 (my birthday) our job was to go and escort a French ship, the *Commandant Duboc* and a little Italian ship, the *Roma,* to a little island called Castle Rossino south of Turkey. I never saw them. I guess they came from out of the clouds. I heard BOOM, BOOM in my motor and it stopped and started smoking. I was at 3,500 feet and used the height I had to build up my speed to about 180 mph. I trimmed the tab forward which meant that if I let my control column go it would automatically go forward even without my touching it. When I put the aircraft upside down, it pushed the nose forward which, because it was upside down, went up and shot me out the other side. I watched the aircraft go over me.

I pulled the ripcord of my parachute and was very nervous at this point. I looked and there were two broken ends. I said, "My God, somebody's taken the silk out of the parachute and put blankets in it and I'm going to die." I look up and nothing's happening. Suddenly, I feel a hell of a jar and the chute's open. There was a hole in the middle of it to let the air out but I thought it was torn. All these things are going through your mind. People say it's a nice ride down. Bullshit! On the way down I was sick and lost my fountain pen, my boots and my watch. You're woozy because you're swinging. I knew NOTHING about my parachute. I think that the British and Americans thought if they taught us too much about it, in a tight squeeze, instead of trying to save the aircraft, we'd bail out.

I landed in the water and the parachute fell on top of me. I suppose I went under about 12 or 15 feet. I could see that the shrouds of the parachute were tied around my legs. I cut them with a knife and I'm holding my breath all this time. When I swam away from the parachute I could see sunshine. I had lost my dinghy, which was part and parcel of the seat, but I had my Mae West which I inflated. So I'm sitting in the water and it's nice—about 70 degrees F. I thought about the last words I heard from my friend who was in the other aircraft, "What are you doing, Louis?" I said, "I'LL LET YOU KNOW LATER." When he saw me go out, he went over to the French ship and directed them to where I was. I was in the water for about an hour and kept thinking, "They're going to pick me up." The next thing I saw was a rowboat coming towards me. I was convinced they were Germans because we were in German waters. Then I heard one guy say, "*Si c'est un Boche, je vais l'assomer avec ma rame.*" I'm listening to this and yelled out, "*Je suis un Canadien-Français de Québec.*" I heard them say, "*C'est un Canadien. Mon Dieu.*" They put me on board ship and this is the unbelievable sequence: the second-in-command came over; his name was Lt. Com. Seymour Frippier. (I found out later that he had been a professor of French at Selwyn House School in Westmount.) He asked me where I was from. I told him, "I'm sorry, sir, but I'm not allowed to tell you. But I can tell you that I was born in Montreal." He said, "Do you know Henri Geoffrion?" I said, "He's my father, sir." Apparently this guy used to play bridge at the St. Denis Club with my dad and got to know him. Unbelievable! Then, trust the French, because it was my birthday, we had a cake with candles.

There was a British liaison officer aboard this ship and, when I arrived, he said, "Oh jolly good, we'll be able to speak English." Because I was in a Hurricane, to him I couldn't be anything but an Englishman. I remember that his face went down quite a bit when he found out I was speaking French with the "Froggies" but his eyes lit up when he saw that this pilot was all out for "God, King and Country." I was on the ship for two or three days and we actually became very friendly. For bailing out I got a little gold caterpillar with my name on the back: "PO LPT Geoffrion, R79021, 30th of October 1943."

A little later, I had another episode over water. I thought I was being very calm but I wasn't calm anymore over water. My CO said that I needed a rest fast. I had fifteen hours to go on my tour and they said, "That's it." They could do that and I volunteered to work with a unit that did cooperation with the navy. I was there for five months and then came back to Montreal on the *Queen Elizabeth.* At the end of each tour, Canadians came home for a month. It was nice to see my family. My little sister that I had left when she was ten years old was now a lady of fourteen and I didn't recognize her. My brother André had grown about two feet. Pierre wasn't home then. He was in the navy doing convoy patrol in the Atlantic.

I met Buzz Beurling up north when I was on leave and did a lot of skiing with him. Every noon, we'd go outside and he'd have me practice. He'd say, "Louis, see that pine tree over there. Try and pick a needle off it and then turn away for a minute and then go right back to the end of that needle and shoot. When you're able to do that, you're going to have to do it in the air in an airplane that's moving." Discipline was a bad word to him but this guy could fly. He was seen flying through the main street of Valletta, the capital of Malta, *upside down.*

I went back to England for a second tour. Now I was with 421 Squadron in the RCAF. I was flying Spitfires, which had a much narrower undercarriage than the Hurricane, and you couldn't see anything over the long nose. When taxiing on the ground, the mechanic had to sit on the wing and direct you to your take-off point. Coming in to land, you had to "sideslip" until you got down to about 10 feet, then you'd kick your left rudder and straighten out. In Europe I arrived first in Belgium at Petit-Progel. Then we were moved to Eindhoven, Goch and from there, a place called Diepholz. In Germany we did a tremendous amount of ground strafing and we shot up an awful lot of trains. We used to get up at a quarter to three in the morning and, on one trip, our CO, Danny Brown, Peter Hart, Peter Nutbrown and I flew in at about 200 or 300 feet and there was nothing to see. Everything was flat. We crossed the Elbe, going north of Hamburg. Suddenly, it started getting light because we were on double daylight saving time. We went to 10,000 feet and started looking at forests. Suddenly, we saw white smoke and knew that it was an engine dousing its flames to hide beside the forest for the day. We went down and shot it up, came back and reported it, had breakfast and we did something similar the next day and again and again. The Germans used to refer to us as "*Bomber Gangsters*" and "*Strafen Gangsters*". We were told to do certain things and we did them. No farmer, German or French, likes it when you set fire to his house or shoot up his cattle. They used to say that we were recruited from the slums and were the children of the Mafia.

We knew the war was just about over. We were fifty miles from the Elbe and the Russians were on the other side. The Germans were on the border and could go nowhere. The authorities had asked for technicians to be sent to the area of the Belsen concentration camp. They took some pilots to drive them down and that's how I got to see Belsen. I saw some generals, and they were crying. I don't think anybody went there without having a tear in his eye or a lump in his throat. There were people walking aimlessly. I was told that one of the prisoners was a former surgeon at the Berlin General Hospital and another one had played with the Berlin Symphony Orchestra. They knew we were trying to help all of them but you know, a blue uniform looks awfully much like the German uniform. Our guards made the German guards dig a big grave and I saw a bulldozer pushing the bodies in. The one thing I can't describe to you is the smell.

The war ended so I never got my second tour. I got maybe seventy-five hours. I was starting to get nervous at the end. This luck that had been with me—bailing out wasn't lucky but the whole thing was pretty lucky. I was starting to come in and land and my mechanic would say, "Hey, Louis, c'mere, you've got seven bullets in your motor." And they were all within half an inch of a vital pipe. And by this time, I was getting tired. My month's leave at home was not exactly a restful one. I was between two flights when the war ended. We were on the jeep preparing to go out on another flight when suddenly all the rifles and cannons are firing in the air. Peter Hart was with me and I told him to come to my room. I said, "These nuts are going to kill us both. I think there were more casualties on the aerodrome that night than we had in the previous month. Nobody could land there. They had to go elsewhere. Peter said, "Get on your knees, Louis." We both did and he said, "God, thanks very much for protecting us." I told him I didn't feel like getting drunk and he agreed because we thought they might need us the next day. What happened with the others I don't know. We packed all the kit bags we could find on top of the three bunks and you could hear the fragmentations from our own shells exploding in the air and hitting the roof. Of course, these little pieces of metal can kill you. The next morning at breakfast I said, "Jesus, what do we do now?" Danny Brown said, "Go pack, Louis, we're going home."

Navy

George Holland

On November 16, 1945, George Holland was demobilized from the navy after having served on convoy and striking force duty. He was under recall for seven years because of the fear that the Allies would possibly be facing a war with the Soviet Union. Before returning to Montreal after the war, he married his eighteen-year-old sweetheart, Kathleen in Halifax. They built a house together and brought up a family of nine children.

I CHANGED MY BIRTH CERTIFICATE to get into the service. I was sixteen and the reason I joined up on May 5, 1941 was because when I went to the movies I used to see *The Eyes and Ears of the World* which showed what the Germans were doing to people in Europe, how they were killing the Jews off and taking all their money and I said that I couldn't live like that. I grew up in Point St. Charles where we were all very poor and my older brother Hubert and I used to fight our way to school and back. We said, "If we can take on Point St. Charles, we can take on Hitler." I joined the Duke of Connaught's Regiment but when my mother found out, she reported me and I was discharged after only a few months. I walked out and half an hour later I went into the navy recruiting office on Mountain Street and joined. My mother was going to tell them that I was underage but I said, "Mom, if you get me out of the navy, I'll go in the merchant navy." She didn't want that because she said that the merchant navy was 90 percent sure death and she would forget about reporting me. My brother joined the army too, and did basic training but was dismissed for health reasons and never got overseas. The navy was very interested in me because I had worked as a locksmith and knew about combination vaults. They wanted me for explosives and fine work.

They were very, very friendly to me when I joined up but the minute I signed my name, someone yelled at me to come to where he was. I walked over to him and was told, "You don't walk. You don't run. You FLY." It was tough but they had a purpose. The first two months of basic training I did in Montreal. They'd march us around the streets with our two big St. Bernard mascots to try to get people to join up. They tried to find out what we were like because in the navy you've got to be a very calm person. You've got twenty-two in a small room. You live, eat and sleep together. You can't fight and there's no such thing as locking anything. There's a trust and if anything ever went missing on a ship, nobody went ashore until they found out who took it and that person was discharged.

They shipped us down to Halifax just before Christmas. I was put on a train with a lunch of two jam sandwiches and we stopped at every outhouse along the way. (laughs) To go from Montreal to Halifax in those days was thirty-six hours. It was very cold and there was no bed to sleep on. We were lucky because the Salvation Army was always there with cookies and hot tea when we stopped. Those were very poor times. When we got to Halifax I was put in A Block which was an awful, old, building that was built during the First World War. To get water to shave I would go to the radiator and try to get some warm water out of it. They made it hard for us but they had a purpose. They were trying to harden us up. You had to wait outside to get your meals and there were so many in line that it took a long time and you were hungry and cold. After two months basic training, we were put on ships to practice what we learned. The first ship I was on was a converted wooden yacht which the government had got from the Henry Birks' family for the war. I wanted to be a torpedoman which is the one who shoots torpedoes and looks after them. A torpedo isn't an ordinary thing. It has a four-cylinder diesel engine which can be aimed at any depth you want. Part of my job was finding submarines and dropping ten-charge patterns to blow them up, making sure the detonators were all put in the wraps right and handling all the electrical work, the gyro compass, the firing of the guns; anything to do with electrical or dynamite was part of my job.

I did my ammunition training—how to blow things up—on Sable Island. I remember one time ten of us went out. We had to make dynamite, put it under the ground and blow it up. My instructor was there and, all of a sudden, we heard a big boom. He said, "Who went over there?" I said, "Bill's over there." He says, "Oh, he's gone." I says, "Well, we'd better go help him." He says, "You won't find nothing." And he was gone. That was the end of him but it was just like a part of living to this guy. I guess it happened many times. He said to me, "Don't make a mistake in what you do because you'll be just like Bill." You just didn't make mistakes.

They can train you so much in Halifax; how to do things, how to let down the lifeboats, how to fire the guns, but they could not train you without good weather so they sent us to Bermuda for part of our basic training. We didn't go ashore that much because we were more interested in getting into the water and swimming. It was beautiful there but there was nothing that big that you could see and we couldn't go to any of the special places that all the wealthy people went to.

I was then sent out to sea as a torpedoman for one year. I was on a destroyer called *Columbia* which was an American ship from the First World War (*USS Haraden*). We were on convoy duty first and then striking force duty with the air force. They would tell us where the submarines were and we would go and try to get them. Once we had to shoot in to Staten Island because the plates on one side of the ship were all exploded off when we were torpedoed by a U-boat so we had to get them welded on. While we were waiting for the repairs to be done, I asked the captain if I could go home to see my mom. He said he wasn't supposed to allow me to go but if I promised to be back on time it was okay. So I went down to the train station and bought a ticket to Montreal. I said, "How much do I owe you?" They said, "Your money's no good here, sailor." So I went to Montreal no charge. Going back, they charged me $18 to go fight a war for my country but everywhere in the United States my money was no good—the Pepsi Cola Canteen, the restaurants, the bars. The Americans were very good to us and they would not let us pay for anything. They would throw parties for us. At one of these parties a young girl sat talking to me for a long time. I didn't know who she was but my friends told me it was June Allyson. She was the nicest lady I ever met. She was only young and did not drink or smoke, not like the rest of them. Frank Sinatra and Bing Crosby were also there. They were having a get-together in New York because of the film, *Two Girls and a Sailor*.

I was sent back to Halifax to become a leading torpedo operator and then went back to the *Columbia*. I loved that ship. Being a torpedoman, I had to do some commando work. We were sent into a French seaport where the German subs would get oil and food before going out into the Atlantic. About eight of us would row out in wooden whalers. Two of us would be wearing rubber suits and would have about five or six time bombs hooked on to our belts. They were little round things about the size of a plate. I would dive down and sneak through the wire nets which were all around the harbour. The bombs were magnetized and we just had to get in there and touch them to the bottom of the subs. Then we'd set the timers and they would turn and click off one hour. By that time we were out of the port, back onto our ship and on our way. If we looked back we could see the sky light up. We did this at night-time and only when it was a dark night with no moonlight. The Free French used to do this but they were losing too many men because the Germans had fences, lights and guards. They never expected us to come in from the water. The first time we got away with it. The second time we got away with it but then we heard from the Free French (they would let us know everything) that the Germans knew we were coming in off ships so we never went back.

On convoy duty we would leave with approximately, say seventy ships and if we got in with forty we were doing good so you can see what the merchant men went through. There were about 900 German submarines in the North Atlantic and their ships were more advanced than ours and they could outfire us. If we found out there was a sub we went after it but if the sub got amongst the merchant ships, we couldn't do anything and they would just load torpedoes into them. When a merchant ship went down, we couldn't stop to pick anyone up. Other merchant ships passing by would try to throw ropes and pull them out but many were left. It was pitiful. I would see them in the water. These ships were full of tanks and other things the English needed because they had nothing. The *Valleyfield* passed us one day heading for Londonderry as we were headed for Newfoundland. A friend of mine was aboard and I yelled at him, "Where you goin'?" He says, "Londonderry." I says, "I'll be there in a couple of weeks. Are you gonna be there then?" He says, "We'll be there for a while." I said, "Good. We'll go out and have a "wet" together." He says okay and away they went. Two days later we were notified that the ship had been hit by an acoustic torpedo and my friend was gone.

As the war went on we were getting different kinds of equipment. Now we had the hedgehog, which was twenty-four bombs in the front of the ship loaded on pipes and we could fire them into the water and they'd get the submarine. Sometimes we would be hit but there wouldn't be much damage. If they got our ammunition or cracked us in half, then we were finished. You're very, very scared. Nobody is not scared. Every time you heard a thump, you thought that was it. I used to sit and look at all my friends after a battle. We'd sit and try to relax and we were all shaking, really shaking, from the oldest to the youngest. No matter how long they were in the navy, they were still shaking for hours. It was a part of life, I guess. It was twenty-four hours a day and we weren't only battling submarines, we were battling the Atlantic. The Atlantic is a very wicked ocean when it wants to be and you could go from, say, fifty below zero to being able to fry an egg on the deck two days later in the Gulf Stream.

Sometimes we'd pick up German or Italian prisoners. We'd try to get them into Newfoundland because they treated them well there. The prisoners all thought we were going to kill them and thought we were lying when we said we wouldn't. No way would we hurt them. You don't kill for the sake of killing. We killed during the war. I don't like talking about killing but you're trained that it's them or us. I didn't find them bad people, but some of the Germans had it in mind that they were the master race. They told us that we were wasting our time fighting them because they were so powerful they were going to walk over us. Most of them could speak English and one captain of a U-boat had been educated at McGill. He was twenty-two or twenty-three and he asked me if the naked lady was still in the man's beard in the picture in Mother Martin's restaurant. They had pictures of the St. Lawrence better than ours. They had planned all this years before. We would laugh at them and sing songs like:

> If Hitler says we are the master race
> We heil, sieg heil, right in the führer's face
> But to laugh at Hitler is a disgrace
> So we heil, sieg heil, right in the führer's face.

We had ways of keeping happy. We had kids from all over Canada and some came with their guitars. We used to sit on the deck when the air force told us there wasn't a submarine for miles. We'd make up songs about everything and tell jokes. The prisoners couldn't understand us and thought we were all crazy. We were singing in the middle of a war but we had to have some pleasure.

There was one officer who picked on me. The rest I could say were perfect but this one was in the gunnery party and he seemed to not like the torpedo party. He was picking on me all the time so when we had a boxing match on the ship I challenged him. If you challenged someone, they had to face you in the ring. If they were bad to you, you took it out on them. Well, I took it out on this man so, after that, he was never bad to me again. This was our even-steven in the navy. An officer was an officer and gave orders but you had the right to challenge them. We were under Nelson's Law in the navy so, if I was late coming back I would get maybe sixteen days of number 11, that's no leave and extra work for punishment. One time in basic training, I got fed up waiting to have my breakfast so I said that I had to go to the washroom so I could be first in line. I shot out the back door and, as I was running by, I passed this officer who had gold braid everywhere. He yelled at me, "Hey you, mate. Come here. I'm a captain and you didn't salute me. Do you know who I am?" I said, "No, do you know who I am?" He said no. I said, "Good" and kept on running. Well, (laughs) he lined everybody up in the parade field and came along. When he got to me he says, "YOU!" He gave me fourteen days number 16 which was two hours extra work and no leave. I had to move a pile of earth and when I was finished, move it back. There must have been twenty truckloads. I saluted an officer after that.

The food was very good. I would go to the galley in the morning to get my breakfast. The cook would put two beautiful eggs and bacon on my plate and you'd swear it was cooked specially for you. He always had a cake for every man who had a birthday which he baked even on the roughest days on the ocean. I had sirloin steak that I never had in my life. (I only had round steak, coming from the Point.) Sirloin steak, baked potatoes, fried potatoes, all given to me by the cook himself. If I wanted more I came back and he gave me seconds. There was no end to it. We had fruit, ice cream and everything we had never seen in our lives. We had it all.

I was on the *Columbia* until we went aground off Newfoundland. We had run out of ammunition and were going full speed through the ice. We lost the whole front of the ship and had to get her into port backwards. Some men were killed but I only had scratches and bruises, nothing serious. I was given thirty-two days survivor's leave and went home. In Montreal, I had taken off my uniform and, one day while I was waiting to meet my sister, a lady gave me a white feather. When my sister saw me she said, "Where did you get that?" I said, "The lady over there gave it to me." She went over and was ready to beat her up. She said, "That's my brother. He's on survivor's leave from the war and you give him A WHITE FEATHER!" I didn't know what a white feather meant. If you looked like you were old enough to fight, they'd give you a white feather. It was a sign of cowardice.

After that I got on the *Penetang* and was on full convoy duty. Once, on shore leave in England, I went up to see my grandmother in Leicester. She had never seen me before because my brother, my sister and I were born in Montreal but she knew me the minute she opened the door. Ninety years old and she had nobody to look after her property which was really run-down. I was with a friend and we had a week off so we fixed up her house. We brought our own food which we got off the ship because they didn't have much food.

I lost my hearing from the concussion of the explosions. I was beside this

12-pounder gun and every time it went off, the explosion would burn the back of my neck and my ears would burn for three or four days. I knew my hearing was going but when I got out of the service they wouldn't listen to me. When they discharged you, it was a ten-minute thing. You marched through a long corridor naked, they stuck things in your ears and mouth, listened to your heart and when you got to the end, you were discharged. I got a disability pension the second time I applied and now, they're very good to me. They (DVA) pay to remove my snow and cut my grass. Anything serious on my house, they pay for. When the Ice Storm was on, they were on the phone right away offering me wood, food and taxi service if I had to go somewhere.

There were seven of us who went in the service and I was the only one who came home. The ones who couldn't get in the navy went in the merchant navy. Terry Dryden survived quite a few trips. He was in London and got on the wrong train. He jumped down on the platform to run across to the one he wanted and got hit by a train. His mother never got over it.

Thomas Seivewright

Tommy Seivewright enlisted in the navy in March 1942. He originally wanted to join the Black Watch to honour his Scottish heritage but his father, a World War I veteran of the naval Battle of Jutland, wouldn't hear of it, so the navy it was. In retrospect, he thinks it might have been a good decision because of the very heavy losses suffered by this proud regiment. Living in Griffintown at the time, he says that many boys from his area and Point St. Charles joined up because there was a lot of truth in the old saying, You joined up to get a pair of boots and three meals a day.

I WENT UP TO THE RCNVR BARRACKS on Mountain Street to enlist and did my basic training in Toronto at *HMCS York*. After that we all got twenty-eight days' leave which I spent in Montreal. We got a telegram saying to report to the barracks in Montreal and then I was drafted to Toronto. I was the only one, of about thirty from Montreal, who was sent to Victoria, B.C. on *HMCS Naden*. The rest of my chums were sent to Halifax and I thought that was a bit of a raw rub, but what can you do when you're in the navy? I went to the Stoker-Training Establishment (STE) for a month's course. I was in the engineering branch of the navy. A stoker learns about the upkeep of the mechanical equipment, the engine and boiler room. You progressed through the ranks, when you had the experience and the time, from second-class stoker, first-class stoker, leading stoker and then to a petty officer. While I was taking the course, there was a notice on the board that they were looking for young men from the ages of eighteen to twenty-five to join a special commando unit so I volunteered. I was accepted and we took preliminary basic training which was supposed to be completed in Halifax. We made friends and buddies during this time but then we were all sent home on leave before joining up again in Halifax.

We were then told there were too many naval commandos so we were drafted to different ships for convoy duty in the North Atlantic run which meant from the eastern seaboard, Halifax and Boston to England. I picked up my ship at Saint Margaret's Bay, just outside of Halifax. It was a brand-new ship that was christened *HMCS Manitoulin*, built here but manned by an all-British crew. Now these men were from all over the British Isles. They were from Scotland, Ireland, and all different parts of England. I didn't know whether I was on an English ship or a German ship because they all had different accents. I was the only one who could speak English on that Limey ship! All Englishmen, but none of them could speak English. They must have given the German prisoners a hard time because half of the Germans could speak better English than they could. (laughs) Some of these men had been at sea for fifteen to twenty years. They were old veteran seamen; some of them were fishermen from all along the coasts of England, Scotland and Ireland. They were the best seamen, I think to this day, in the world. Older men, doing a young man's job. I was the youngest man on board. I was eighteen.

It was hard on me because I was getting Canadian wages and I was the "lowee of the low". I was a second-class stoker and I was making more money than the first lieutenant officer and it was hard for them to get used to that. We got paid every fortnight and when I went for my first pay, they didn't have enough cash so they paid the other guys and then called me over and gave me a check. That didn't go over very well. I was damn near a millionaire compared to what they were getting and that caused a bit of dissention. When we went to the wet canteen at *HMCS Stadacona* after work, I didn't let them buy a round. I was the big shot that day. I bought them two pints or two glasses each, whatever they were drinking so I wasn't a "bad topper", as they used to say.

We were a mid-ocean escort ship. We took the convoys from Halifax, Boston and New York to the middle of the Atlantic where they were met by an

English convoy of war vessels. I did my job in the boiler room, four hours on, eight hours off. It was bad. The North Atlantic is a terrible place at all times but in the winter you can't explain it. I never thought the sea could be so strong. It could take a two-inch metal bar and twist it like a pretzel. I didn't get much sleep because I had a bunk which was bolted to the bulkhead so when the ship moved the bunk moved with it. I thought we were more of a submarine than the submarines because, in a rough sea, when we went down, I was afraid that we were never going to come up because there was so much water. When the bow broke the surface and then had to crawl up through that wave, you're pitching and rolling at the same time. I was so seasick one day that I was praying that the ship would sink.

We had some close calls. The U-boats were there in force; "wolf packs", we called them. The ASDIC (Anti-Submarine Detection Investigation Committee) would send out a ping and we would know by the screech and loudness when we got the ping back how close the subs were and go into action stations. We'd drop depth charges and try to surface the sub and sink it with gunfire. Of course, they were doing the same to us. Sometimes the escort vessels had to separate, so if they saw us through a periscope and knew we were alone, they'd take a pot shot at us to get us out of the road because they didn't want to get pinged. It's always in your mind that the ship might be hit. Lots of times I'd be looking up through the skylight and thinking that I could scramble on top of the engines—if they were still there and I survived the explosion—and go through the skylight. Another way to escape was up a ladder to the upper deck. There were two boilers, each with 125 pounds of steam pressure. If you weren't killed with the explosion, you were scalded to death. When my watch was over, I always ran up the companionway to the upper deck where I felt safer. Our ship was never hit but we did kill a lot of fish with the depth charges. They came up to the surface, all kinds, cod, mackerel, everything, you name it. If there was no scare then we had "relax action stations" and all the guys would get nets and we'd have fish for a week.

At the end of 1943, I was drafted back to barracks. I was a first-class stoker and had the time in now to go for my leading stoker course. I knew I would pass the exam because I was practically a leading stoker already. You had to do three months at the MTE (Mechanical Training Establishment) in Halifax. I was thankful in one way because it meant I wouldn't have to go in the North Atlantic for three months but I missed my friends, my buddies—the English crew. They used to call me the "crazy Canuck" and a lot worse names. (laughs)

I took the course, passed the exam and was waiting for another ship. I had fourteen days' leave this time but I took more than fourteen days and, in the navy, they call this being "adrift." I went adrift for about ten days. I had a girlfriend in Montreal and, being a sailor at sea for a long time, you know. I was about nineteen going on twenty at this time. Montreal was a wide open city and I was uptown this night with a couple of my buddies who were in the navy. When I got home and opened the door, I could hear voices in the front room. Dad said to me in his Scotch accent, "Is that you, Tom?" I said aye and he says, "Come in here. I've got a couple of visitors waiting on you." I walked in and there were two MPs waiting for me. I wasn't trying to desert. I just wanted extra leave to have a good time. All the military outfits had this problem, even the air force. (We used to call them the Brylcreem boys, you know, the cigarettes, their hair glued down. You'd think they were going to Hollywood!) They didn't have any space for me at *Stadacona*. It was filled. It was around Christmas time so there were a lot of "birds," as we called them. The jailhouse in the army barracks at Longueuil was filled up too, so they took me to No. 1 police station in Montreal and I stayed there for three weeks. They put me in what they called "the cage" with all the guys awaiting trial. What a bunch of rubby-dubs! I saw a lot in the navy but these were guys living off the street.

Because I was working for His Majesty's government I was treated like a king. I got three dollars a day for food so the restaurant guy would come and I'd order from the menu. Food was cheap at that time, you know—what you could get. You couldn't get eggs and everybody was rationed, but I could buy cigarettes, tobacco and everything. I was quite the guy there because all the rubby-dubs were bumming cigarettes off me. They'd come around me at 12 o'clock when this guy who worked in the corner restaurant would come in and take my order and I'd order them a Coke once in a while. The MPs came for me this Monday morning and told me I was going to Halifax and to get my gear together. I'll never forgive the navy for doing this: they put me in HANDCUFFS to take me to Bonaventure Station. I told them they didn't have to do that but they said, "It's the rule just in case you try to make a 'flyaway.'" I told them I was going back to Halifax but they put me in cuffs anyway. It wasn't too bad in the police car, but walking through the station with everybody looking at me ... You'd think I'd killed somebody. That was a little hard to take. When I got on board train, they took the cuffs off, but if I had to go to the bathroom, one of the MPs would follow me and stand outside the door until I came out to make sure that I didn't break a window and jump through.

I figured I'd get about fourteen days' extra work but I only got seven this time. This was strike two for me. One time when I was taking my course, an officer called me something I didn't like so I told him, "If you ever do that again, you'll wish your mother had crossed her legs or strangled you at birth. I'll beat the goddamned shit out of you." So I got fourteen days in cells in Halifax picking oakum. They give you six bars. They're about two inches wide and about six inches long. It's like tar rope and they use it in ships to keep the water out. You have to shred it and it took me about six hours to do it. They come in with a scale and weigh it and, if you haven't got three pounds—and it's very light—they put it on your next task. I had about two extra ones to do. This guy in the next cell told me a way to do it fast. He was an old-timer. (laughs) I had no trouble after that and could do it in an hour and a half. The second time in cells, they gave me the same job but I was a vet by this time. I knew what the job was all about. (laughs)

In the navy, if you didn't sneeze right … naval discipline was pretty tough and there were a lot of silly little rules but you had to obey because it was the navy. The navy could be snobbish but when new officers came aboard, we brought them down if they were snobs. Some of these seamen, especially on that English ship, wouldn't stand for it. They'd throw him overboard the first stormy night. That's true. They'd bang his head against the bulkhead and throw him overboard. Lost At Sea. That was it. That happened many times. A buddy of mine did it but the officer was very lucky because the back of his heel stuck in one of the guy lines and he didn't go over. He was dangling there and shouting till one of the seamen got him. They never got the guy. Everybody knew who it was but nobody squealed.

Halifax was strictly a navy town. You couldn't throw a brick without hitting a sailor. There were no bars where you could go for a beer or places to blow off steam on shore leave. You had to go to the wet canteen or buy a bottle of Scotch. Bootleggers were all over the place. I was in barracks for about a month and was getting tired of it. If you coughed the wrong way, you'd get extra work. There was always someone on top of you. Barracks life is simply discipline. In early 1943, my buddy Frank Parsons and I were getting fed up with lounging around in barracks waiting for a draft so we went to the petty officer and told him that we wanted to get out of the goddamned barracks. We both got a draft to the same ship, the *HMCS Moose Jaw*, which was in dry dock in Shelbourne. In the meantime, I had passed my MTE course and qualified as a petty officer but it was never confirmed. I did the work of a PO but was never paid or recognized as such. Everyone on the *Moose Jaw* was Canadian which was new to me. We went to Saint Margaret's Bay again and we did our WAPs (Work Assignment Procedure). We'd take the ship out and the torpedo crew would try all the guns.

We went from Halifax to Londonderry, Ireland, and were based there for nearly a month having exercises every day, and screening out the ones who didn't fit in. They would be drafted to other ships or sent back to our barracks in Scotland to retrain. Wireless operators, telegraphists, torpedo operators: if you couldn't do the job, they sent you back to school. After training, our base was in Milford Haven, a beautiful little seaside fishing town in Wales, and we stayed there until the end of the war. We went out on what they called the E-boat alley. The Germans had E-boats which were low-slung motor torpedo boats. They carried two torpedo tubes in the back and two in the front so they could do a lot of damage. We did runs protecting the convoys from Wales right up to Scapa Flow, which is north of Scotland. France was occupied territory at the time—it was all occupied territory—and, if you were unlucky, you got a ship to Murmansk. Half the guys who went to Murmansk never came back. If the rough water didn't get them, the subs did, because we had no air cover and the German air force had control right up to the Arctic. That was a death run, actually. We knew the invasion was coming because we had the radio on and you put two and two together.

D-Day, we were off. We escorted the American troops to Omaha Beach from Milford Haven. We had to go from Wales, around Land's End and then cross the channel to France. It was true what you saw in the film, *Saving Private Ryan*. We were there too early to land and these Americans, they were all kids, too, eighteen or nineteen and they were circling around us for about an hour and actually they circled for about six hours before they landed. These kids were so seasick they were wishing to die. We were on a corvette and it was less choppy for us but they were in landing crafts which held about 150 men. They were like big shoeboxes, flat-bottomed with no keel. Huddled in there about 150 young men, all armed and weighted down and when they jumped off, you know, half of them sank. Time and weather went against the invasion. They were lucky they were able to land. I can only visualize what they went through. Our orders were to drop the troops and return. We were attacked with aircraft but we never got a scratch. You're too busy to be terrified. We gave them supporting fire as soon as we got within range and we had the big boys in the British navy about twenty miles behind us with their long range guns. Every time they fired, I thought my scalp was going to come off. We returned for more troop carriers. There's so much confusion. The landing crafts would come close to us and then we'd know that we were going in with this bunch. There'd be maybe some English frigates and Canadian corvettes like the *Algoma*. Then we'd get the signal to move and they'd move in ahead of us and we'd branch out, maybe one in front, maybe two in back, two or three on each side but the landing crafts would be in the middle. We were like a sheepdog herding these sheep and that was it. We went two times and then stayed overnight at Milford Haven. By the next morning they had a beachhead. Omaha. That was terrible. We dropped them off there but that was our job. Done.

In the navy, the officers had what they called "up spirits" at 11 o'clock. Every sailor got a tot of rum. That was navy rum, dark and powerful and if you weren't used to it, one tot would put you out. And there was also, "Splice the main brace." They'd give you a treat for some special occasion like getting a submarine, shooting down a plane or doing something out of the ordinary. Sometimes they were double tots, about three ounces. We had plenty of rum. I used to bottle it because you didn't feel good when you drank rum at sea. You get into a rough sea for a week and, even if you were at sea for twenty years you didn't feel one hundred percent so all the guys used to save it and when we got into port we'd drink it. Sometimes we'd have six or eight quart bottles of rum in our lockers before we hit port.

When the war was declared officially over, that was when "Smith" got it. We were celebrating in port. It was "splice the main brace." I must have had about twelve quarts of rum, no kidding. Smith had a pal on the corvette next to us. When I saw him I said, "You'd better take it easy on the juice. You're gonna get pissed and you won't be able to walk over to the other ship. We'll have to carry you." There was a small gap between the ships and Smith went down. He was a sailor, but he couldn't swim a stroke. But he could have yelled. He must have hit his head against the bow. About an hour later his buddy came looking for him. We told him that he had gone over to the other ship but he said that he hadn't. We searched everywhere and piped it over the ship. The officers got notification and they sent out search parties to check the pub and all the shops along the dockyard. He wasn't in the pub; he wasn't in the dockyard so that was it. A small crew put down a whaler and rode about a mile down the current and back, searching for about an hour. No Smith. What a way to celebrate. What a way for his mother to get a telegram after the war. Of course, they'd never say he was drunk and fell overboard. You don't put that down. He was gone, not killed in action, just gone. Killed In Naval Operations, that's the way they put it. We all had leave the last night so we went ashore and got drunk and everybody forgot about Smith. We were about two days outside of Halifax when we got notification that his body was found in the torpedo net about four miles down the river, just before the open sea.

When we were on shore leave in Britain, we didn't go to a church social, have tea and crumpets and walk the girl home. No way. You're with a bunch of guys, nineteen or twenty years of age, three, four weeks a month at sea and always hearing guy talk. Every other word was "f" this or "f" that. We'd go to a pub, have a few pints and check the joint out. Don't forget, there were a lot of British girls in the services. We would go to the military girls first because they knew what it was all about. It was wartime, things were let down. I started to grow up in my thinking about girls. When you're fourteen or fifteen, you're scared of girls. You don't know what to talk about. I found the English girls so different than the Canadian girls. They called a spade a spade. If you got too fresh, they would let you know right off the bat. "You're not going to win bingo here tonight, laddie." A married woman would tell you that her husband was overseas and that was that. Some of them, though, had husbands who were gone for three or four years and, if they got a good-looking guy or some one they liked to talk to … it worked both ways. We could tell the good gals from the "prosties", as we called them. Don't forget, no penicillin in those days. If you got a dose of gonorrhoea they gave you what we called the "hockey stick treatment." It was a surgical instrument like a pen and the doctor pushed the end of it up your penis and then he pressed the button and thin blades branched out like an umbrella and then he pulled it down so that it scraped all the sores which held pus and broke them open so they could be discharged and that was painful. You could hear guys screaming. They also gave you sulpha drugs and told you to drink a lot of water. They issued us condoms and many women in Britain wouldn't let you get close to them unless you had a condom. Many guys wouldn't use condoms because they said it was like washing your feet with your socks on.

I have the greatest respect for the German army and the seamen. They were like us. They were caught up in a war. The average German kid had a lot of propaganda with the Hitler Youth Movement but we had our propaganda too. We were the good guys—they were the bad guys. I didn't hate them personally. I was fighting for a cause. We had that patriotism and when your country goes to war, you go. I didn't want no German telling me what to do or

(Above)
George Holland says goodbye to his widowed mother,
Rozel Street, December 1941.
"If we can take on Point St. Charles, we can take on Hitler."

(Below)
On board the *Columbia*, 1943.
"Songs and jokes, and sometimes shaking for hours."

(Above) Georges Malouin in front of his aunt's house on Rachel Street, 1941.
"The navy was hell."

(Below) Tommy Seivewright in Victoria, B.C.
"You grow up fast in a war."

getting pulled out of bed in the middle of the night because I was a Jew, if I was a Jew. That rubbed me the wrong way. Don't forget too, all the guys who were in the military, we were Depression kids and grew up when ten cents was a lot of money. You could go to a show with a quarter; buy a pop and everything else and still come out with a nickel. Can't do that today. You could go uptown if you were old enough and buy yourself a woman for 50 cents.

I had two friends who were German boys whose families had immigrated to Canada before the Second World War. One was Tommy Brehn and the other was Ernie Frank. Ernie Frank's parents packed it up here in Montreal and moved back to Germany in 1938 or 1939 because Hitler said that things were going well in Germany. When war broke out, Tommy Brehn joined the RCAF and his brother Edgar joined the army. Tommy got a letter from Germany saying that Ernie Frank had joined the air force. Wouldn't it be ironic if these two guys met one another, one in a Messerschmitt and the other in a Spitfire, who went to school together and were now fighting against one another in the skies above the English Channel, France or Germany? Edgar survived the war but I lost touch with Tommy and never heard from Frank after that. (Note: We found out later that Thomas John Brehn was killed on November 24, 1943. He has no known grave and is commemorated at the Runnymede Memorial in England.)

You grow up fast when you're in war. It was a good experience and a good way to get an education but I hope nobody thinks that it was an experience I would like every guy of sixteen or seventeen years of age to go through. War is hell.

Georges Malouin

Georges Malouin joined the navy in 1941 for all the usual reasons, but left it realizing that he did not have a country. He has spent most of his adult life receiving psychiatric help for the emotional trauma he suffered while working as an ordinary seaman.

I JOINED because my two older brothers were in the navy and, not knowing the mess I was getting into, I wanted to see the world. The navy to me was hell. I joined up with the French section, Cartier, thinking that it would be something French but Montreal and Cartier section was the same thing—all English, not even a word of French to show that we existed. It wasn't so bad when I first enlisted because they were mostly French in my division although those who joined the navy could speak English. My two brothers had worked for English companies so their English was perfect. My oldest brother was a petty officer, so he never had any trouble, and the other one was a wireless operator.

Training? (laughs) It was in Montreal and I understood nothing. The only thing I could say in English was: "Me, English, not much." I didn't even always understand my name because I've been called Malquin, Maloroom, Mal, here, Mal, there. When they gave me the course in armaments and explosives, I understood nothing and just scratched things on my paper in the tests. They didn't pass me and thought I was probably in the lower range of intelligence. I couldn't speak English so I was not intelligent.

My first ship was the *Lethbridge* in Halifax and the guys didn't like very much the fact that they had a Frenchman on board so they were watching me. Once I was on watch at the end of the ship and was seasick because I was new in the service. I was vomiting overboard and they came and put me in cells for two weeks thinking I was sleeping on duty. I saw the look of hate on the faces of the officer and the rating who was with him. That's when I began to be angry. I never forgot that and thought, "Do what you want. I don't care." I was in jail and didn't even know why and that's when I became a rebel.

So after I got out of there, they sent me to Newfoundland. Because of a mix-up with names, I didn't get any pay for eight months. I got mad because I wasn't in the service for free. Anything that was English then became my enemy. I used to say, "If I could put my hand on Churchill's cigar, I'd make chewing tobacco with it." I began to admire the Germans and while I was in Newfoundland I took a course in German and that was against me. (laughs) I also wrote things against the navy and they thought I was a spy. I was told I was going to be shot. Just imagine a young fellow in the barracks, Christmas is coming and being told he was going to be shot. I was eighteen and naive and believed it. I managed to get myself in jail again. I was no criminal but, speaking only French, could not defend myself. They sent me an interpreter but he said he couldn't understand my French although I spoke it better than most. So I spent months in His Majesty's jail considered an enemy of the country.

At Niobe, the barracks in Greenock, Scotland, I was waiting for transport to *HMCS Teme* and we had permission to sleep at the YMCA. Around midnight four sailors arrived and went to another sailor named Drolet who wasn't too hefty, being short and weighing about a hundred pounds. They asked him what he was doing there and he told them he was waiting to go on a ship. They said he had no business there, beat him up and threw him out the door. I told myself that if they came to me and behaved like that, I would have some fun with them. They came and surrounded me and asked me what I was doing there. I wasn't afraid. I had my two hands and was a husky fellow. I said, "It's none of your business." One of them told me that he was the killick of the watch. Killick is like a sergeant. I said, "If you're a killick, you have to wear your uniform before you tell me what to do." He told me that I had to get out. He made the mistake of grabbing me and I gave him a punch. The three others jumped on me. At the end, three were on the floor and the fourth one got away. I made a massacre of them. I'm not the kind to look for trouble but I don't run away from it either. So the Military Police came and one said, "I hear you had problems." I said, "My problems are over there." (They were still on the floor.) They quickly understood the situation and told me that these guys were already on punishment and forbidden to go to the canteen and drink. An officer told me that I could press charges because I was the one who had been attacked but, if I did, I would miss my ship and these guys would never forget it. Well, I didn't want that and told him to let it go. When I went on *HMCS Teme*, these guys came alongside the ship and told my shipmates all about their adventure with me and said that I was responsible for making them go to jail. They didn't tell the truth, but that's the reason the hell started. I didn't want trouble but I had trouble. People with racial prejudice—do you think they need a reason to hate? The fact that I spoke French and couldn't speak English was enough. We had all kinds. I met some Ukrainians on a ship and tried to be friendly with them but, if a fellow comes to Canada and he's not French, right away he's English. In every port I visited, I made friends with Europeans and had no trouble.

One good thing happened at Niobe. One day they sent me to make a hole in the wall for the post office and I told the fellow working with me to go on one side to do the job. He said, "Goddammit, I've been here five minutes and already you're giving me orders." I told him I thought I had to tell him what to do. The next day he apologized and told me that he had had a bad night and we became friends. He was an English fellow from New Brunswick, Robert Rowe. When you have a friendship you always find a way to communicate. Bob was always reading comics and telling me jokes and I was starting to learn English a little. The day after my run-in at the YMCA, I got on the *Teme* and, to my great joy, Bob joined me there.

I was on the *Lethbridge*, the *Qu'appelle*, and the *Kincardine* but *HMCS*

Teme was the worst. That's when I started to hate. Since it said on the papers that I couldn't understand much and wasn't good on the upper deck, they made me an officers' servant. I was good at needle and thread and I took care of their clothes. The officers were not so bad. During the day it was okay because I was working for them but at night I had to hide. Somehow or other, one of the officers knew I was friends with Bob so he put us on the same watch. (That's the only good thing they did in the service.) One day, Bob came to me and told me that he overheard some of the guys say that the first chance they had they would throw me overboard. I knew from my brothers and others that it *did* happen and that the law of silence would mean that they wouldn't stool on each other. So I was waiting for them. I had bought a gun, a .45, from a fellow from Rosemount who was on the ship and every time one of them came near me, I would tell him I didn't want to see him around me. I was really mad, you know. I wanted to use a machine gun and machine gun all the crew. The only thing that stopped me was having my friend Bob. I knew where the guns were and I only had to cut the chains to use them. I even had maps and knew exactly where I was going to land after I sank the ship. Bob told me that they would take the gun away from me when I was asleep so, every night for three or four months, I had to sleep in a lifeboat. Do you know what being afraid is? I was afraid and shaking with cold and fear and hunger. I had nothing to eat so Bob would come and give me some food. Sometimes it was frozen potatoes or potato peels, which made me sick, and I had diarrhea but couldn't get out of the boat. I couldn't bathe or anything. It was hell. I was living a nightmare and was delirious. For Christmas Bob brought me a chicken leg or some ham, I don't remember exactly, but I do remember the piece of apple pie and a jug of hot chocolate. That was my Christmas. I couldn't eat in the mess because even in daytime they would throw me overboard. Many times I wished I could die. All the things that happen on a ship—nobody sees a thing. They were just like hoodlums, like bandits. A percentage of the people were neutral but there were about five or six that were bad. I'm husky but against five or six? The three worst were from St. Catharines, Ontario. Whenever they would meet me somewhere they would give me a punch. These guys were not civilized people. At the end I was so mad that I probably would have worked for Hitler. The guys who were supposed to be fighting on my side were fighting against me. I had two wars. I was fighting against the Germans and watching for my life on the ship. The enemy was not only below the water. They were on deck with me. Sometimes I was sure that I had lost my mind. I was dreaming all kinds of things, like an army of liberators would liberate me. I was out of my mind.

We got torpedoed by a U-boat near Falmouth on March 29, 1945 at 7:45 in the morning. The explosion knocked sixty feet off the stern and my friend Bob got killed. (sighs) That was the worst thing that could happen in my world. There was no chance of a funeral or anything like that. No mourning. Nothing. He just disappeared. He wasn't my best friend—he was my *brother*. I got hit with shrapnel in my face and chest and one eye was affected. The guys came around and said, "You bastard, how come you're still alive? It's always the good ones who die." The ship was towed to Falmouth. While I was taken from the ship to the harbour, I was in a basket and the two guys holding the cables let them go. I was drunk with morphine but I still remember it. It's a good thing the captain came or they would have drowned me. On the 13 of April, I had to go back on the ship to pick up the ammunition that was lying around before the ship was scrapped. Not knowing what I was doing because I couldn't understand the ammunition course I took, I picked up an explosive and it blew up. I lost the thumb and three fingers of my left hand. I was in the hospital when two officers came to see me and told me that they had found a gun in my locker and I was going to be court-martialed. I told the doctor that I didn't want to see them again and that was it. I never heard about it and I think the officer kept the gun for himself.

I was a jailbird, that's what we were called in the service. I spent four or five months in jail altogether because I had a reputation as a rebel. You sleep on a bed made of wood. I don't think there was a mattress. (I can sleep anywhere now.) I was always alone in my cell. I had a Spanish book so I learned Spanish. I sang and talked to myself. Dinner when you had it was a biscuit (hardtack) with a jug of tea. You put the biscuit in the tea but, by the time it got soft, the tea was cold. But they give you a lot of tea, eh? When you threw this biscuit against the wall, sometimes it would break and sometimes it wouldn't. I used to kill the cockroaches with it. On Sundays we had a meal but if they decided that your cell wasn't clean enough, you had no dinner. They broke my spirit and I lost my mind after the *Teme*. The first thing I said when that happened was, "I won't have to pick oakum anymore."

At the end of the war, I wanted to go home on the first ship, a rowboat or anything going to Canada. I was on the parade ground at Greenock when an officer called me inside and asked me when I was going home. When I got back, my name had been called but I wasn't there. They did that four times.

Tell me that it was only a mistake! The fifth time I lost my patience and they placed me on the first ship in the direction of Canada.

A few days before coming back, some guy attacked me because I was French but there were some guys from out West, Manitoba or Saskatchewan— probably Ukrainians—and one of them said, "The guy is wounded. If you touch him, you'll have to do it over my dead body." On the ship coming back over, I had to sleep on the floor. I was sick and wounded and imagine how nervous I felt when they decided to get rid of all the ammunition on the ship, the depth charges, the 4-pounder guns and everything. They took me to Newfoundland. When I left the ship, I had my two hands bandaged and asked someone to take my luggage ashore. They threw my kit bag overboard so I couldn't change clothes and had no hat or anything. I was charged a lot of money to replace my kit. When I went to see my brother who was in Newfoundland already, I was crying and he told me I didn't look so good.

My brothers had good experiences in the navy. One brother didn't believe what happened to me and we didn't talk for a few years. I couldn't understand because every chance I had to see him during the war, I would tell him about my bad treatment. When I came home I thought that if I kept on with the feelings of hate and vengeance, I would kill myself. I got rid of the hate when I got married. Just having my wife with me was enough because she's something special. When I married her, she was seventeen years old, a little girl from the country. She never had any courses in psychology or anything like that but she amazes me by the things she comes out with. Not only do I love her, I couldn't do without her. She takes good care of me and knows what I want even before I do. I'm bitter though and I don't believe in people as much as I did. I love people and that's the reason I learned many languages. Whenever I go into a store with a Chinese owner, I say a few words in Chinese to him. To love people you must speak their language. But some English—it seems a way of life for them to hate the French just in case we take over. I don't understand this fear of being invaded because what are seven million people surrounded by three hundred million? Every time I spoke French outside of Quebec, I was told that Canada was an English country. I cannot keep on being hated like that. I wish we could stay in Canada but I have no reason to believe it. I am a Quebecer.

(Above)
Velma Burt Lee.
"I would have liked to stay in the service and work my way up."

(Below)
Twenty-seven merchant seamen being rescued
by HMCS Columbia and taken to Newfoundland.

Official military photo of a merchant ship going down in the Atlantic.
Courtesy of George Holland.

Velma Burt Lee

The navy was the last branch of the service to accept women in its ranks. In one famous story, a Canadian commodore announced, "I will not have women in my command. I don't want them, and I won't have them." "But Commodore," a Wren said while tapping her forehead, "our Wrens have something up here." "I don't care where they've got it," he retorted, "My sailors are sure to find it." He lost. In July 1942, the Women's Royal Canadian Naval Service (WRCNS) was created and more than 6,000 Wrens, as they were called, served until they were disbanded after the war. Velma Burt Lee grew up in Ville Émard and loved her time in the navy.

WHEN I WAS A YOUNG GIRL, I used to love to go down to Angrignon Park (it was only a field then) and look up at the sky and watch all the airplanes going over. The war came along and I wanted to join the air force. I went to sign up and lied about my age. When Mom found out, she phoned them and told them that I was only fifteen so that cancelled that out. We didn't think the war would end as soon as it did so, on February 8, 1945 two of my girlfriends and I went to enlist at *Donnacona* on Drummond Street and two of us were accepted. My mother had heard a lot of bad gossip about women in the service which wasn't true at all. I said, "Mom, if I want to be bad, I can be bad without a uniform and I don't intend to be bad." She gave her consent and I went off to Galt, Ontario for basic training.

In training, we had to do everything: learn to make our beds properly, keep our uniform tidy, wash floors, do dishes and all kinds of other duties. It was very good training, hard but good, and I liked it. Our pay, I think, was $1.06 a day. When our training was done, they sorted us out and, since we were one of the last batches of girls to enlist, we got the tail end of the jobs which is kitchen duties. (laughs) We worked in shifts and had to do all the kitchen work like setting the tables, washing the dishes, keeping the tables and chairs clean, sweeping the floors and whatever. Six weeks later, we were sent to *Stadacona* in Halifax. We lived in a separate barracks from the men in the Wren block. My duties were the same as in Galt. I got up at four in the morning to start work at five and worked until three in the afternoon. The work wasn't anything too interesting. It was more like housework, shall we say. (laughs) I invited my mother to come to *Stadacona* and she visited for a week. She came into the barracks and saw how we lived. She met my friends and ate dinner and supper with us and I think she was content after that.

We had leisure time and we used to go to movies and restaurants in Halifax. The Knights of Columbus had dances and that's where we spent most of our time because their dances were well organized and well supervised. Civilians and people in the service would go. We had no problem with the people in Halifax. They treated us with respect wherever we went. We'd also be driven by truck to another base for dances. I had a boyfriend at the time. He was an army man who had been overseas for three years. He fought at Dieppe and in Sicily and had been discharged. I met him just before I joined up and we kept in touch. He worked on the trains and when he came to Halifax, we would meet and have dinner. He'd come to the base but we had strict hours and, of course, we weren't allowed to bring anybody into the barracks.

On VE-Day, May 8, it was announced over the P.A. system that the war was over. We were allowed to go out, but everyone had to be back by eleven o'clock. I was on duty that morning so I went out about two or three o'clock. I walked around with a sailor that I knew. The churches were wide open and the bells were ringing. Outside of that there was nothing. They didn't have a big parade or anything because they didn't have time to organize one. I was on Barrington Street and I would say that about 50 percent of the people of Halifax were out on the streets. I saw a lot of people smashing windows and carrying things out of the stores. I couldn't understand why they were doing it but maybe they were poor people who couldn't afford much. It was sad because the storekeepers couldn't do anything about it and I didn't see any police at all. The navy was in there too, breaking windows but they weren't carrying any goods. What could sailors take and where could they take it? They couldn't bring boxes, clothes or furniture into the base or back to a ship. The people blamed it on the navy but it wasn't the navy. I would say the sailors were only after booze. The war was over and they were celebrating and got drunk. My friend and I weren't drinking (I never drank or smoked) so we found a good restaurant where we ate and spent some time and then I went back to barracks at about ten o'clock. I was so glad the war was over.

I met some very, very nice girls in the navy. Excellent friends and I'm still in touch with them. My life in the navy wasn't long, just a little over a year, but I loved every bit of it. I learned discipline and how to live with others and to "get on with it" and not take your time doing things. If I had not been engaged to my husband, I would have liked to stay in the service and work my way up.

Army

Patrick Poirier

The Royal Rifles of Canada of Quebec City recruited from Quebec City through the Gaspé to the Eastern Townships and about 35 percent of their members were French Canadians. What awaited these young men and the men of The Winnipeg Grenadiers after bravely staving off the surrender of Hong Kong until December 25, 1941 were torture, starvation and maltreatment at the hands of their pitiless and brutal Japanese captors. One of their guards was Kanao Inouye, a Japanese Canadian who had suffered racist rejection while growing up. The Canadians were to suffer his special wrath. Of the 1,975 Canadians soldiers who took part in the first commitment of the war, 550 never came back. Nearly half this number died in prison camps. Patrick Poirier was born in Nouvelle, Quebec and served as a medical orderly with the Royal Rifles. At the age of eighty-five, (2002) he still walks with military bearing and speaks the fluent Japanese that he learned under inhuman conditions. He is a very caring man and this interview was a painful revisiting of those black years.

MY MOTHER'S BROTHER, Angus Duguay, had been a prisoner of war of the Germans in the First War. He had been gassed and mistreated and when he came home he became a real devil. Whenever he took a drink he would break everything in the house. When my parents came to see me leave at Matapédia, my mother said, "I don't want you to be taken a prisoner of war. I would rather you died at my feet right now." She was crying and made me cry too. (emotional pause) On the train from Valcartier we stopped in Winnipeg to pick up the Winnipeg Grenadiers. We got on the *Awatea* and had no idea where we were being sent. We thought we were going to China, Japan or Europe. We didn't know anything—it was a military secret. We first landed in Hawaii and then Manila. I was seasick for twenty-one days until we reached Hong Kong on November 16. In Hong Kong, we were about 8,000 troops, British, Indian (all big men), Hong Kong volunteers, Australians and about 2,000 Canadians.

I was a medical orderly. All the bandsmen were. We could never imagine when the war started what would happen to us. One night I was called at 11 o'clock, "Medical orderly, wounded man here." I went down the road and when I got close to this man's head, a burst of hot blood hit my face. It was my first battle experience and I felt so bad. I thought, "I don't think I'll be able to do this work. It's impossible for me." All of a sudden, everything cleared out and I did my job after that. I put a bandage on this guy and we brought him to an ambulance. The ambulance was fired on by the Japanese and when I got to the tent where the doctors were, I opened up the ambulance door and there was about an inch of blood on the floor. We had to take all those guys out and some of them were dead. Yeah, it was awful.

Dr. Lynch sent me down a gully with a stretcher and a Chinaman. We got to an Indian soldier and all he could say was, "Stop blood. Stop blood." I got him on the stretcher and this Chinaman was too frightened to hold the back of the stretcher because he thought he would be machine-gunned. I took the back and we brought him up. I ripped the shirt off this Indian and there was a layer of blood on his chest just like Jello. I put a bandage on him but he had to wait a while because there were a lot of patients. One guy needed an escort for the ambulance to go to the village but Dr. Lynch said I had to stay with him because he needed me. The guy who took my place in the ambulance was fired on and died. If it would have been me, I would have been gone. We also found one of our men who had been horribly mutilated. When the boys found him, you can imagine how they felt in their hearts.

We fought from December 8 until we were taken prisoners of war on December 25 at three o'clock in the afternoon. We had no more ammunition, no more food, no more water and we just had to give in. The Japanese fired machine guns over our heads to see if anybody would run so they could shoot them as escapees. Our officers told us not to run and, if we died there, that was all there was to it. They drove us to a big garage for buses where we all sat down. During the next hour, an interpreter came in and told us about four or five times that they didn't take prisoners and we were all going to die. You can imagine our boys, some wanted to yell or run away or something but we had to sit there. When the hour was up, they came in with machine guns and walked us to buses and drove us to North Point Camp which was a refugee camp.

We were sent into one hospital at Stanley to get the patients. The walls were thick with blood. The nurses had been raped and killed. It was a real disaster, a slaughterhouse. The Japanese just walked through there and put bayonets through the faces and bodies of the patients in their beds.

We stayed at North Point Camp for about seven months. All the windows and doors were busted. We had to lie on cement and were so tight that we had to lie sideways. We had lice, bedbugs and mosquitoes which, if they pick you, can give you malaria for seven years. With the lice and bedbugs you scratch and can get an infection and we had very few medical supplies because our camp at Sham Shui Po had been bombed. We ate rice, which wasn't too good, and then it got worse, we got Korean rice which was pink with worms in it. Even the worms were pinkish white. When it was cooked it smelled like old hay. Our doctors said that if we wanted to go back to Canada we had to eat it and that they were eating it themselves. We'd get animal guts, cut them in pieces and put them in water for soup but we had no salt or anything. We got 395 grams of food a day, divided in two. When we came back, our stomachs had shrunk to the size of a four-year-old child's. I didn't get a single Red Cross parcel or a letter from home in all that time. After the war, the Japanese showed our doctors about a thousand parcels but nobody wanted to touch them in case they had been poisoned. They would steal the chocolate and other things but they didn't know what cheddar cheese was and tried to use it for soap.

We had some bandages and tape which the Japanese furnished and peroxide by the gallon. We had to treat boils, abscesses, malaria, diphtheria and dysentery. Dysentery is death. We had no medicine to get the germ out of the bowels. Our guys were dying all over the place—some in the yard and some sitting on the toilet. They were pale and had terrible cramps and used to go to the toilet twelve times in twelve hours until they were cleaned down to blood and mucus and that was the end. The boys would ask for vitamin injections and one medical secret was that we would boil water and inject about 140 people a night. We called it Vitamin B but it was just water. The doctors ordered that for morale reasons. We were able to get some calcium so, any guy that was run down, we would give him 2 cc. of calcium liquid intra-venously. This gave him energy and the next day the guy was peppy as hell and felt like jumping over the fence. He was like that for three or four days and then would be falling down again.

We were made to go out to Kai Tak Airport and weed the grass. There were two or three Japanese guards and maybe a couple of hundred of our boys. They made them kneel down and weed the grass that grew between the cement squares. Later on, they made them go up a big mountain and bring down clay to widen this airport. They had bare heads and the temperature was about 103 degrees F. Some of them got what we called brain fever. The guys would pass out and I had to get them to the camp. They were out for a month and a half. They'd look at you with no reaction. My job was to force them to drink water. I had a little glass with a beak and, if it was a big guy, two orderlies would help me hold him down and I'd grab his nose and force his mouth open and give him some water until his Adam's apple moved. They had to drink a quart of water a day to stay alive. It was hard work and I used to say to myself, "If there's a God, why should I have a job like this?" Dr. Reid used to tell me that I was saving their lives. About a month and a half later, they would wake up crying and not know where they were.

After a while, there were so many soldiers sick that they opened up a hospital in the big administration camp at Sham Shui Po where our camp had been. It was divided into rooms and we cleaned it out. The Japs had no choice. They were frightened themselves of getting sickness from our boys. We had about three doctors. It's hard to guess how many patients there were, but there were more than one hundred. In my room I had sixteen patients and, every morning when I came in, there was always one gone. We called the doctor, wrapped the corpse in a blanket and then they brought him to the city to be cremated. Eventually, all the prisoners were moved to Sham Shui Po from North Point Camp. I caught diphtheria there, myself. The doctors had enough antitoxin to give an injection to the medical orderlies. You couldn't move for three days after this needle. I was curious and asked Dr. Reid (he was like a father to me) what was in it. He told me that they used sperm from a stallion and we weren't supposed to move because it was too hard on our hearts. I couldn't stand being in bed for three days without moving so I went upstairs to see my friends and, before I got to the top, I fell backwards and was half-conscious. A guy carried me back to my bed. I was also operated on for hemorrhoids while I was wide awake.

The Japanese were in charge and the hospital was like a butcher shop. We did all our operations with our patients fully conscious. We would tape their mouths and tie their hands and feet. I had to check their pulse. The guy would be so clear about what was going on. I used to say, "If there's a God above, why doesn't He let him die on the table instead of going through this torture." Every day, the guard would open up the door and yell, "EE KURA KONJE?" (How many patients?) and then, "NETSU?" (fever?), then "NIAKU?" (pulse?). They had papers and were writing all this down. The next guard would come in and yell and do the same. There was only one guard through all the three-and-a-half years that I met who was decent. A little Japanese, good-looking, short and tubby and *very* polite; he'd knock before he came in and bow to me and then ask the same questions as the others. He was so polite that I couldn't understand that he was Japanese. He always left me a little ball of rice. Captain

Reid told me never to eat any rice given by the guards because it might be poisoned. I said, "Captain Reid, I'm so hungry and the ball of rice looks so nice and white that I'm going to take a chance." For the one month that he was there, he always talked to me and gave me a ball of rice. He told me that he had lived on a farm with his parents and one day an army truck came and took all their vegetables and they took him too and sent him in the army. When he talked to me, I always said, "I don't know," because you couldn't trust them at all. This guy was decent but you couldn't take any chances. If they brought you back to a guard, you'd get a hell of a beating; they'd half kill you.

I was beaten. We were all beaten. Once a Japanese doctor came in with two guards and the interpreter asked us all to take a step forward if we were doing our best to keep our patients alive. So we all took a step forward. He didn't seem to like what we did and then asked his interpreter to ask us to take another step forward if we were doing more than our best to keep the prisoners alive. We did and the doctor got mad and started swinging his bayonet. He got one of our guys to kneel down and was swinging the bayonet over his head. Then he took a water hose, doubled it and beat the doctors and then started in on us. He hit us so hard across the face that we had marks for two or three days. Dr. Crawford then said to the interpreter, "Hold on one minute, please. I want to talk to you. What you are doing right now is an insult on medical life all over the world. We were asked to take a step and we did it and this beating is unacceptable. If ever this war is over, somebody will pay for this because it is unforgettable what you are doing." So he stopped. Dr. Crawford could have been killed right there.

We couldn't talk to each other too much because the Japanese wouldn't allow it. There was a large parade ground and every night before we went to bed, we had to go out and walk for ten minutes. We had an RC priest with us, Father Deloray from Toronto who used to hear the boys' confessions and give absolution as they were walking. He said mass at the beginning but they thought we were gathering to plan an escape so they stopped that. This man came with pitch-black hair and within six months, it was as white as snow. I used to pray a lot and ask myself what was going wrong. If there was a God up above seeing all this, why didn't he stop what was happening? (said emotionally)

When you're caught in a place like that, you just have to try to learn the language. I learned Japanese and never forgot it. It would get you out of a beating. If they spoke to you and you didn't answer in Japanese, you'd get a bang on the head, maybe two. They were pleased as hell if you spoke Japanese. They were very, very impressed with me and used to say to me, "Poirier, you have a good head." I would say, "Thank you very much."

I saw torture in Hong Kong. They had big announcements for the Chinese to walk on one side and, most of them didn't pay attention to these signs. The Japanese would see them coming and kill them right there with machine guns or torture them. Our camp was close to where the tide would come in. I saw an old lady with a kid on her back. She went to get fish when the tide went out. One guy saw her, BANG, and the child was alive until the sea came up and took it. I've seen so many things that it's hard to ... .

In January 1943 we were shipped to Yokohama because there was a lack of food in Hong Kong. When we first got there, they gave us big plates of barley to eat and we thought we were in heaven. It's good for you but too much gives you an allergy and you have big itching sores all over your body. Our doctor told them to make it half-and-half. They didn't want that so we went back to the rotten rice with worms in it. At the shipyard they built gunboats, destroyers and submarines. There were 105,000 Japanese working there. We were about 450 prisoners and were doing all kinds of work. Each guard had maybe five or six men and he had to find work for them, even the officers. Every second day I worked as a medical orderly. If anybody got wounded (it happened many times) the guard would come and get me. I'd patch him up and, if he was too badly injured, we'd have to bring him to the hospital. I worked in the paint shop and we had to paint the ships. We'd go through five gallons of paint in the morning and five in the afternoon.

We had Inouye (Kamloops Kid) in our camp at Yokohama for not even a month. We told the interpreter to get rid of that guy because the boys wanted to kill him. He would make everybody get out, 450 men, and scream at us, "YOU SONS OF WHORE BASTARDS. YOU'RE IN THIS CAMP AND YOU'RE GOING TO PAY FOR IT. WE HATE THE FACES OF THE WHITE MAN. WE'RE GOING TO TORTURE EVERY F——— ONE OF YOU." Talk like that, you know. We used to say, "Where the hell is he coming from?" He was mentally sick and had no brains whatsoever. Torturing us to death and killing us was all he wanted.

When the Americans started bombing Yokohama (they used to bomb the hell out of us) we had to go to work in the mines at Sendai. Of the men who were able, we worked in three shifts with maybe seventy men in each shift. That winter, there were seventy-five boys with pneumonia and some died.

Others had water on their lungs and Capt. Reid used to puncture their lungs with a long needle and take the water out. I had a pretty good job because I was an orderly. They gave me the job of bringing down the empty coal cars and bringing up the loaded ones.

One day, just as the second shift was preparing to go down the mine, everything stopped and the interpreter called our officers into the office and they heard that Tojo had given up. Our officers were frightened in case our boys would run wild so they came into our huts and told us the war was over. We were told to be quiet and polite and not to get excited or be friendly with the guards. The civilians outside wanted to kill us because we were eating their rice so our officers asked the Japanese commanding officer to leave guards with loaded rifles around our camp. The Japanese guards would try to talk to us but we had spite against them because of what they had done to us and to all our friends. The Americans would fly by and drop notes to us. One note said that a C-54 would be dropping barrels of food so we were told to get away and go close to the woods. One day we got a note asking if a certain guy was in our camp and, if so, to make a YES on the ground with stones. The next day, two pilots came down and waved their wings to salute their friend but they went too close to the flagpole and crashed and burned right there. Nobody could get close to the plane and it was a pitiful day. Everybody was in mourning and did they ever cry.

We were kept in Sendai until we got on trains to go to Tokyo. The American army was there with bands and everything. My God, we thought we were in heaven and *so glad to be free.* (said very emotionally) We had come in coal cars and were all black. As soon as we got off the train, there were American orderlies who washed us with disinfecting soap and sent us to doctors. They had seven or eight doctors. We went on board the huge battleship *Wisconsin.* There were 3,000 sailors on board. General MacArthur was standing there with the admiral. They shook our hands and said, "Well done, boys. We're glad you're aboard." There were 128 of us and each one of us had a sailor to take care of us. The sailor who took care of me was (I'll never forget his name) Leonard Woznick from Ohio. He said, "You look just like my friend. Anything you want, just ask me." We were dressed all in white like sailors and used to eat and sleep on the deck in big hammocks with nice navy blankets. It was just like paradise. The band used to come and play for breakfast and dinner. We couldn't eat much. Most of us would go for ice cream and they had lots of that. We were allowed anything we wanted except liquor.

We got on a plane in Tokyo and landed in Guam where we spent a week with more medical tests. From there we went to McDowen Island near San Francisco. Government people from Ottawa, all the big shots, were there and shook our hands. They gave each of us an envelope with $100 from "the people of Canada" to spend. We then took the train and landed in Seattle. Then it was a five-and-a-half hour boat trip to Victoria. I thought it was a beautiful place with nicely kept trees and flowers and told myself that I would make my home there but I never did. I couldn't leave my parents. We took the train from Vancouver and nothing was missing. We had porters at each end and, whatever we wanted, they would give us. We stopped at each station to let some of the boys off. At every station there were big crowds, big bands and signs, THE BOYS ARE BACK FROM HONG KONG. There were volunteers to take us around each city but most of us didn't want to go. I was weak and not feeling too well. We were really run-down and couldn't eat much.

Then we got to Quebec City. There were thousands of cops, hand in hand, holding back the people who wanted to grab us, kiss us and talk to us. They had a great big banquet for us at the Château Frontenac but none of us wanted to go. We all felt the same, we were just anxious to take the train and go home. I wasn't interested in what they were doing or how polite they were. I just wanted to go home and the closer we got, the more excited we all got and we cried and everything. I felt a bit shy about reaching home. I didn't know if anybody had died or anything and I had a big ball of fire in my stomach.

At Campbellton, my parents were there to bring me to my sister's house. She had a big sign, WELCOME HOME, PAT, FROM HONG KONG. The worst thing for me after working in the hospital was going through towns and meeting people from New Richmond, Cascapédia and all along the Gaspé coast. They asked me about their sons. "My son Maurice. What did he die of? Did he suffer?" I cried and cried. I couldn't help it. (said emotionally) Some of these guys had died in my arms. It was too hard on me and I couldn't take it.

My mother went blind worrying about me. She went for days at a time without eating and my father got really uneasy and thought she was going to go nuts. She'd send my father and brother to the barn and, when she was alone in the house, she'd cry and scream. When I came back, was she ever happy to see that I was normal! She couldn't see but touched my arms, legs and face. I talked to her and cried and cried. I just can't tell you how it felt to be home. I couldn't realize I was home and it seemed like a dream.

We were no sooner home than we got a ticket to go to St. Charles Hospital in Quebec City. They had a special place there for "Hong Kongers". We had to go on account of our pension. If you refused, you could be cut off. They kept us for about two weeks and we were punctured with all kinds of needles, vitamin B and all the other vitamins. When I left I weighed 155 pounds and when I came back I weighed ninety-five. We got impatient with all those damn needles in us and finally the doctors let us go home. For about six months, I used to go to sleep and dream and then BANG I used to throw myself off the bed. I thought somebody was after me with a bayonet and thought I was going to die in my bed. Everybody would get up and find me on the floor. They'd ask, "Are you in pain? What's the matter? Are you sick?" I knew that I was making my family uneasy but there was nothing I could do.

It's unbelievable that I'm here today at my age and there aren't many of us. Out of 2,000, there are about 125 of us left. This experience changed me and it stayed with me. I saw torture in front of my eyes. The Japanese had no respect whatsoever for Canadians or any white man.

David L. Hart

The Dieppe raid of August 19,1942 was planned for many reasons: to provide war experience for well-trained and avid Canadian troops; to provide practice for the huge invasion of France which was to come; to appease Allied public demands and to answer the Russian request that we do something to take the pressure off their imperilled troops. Of the more than 6,000 troops involved, nearly 5,000 were Canadian. When it was over, 907 Canadians were dead and nearly 1,900 had become prisoners of war. It was the costliest day ever in our military history and its value is still being debated today. If there were many victims on that day, there were also many heroes and Sergeant David Hart was one of them, winning the Military Medal for bravery in the field. On August 26, 1939, the future accountant closed the two ledgers he was working on and reported to his armoury, and that was the last he saw of any accounting until his discharge in June 1945. During the war, he served as a signalman with 2nd Divisional Signals. He ended the war with the rank of lieutenant and is still active in the military, having been appointed honorary lieutenant colonel, 712 Communication Squadron in 1976, a position he still holds.

IN 1938, you could see the clouds of war coming and I was anxious to do my part for my country. I was in the 4th Divisional Signals in the reserves and when war was declared, they asked us if we wanted to go active. Of course, everybody said yes and I was brought to the Sun Life Building for a medical. Everything was fine except that the sergeant told me I was too short and wouldn't accept me. I made such a noise that the medical officer came out and asked what was going on. The sergeant told him, "This soldier won't accept his rejection. He's half an inch too short." So he looks at me. I was very well built and in all kinds of sports. He says, "What's your name, soldier?" I told him my name was Hart and he asked if I had a brother Paul in the McGill COTC. I said, "Yes, sir." He said, "Paul and I are fellow officers and we must have measured you wrong." He ruffled the hair that I had in those days and that's how I got in.

I spent two years in England and then they decided to take two brigades for the training for the Dieppe raid. The 6th Brigade, which was comprised of the South Saskatchewan Regiment, the Cameron Highlanders of Winnipeg, and the Fusiliers Mont-Royal. They also took elements of the First Army Tank

Brigade. Now, the 4th Brigade—which is what I was in—consisted of the Essex Scottish, the Royal Hamilton Light Infantry and the Royal Regiment of Canada. I think the Fusiliers had one company of the Black Watch. We also had engineers with assignments to blow up various things. We also had a chap who was a radar specialist from the British air force whose job it was to land with the South Saskatchewan Regiment, and twelve people were assigned to him. His job was to find out how their radar worked and the twelve people with him were to protect him but if he was captured, they were to kill him because he knew so much about our radar. We took full commando training for the raid and I was in the best shape ever in all my life.

We didn't know what we were doing until we got aboard ship on July 2, 1942 and Brigadier Lett, who was the brigade commander, gathered everybody up on deck and said, "Men, this is it. We're going into action." You never heard such a sustained cheer in all your life! It took about five minutes before he was able to quieten us down. He told us that we would be briefed later in the day. The ship's captain came to him just before supper and told him that all the table knives had disappeared. You know why? All the fellows went down to the ship's armourer and made commando daggers out of them. That's the kind of zeal we had. We were trained extremely well. We knew the locations and the objectives and were given maps that we could sew into our jacket linings. We had buttons on our trousers which, if you put two of them together, would make a compass for escape purposes. We were also given French money. The weather was beautiful but the winds were so strong that the paratroopers (who were to secure both flanks) would have been dispersed all over and wouldn't have been effective. We stayed aboard that ship until July 9 when we were told that we weren't going to go in but would stand down. We were also told not to talk about it.

All of the 5,000 troops went from the Isle of Wight back to the mainland. Now, we had all been permitted to write last letters with the idea that, if we went in, they would be posted and, if we didn't, they would be destroyed. Somehow or other, some of these letters got posted and I, as a signals superintendent, was fielding calls from girlfriends all over England asking, "What Dieppe raid? We didn't see anything in the paper." So, I'm positive the Germans knew. When we were given the planning on July 2, our intelligence was that they had 1,000 troops there. We were going in with 6,000 troops so the planning was okay. Montgomery overruled Mountbatten and said that we had the firepower, the battleships, the heavy bombers and a six to one advantage to attempt a frontal attack. The pressure by the Russians to do something was so intense that, on August 18, we went in. I must emphasize that, by the time we did, the Germans had reinforced the area and now had 6,000 troops so now we were one to one. A principle of war is you never attempt a frontal assault on a beach on an equal basis. You must have at least a three to one superiority, which we didn't, but nobody knew that. Secondly, the navy had pulled off the battleships and "Bomber" Harris took away the heavy bombers because he said he had better targets to hit in Germany, so we were left sort of defenceless except for the Mosquito bombers that came in at dawn.

I was awakened at six o'clock in the morning on August 18 in my barracks and my commanding officer, even then, didn't tell me that the raid was on. He said we were going on an exercise of movement and that I had to rouse the men and make sure that they took their weapons, kit and equipment with them. I said, "Another goddamned exercise." So I went and woke the men and I got an even worse reaction from them. Nobody took their weapons because they thought they didn't need them for an exercise. In my backpack, instead of putting stuff that I needed, I put 1,000 cigarettes that I had received from Montreal. We arrived at New Haven at six o'clock at night and that's when my commanding officer came over and said, "Sergeant, this is it. We're going to do Dieppe again." I said, "WHAT!" He told me to brief my men and then we loaded our gear onto a tank landing craft (which neither I nor the guys had trained on) and we started off in convoy. There were about 287 boats of all sizes going across quietly until about three o'clock in the morning when the Number 3 Commandos met with an E-boat patrol which gave the whole show away. Not only that; on that flank, the Royal Regiment was 15 minutes late and, instead of landing at first light, they arrived at dawn. This area was absolutely sheer wall and they had enfilade fire from the side and enfilade fire from the top. In addition, the Germans on the top of the cliff where the fellows were taking shelter against the sea wall would pull grenades and just drop them over on them, just like that. So the poor Royal Regiment came back with about twenty-three men out of 600. The Essex Scottish came out with about thirty-five men. A terrible disaster. The Royal Hamilton Light Infantry had a little more success at the Casino. The South Saskatchewan Regiment and the Cameron Highlanders went in about three miles and had quite a bit of success. The commanding officer of the SSR, Cecil Merritt, got the VC for showing the fellows that there was no problem crossing a bridge. The 4th Commando had tremendous success, too.

It was quiet as we were going over. The Royal Regiment on "Blue Beach" and the South Saskatchewans on "Green Beach" were the first to land. We were to land at dawn at the main beach which was called "Red Beach" (very well-named!) and when we did, the Essex had already dropped off their men. As the ramp went down, the steel of the ramp was replaced by the steel of the bullets that were coming in. We took whatever shelter we could and the tanks went off one by one. As each tank went off, the ship moved a bit farther back so the last tank landed in about four feet of water. The ship moved back until there was six feet of water. Then the landing ship moved back a little farther and the next thing I knew a shell had severed the chain that held the ramp so the ramp went straight down and embedded itself in the sand and we were stuck. We were moving this way and that and, of course, whichever way we moved we were being shot at. I didn't think of the dangers because I had a job to do. Then the motor got knocked off by the shellfire. If they had ever hit the helium pipes for the barrage balloons that we had above us, then all of us would have been gone but fortunately that didn't happen.

I had to drag my radio set on what we called a "baby dolly" which had two wheels and was necessary because in communications we also had to lay cable. You hang the cable on a pole and roll the cable out so we adapted this for our 19-set by making a box and putting this box on this dolly. Three of us had to haul this thing because it was so heavy. The 19-set was experimental at that time but it proved its efficiency and that's what was used for all communication until the end of the war because it had two main frequencies plus an intercom with a range of about five miles. The set was on top and underneath were two 185-hour ampere batteries which were big and heavy. We also had about a thousand rounds of ammunition on it for our troops in case we were successful. It was ideal for tanks because the intercom was within the tank. One frequency was from tank to tank in the squadron and the other was for speaking to headquarters so it was very efficient. (Matter of fact, they were made here by Marconi in Montreal and the Russians got a lot of them from us as well.) We wore earphones so we couldn't hear the noise as much and we also had to concentrate because in those days we didn't have pinpoint accuracy and had to "net" the radio set. Nowadays you just press a button and you're bing on but with a dial, until you get it exact you have distortion and don't get it right.

I don't know what happened to our intelligence but it was terrible. A Churchill tank can surmount a low fence about three feet high but the fence was seven feet high where we were, so the tanks would come up and get knocked off when they were hit in their underbelly which wasn't reinforced. Their tracks also got knocked off by the shale of the beach. There were cliffs on the right and the left and that's where the Germans had these batteries of 6-inch guns firing at us. We had destroyers that were providing answering fire but they only had 4-inch guns and even 6-inch guns don't have the same power at sea as they do on land. So we were outgunned and our casualties were absolutely frightful. I passed one message to Brigadier-General Churchill Mann, who was the general staff officer 1. I told him that twelve men of the Essex Scottish had reported that they had penetrated the town. He took that to mean that the Essex had penetrated the town and that's when he committed the Fusiliers Mont-Royal. I got on the air and said, "What the hell are you doing? There's a disaster here." He told me that they were already committed and it was too late.

We were supposed to come back at eleven o'clock in the morning. That was the planning. At about 10 o'clock our people realized that it was an absolute disaster and they decided that the only way they could get survivors out was to send the boats in sooner. They gave the orders through me and I was able to get the order out to the Essex and the RHLI. By this time, the Fusiliers Mont-Royal were also committed. The way you work is when you're on the air operating a radio set you always have a controller at the other end. Headquarters was trying to contact 6th Brigade with the South Saskatchewans and the Camerons but they were too far away. So I got on the air and told them that, with my overlapping frequencies, perhaps I could contact them and give them the order. They told me that I was the only one in communication and they didn't want me to get off the air. I promised that I would be back in two minutes and they said okay. So I got off the air and I had to search. It's not like where you have an instant frequency. You have to tune a dial and the 18-set is very sensitive. I was communicating about three miles away to the SSR and the Camerons. I contacted them, gave them the order to come out and was back on the air in about half a minute. I told headquarters that I had given the order to these people to come out and, as a result, we got at least 600 people out of there, which I didn't know until I got back.

It took until about 11 o'clock before everybody who could got out. Our landing craft was left there and we couldn't move. I was resigned to becoming a prisoner of war or being shot. We could see prisoners being dragged off. I had my revolver out at one point wanting to shoot at the Germans if I could but a revolver at that distance would do nothing. Then the navy came in with two motor launches, hooked themselves one on either side of our craft and towed us all the way back to England. As we were being towed back, of course, we were being attacked by dive bombers all the way. I don't understand why they didn't knock off the barrage balloon that we had and they wouldn't have had those chains and wires to avoid. We had all kinds of wounded men because we were the last ship going back and got splashed as bombs dropped on both sides of the boat.

We didn't get back to Brighton until three in the morning on the 20th so effectively, I hadn't had any sleep or food since six o'clock in the morning of the 18th. We had been toughened up because part of our training was being given four hours sleep and one meal every forty-eight hours. I went in with twenty-five men and came back with eight. I was the second-in-command as a sergeant and, since my commanding officer had been wounded and shipped off to hospital, they wanted to debrief me before I could get some sleep. They said that I must be very thirsty and I said I was. So they gave me a big mug full of navy rum. My crew and I had smoked about 700 of the 1,000 cigarettes that I had with me. My throat was so raw that I didn't feel the rum going down as I "chuggalugged" it. To this day, I can't tell you what I told them. (laughs) Then I got piled into the back of a truck and they trucked me back to my barracks.

The men acquitted themselves absolutely fabulously. One of my people, Jim Crosby, was with the Essex Scottish. He was a signalman, just a private, in other words, and he was reporting back to me on the radio set. The first thing that the Germans were shooting at was the means of communication, not the officers. Crosby's radio set was knocked off and he couldn't communicate. He looked around and saw a dead signaller with an 18-set. He got it to work and helped Colonel Jasperson by giving him communication and calling for air force fire on their position to protect them. He was taken prisoner but subsequently, on the basis of my report, got an MM as well because he saved a lot of people.

The raid might have been successful. It's true that 5,000 Canadian soldiers were involved and it looks, from our point of view, like a Canadian show with all the Canadians being sacrificed, but we had Royal Marine Commandos and fifty American Rangers with us. I feel *terrible* about the men who were killed but, if we hadn't done it, we would have gone into D-Day with the same kind of thinking, committing 250,000 to 300,000 troops who would have suffered the same casualties. The lessons we learned were that we needed heavy air and naval support (16-inch guns do an awful lot of damage) and self-propelled artillery. They realized that you can't go into a heavily defended port because in most cases they have cliffs on either side and, coming up the middle, you're going to get knocked off. With the mulberries (artificial harbours) they were able to get in on the open beaches.

I was with my unit doing my signal office duties when my former commanding officer who had come back from the hospital, came racing up the stairs at the billet one day and said, "Sergeant Hart! Good news! You just got awarded the Military Medal and you're going to Buckingham Palace to get it." I knew that I had gotten some people out but I didn't realize how many I had saved. I was able to contact my two brothers, Paul, who was the adjutant of the Royal 22nd ('Van Doos'), and Eddy, who was with the Second Corps Signals. They were both in England and were able to get leave. So the three of us went to Buckingham Palace and we went into the Gold Room. I've never seen such a beautiful place in all my life. There was a group of us there—various air force types and many from the Dieppe raid. Each one of us went up before the King and he spoke to us for a couple of minutes. I was much more nervous than he was. He was interested and asked a lot of questions about Dieppe and what I did and so on. They claim he used to stutter but I didn't notice that at all. Then my brothers and I went to a restaurant and had a meal and something to drink.

You used to be able to get out of the army with points. You got fifteen points for every month you were overseas and, with fifty points, you could get a discharge once the war was over and you were back here. I had 217 points and couldn't get out. I was stationed in Longueuil as a lieutenant in the appraisal wing which had a number of people coming through to be discharged. One day, my commanding officer—who started as a private and became a major without leaving Longueuil—got a call from the second-in-command of the base to come down to the medical inspection room because the Black Watch were rioting. The Black Watch were waiting to be discharged and were mad as anything at their treatment and were starting to smash up the place. This major was not going to go in and neither was this captain (who got promoted the same way as the major). The captain looked around, saw me and said, "Hart, you go." So I went up there. The guys had benches in their hands and were starting to smash the walls. I could hear them say, "Kill the little bastard. He's not going to stop us," as I worked my way to the front. I got up on a bench because I'm a little guy and put my arms out for them to stop.

These guys were infused with anger. They had been through hell and back; they hated the army and just wanted to get out. The guys in front saw my medal and said, "He's been overseas. He's wearing the Military Medal and has 2 Div. patches." The Black Watch were 5th Brigade and came from 2 Div. so they all stopped. I said, "What's the problem?" The problem was that a French sergeant was processing the Zombies ahead of them. In addition to that, they said that they couldn't understand him when he called their names because of his accent. I told one of the sergeants to call their names and to let them go first to be examined. At that point, everything was quiet. The major, who was second-in-command of the base, was lurking in the background and the medical officer, a captain, came out and told me that I was only a lieutenant and was not going to disrupt his work. I told him he had created a riot and he would do it my way. At that point, the major came out and told him to do what I said. So, because I stopped the riot and was doing a good job, I couldn't get my discharge. I wanted to get back to my accounting career and so one day in the mess, I got the second-in-command a little loaded and gave him my story. The next day, June 28, 1945, I was discharged. I handed in my first assignment on a correspondence course in accounting the next day and I finished two year's studies in five months, coming in seventh in the province.

As far as I'm concerned, the military part of my career has been very satisfying. I've never had any problems (aside from the dangers involved), made marvellous friendships and have had a better look at Canada. I still feel that if we, as Canadians, got our children to go into the service for two or three years, it would be good for them. I have a very strong feeling about reservists. They are twice the citizen because they work during the day and volunteer their time at night and on weekends. Our reservist communicators have been in every peace-keeping duty that we have had. Cyprus, the Golan Heights, Kosovo, Bosnia, Kuwait, you name it—they've been there. Until recently they weren't allowed to shoot back as we were and that takes a lot of guts, so I'm really proud of our military people and try to promote them as much as I can.

Even Rover could help with the war effort by donating his bone. Glycerine in fat and bones was extracted for war use.
The Point News. Courtesy of Frank Monroe.

Arthur Fraser

When Arthur Fraser (a bilingual francophone in spite of his name) left his five-dollar-a-week job in a grocery store to join Les Fusiliers Mont-Royal with five friends, he had no idea what lay before him. What the future held for this seventeen-year-old was: surviving the Dieppe disaster; becoming a prisoner of war until 1945; spending about fourteen months in shackles and, in the dead of winter at the end of the war, being made to endure a three-month forced march. He is the president of the Dieppe Veterans' Association and still has a pair of handcuffs used by the Germans to shackle the Canadians. Because of his experience, even today he will not, if he can help it, buy products made in Germany or Japan.

WE WERE THE LAST BATTALION to land at Dieppe. We landed at seven o'clock in the morning and our job was to stay on the beach and protect the troops as they were coming back from the town and getting on boats to go back to England. So we were the last to land and we were supposed to be the last to go back on the ship but it didn't happen that way. It was really terrible to see all the wounded fellows and the dead bodies. These fellows had been pinned down and couldn't go any further. The water wasn't green. The water for about three or four feet out was red with the blood of our comrades.

There was an officer who was wearing a Scottish cap, not a helmet, and smoking a cigarette with a holder. When I passed him, he said, "I told them to tell you not to land." I don't know why this officer didn't get shot because he was walking up and down the beach like there was nothing. At a quarter to three in the afternoon, we were told to stop shooting and the officer asked for one volunteer to go and stand on a sunken landing craft with a white flag. So one soldier went up with a white flag on the end of his rifle and the Germans shot him. The same thing happened to a second volunteer. Next the officer sent up a German prisoner so they stopped shooting. We raised our hands and the Germans made us take off our steel helmets and throw them on the ground. I was mad and I'm sure I wasn't the only one. We were very well trained and it was our first time in action.

We marched to the Dieppe Hospital with our wounded. A German doctor came out and said that he wanted different blood types. One of our officers told him that we didn't have blood types in our army and the doctor said that he didn't have time to take blood tests. Because of that, I'm sure that many of our soldiers passed away in the yard of the hospital and, for those left on the beach, it was the same thing. The German steel helmets made an impression on me and I noticed that the soldiers that were there were older than myself so they must have seen other action during the war.

We stayed there for maybe an hour or so and then they made us get up and walk fourteen kilometers to Envermeu. They took us to a plaster factory and the officers were taken to a church across the street. The Germans gave us a piece of black bread which to me, eating black bread for the first time, tasted sour. We hadn't eaten since the night before so we ate it. They gave us tea or coffee but we didn't have anything to put it in. The next day we walked to the railroad station and were put in boxcars and taken to another camp which, I was told, was about forty miles from Paris. They interrogated us but that was nothing to talk about. They asked us our names and numbers. One of the interrogators told me, "We've been waiting for you. Eleven days we've been waiting for you." Of course I didn't answer. I think we stayed there for a week but I'm not sure. It was a long time ago. The Vichy government gave us French Canadians some cake and two packages of Gauloise cigarettes each. The officer in charge said, "We all fought together and you should share what you received with the English Canadians." We all agreed to do that. When I opened my package of cigarettes and took my first puff, I fainted so I gave my cigarettes away. From there we took a boxcar again. This one had straw on the floor and a can in the corner. Three fellows escaped from the boxcar and jumped somewhere in France: Dumais, Cloutier and Vermette. I was supposed to be one of them but they told me not to go between the cars because they couldn't hang on very well.

Our next stop was Stalag VIII B in Silesia. There were many nationalities in that camp: English, Australian, New Zealand, Hindus, Jews from Palestine and others. I didn't care for the fellow who was in charge of the French Canadians so I went with the English Canadians. The Germans put a rough string around our wrists, which were crossed in front of us, and we were tied like that for twenty-four hours a day for three months. I slept on the top bunk and the lights were on all night. So to cover my head with the blanket, I undid my string. The guard saw me: *"Kommen Sie hier."* The punishment was that I had my hands tied behind my back and had to stand with my nose and toes touching the wall. If you moved your nose away from the wall, they would slap you. I was lucky. I only stayed there for about half an hour and then they changed guards. They could have made me stand like that for three hours. We got all kinds of sores and blisters on our hands from the cord and when the Red Cross came and saw us, they told the Germans they would have to do something else. Then we were handcuffed from eight to five o'clock every day. We were shackled like that for about fourteen months.

When the Germans shouted, "'*Raus, 'Raus*," we all went into the yard for roll call. Sometimes they just counted us and other times, especially in winter, they made us stay out a long time. We didn't speak to them and they didn't speak to us. They changed them often too. There were courses in English and other things that we could take but since I didn't know if I would be alive the next day, I didn't take any. I spent two Christmases in that camp and I couldn't make myself believe that I was going to come back and see my family again. I lived from day-to-day and didn't pay any attention to anything. There was no future for me that I could see. I knew if I lived that long, that I would be released but I never really believed it because if a bomb drops on your camp, you're dead, that's it. From the time I left Halifax until I came back in May 1945, my life was never sure. There was one fellow in my barracks from out West whose hair turned white in three months. He would always walk with this other fellow. One day I asked his friend, "What happened to him?" He told me that he had received a letter from a neighbour saying that his wife was going out with somebody else.

If you had something to do, it wasn't too bad. I got involved in the black market. All these prison camps have a black market. The first prisoners to arrive at that camp were the English who were captured at Dunkirk. Since they were there before us, they worked in the kitchen and had control of everything. They would swipe or buy bread from the Germans for, maybe twenty cigarettes and sell them to me for fifty cigarettes. We were divided by a barbed wire fence that was ten feet high. When I saw that the guard had his eyes somewhere else, I used to jump the fence and go and pick up my bread, pay the fifty cigarettes, put it in my tunic and jump back over the fence. I also got potatoes, sugar and boots and the money was always cigarettes. With cigarettes you could buy different things.

Most of us fellows, if we are alive today, it is because of the Red Cross parcels that we got. The box would weigh about ten pounds. We'd get cans of Kam or sockeye salmon which we would eat with our German potato rations. We used to get Kraft cheese in a cardboard box but, by the time we got it, it was no good. Sometimes, we got English parcels. They were good but the portions were smaller. We were allowed one letter a month which we wrote on waxy paper. There were about twenty-five or twenty-eight lines on these sheets. If you said that you weren't fed enough or something else that they didn't like, they'd cross it out with a black pencil, so you couldn't say very much. As you know, a lot of the ships were sunk so mail from home was not regular. We had entertainment in the camp. Once we had a vaudeville show; all the fellows were dressed in dresses with red lipstick and makeup and were kissing each other. Oh geez! I said to the fellow beside me, "They're kissing. There are women here." He told me they were all soldiers.

As a soldier, you're supposed to escape. The only way we could escape was to take our chains off and change identity with somebody else. There were some Jews from Palestine who were sent to work in coal mines every day so a few of us changed identity with them. They slept in our barracks and we went to work in the mines. When we got there, the Jewish fellow in charge knew damn well that we were not Palestinians. He offered us a cup of coffee and, talking to him, we had confidence in him so we told him that we were trying to find a way to escape and needed a contact with a Polish civilian. We never got one. They mixed us in with a Polish group and every day we were supposed to fill sixteen boxcars but we didn't want to work too hard for the Germans. The Jews told us nothing so we didn't know that if we didn't work hard, the Poles had to do our work. Of course, the next day we started to work. We also didn't know that the Poles had nothing to eat and when we ate our sandwich at noon, these guys were "eating" with us. Every time we opened our mouths, they did the same. The Poles had nothing to eat. *Nothing.* After that we stopped bringing our lunch and worked our eight hours without food. The Jew in charge stooled on us to the Germans, saying we were Canadians who were trying to escape. For that we got a one-week detention in a tin box which was like an oven in daytime but freezing at night. We only got bread and water that week.

We were sent to Stalag IID, another camp in Stargard (then Germany) in April 1944 and stayed there for about a month. In that camp there were some Russian POWs who were really badly treated. We used to give our soup to them because they had no food and were dying. The fellows who were still living would take dead men out and squeeze them between them so they could be counted at roll call and get their rations. I personally saw this and I'm sure others did too. Then it started to smell and the Germans found out what they were doing. So they got a wagon and filled it up with the dead bodies of these Russian soldiers.

Then about forty of us were sent to work on a big farm with about 500 acres.

When our officer saw where we were supposed to sleep, he asked them to take us back to the camp. It was filthy and terrible. The German in charge, a civilian wearing a Nazi button, was going to hit us with his cane. We all got around him and told him that he was a civilian and, if he raised his cane to us, something would happen to him. Then he asked the three German soldiers to hit us and they said that we were special prisoners and were not allowed to be hit. We were then given whitewash so we could paint the place and new hay for our palliasses. The German CO told him that he couldn't push us and, as long as we kept moving, that was all right. This guy didn't want us but he had to keep us.

For us the march started on the farm which was near Leipzig. The Russians had invaded Germany and at two o'clock in the morning on January 1, 1945, the Germans came and told us we had to leave. We made ourselves a little sleigh and put all our stuff on it. Working on the farm, we were able to swipe cabbages and potatoes. We knew the war was coming to an end and maybe we wouldn't get any more rations or parcels. And it happened; from then till the end of the war, we didn't get any Red Cross parcels. We left at six in the morning and there was snow up to our knees. Every day we walked and one time we crossed the Autobahn about three times so we must have been walking in circles. We called it, "The Death March" because, if you fell, they would shoot you. At night we used to push the snow away and sleep in fields, three or four of us together to keep warm. All the names of the towns and villages had been taken off so we didn't know where we were. One time we saw three people that were hanged and a civilian told us that it was the mayor and two town executives who had decided to run away so they grabbed them and hanged them. The guards were walking too and at night, they had to guard us so we had a few breaks so they could rest. When we started, we were about forty and, as we walked the group got bigger and bigger.

On April 23, I escaped with Jacques Buteau and a fellow from New Brunswick because the Germans gave us one loaf of bread for forty men. We thought that there wouldn't be any food at all the next day. In Germany the winters are not as tough as here and the German farmers used to cover their vegetables with hay so we knew we could swipe food. At night we left the gang and started to walk. We found a barn, went in and slept very well because we were very tired. The next day we started walking and met six French POWs who were working in the area. Three of them wanted to help us and three didn't. We asked them where the front line was and they told us it was on the other side of the river. They told us to stay in the bush and they would feed us. They brought us water too, but not very much and that's what I suffered from the most and my tongue was swollen. We stayed eleven days in the bush, which is a long time. We dug a hole and slept below the surface. One morning, we woke up and heard shooting. We went to the edge of the woods and saw a big tank with a red star on it which meant they were Russians. Later in the afternoon, watching again, we saw seventeen Russian soldiers walking in single file and carrying Tommy guns. Following them in a car was a Russian officer. When we saw them, we came out of the bush and went to the French hut and told them. The Russians took the village over and the French told them that we were Canadians. They didn't understand but then he told them that we were Americans. "*Kamerad, Kamerad.*" They shook hands and brought us to an officer who had five watches on his arms. They weren't working. He didn't know that the pin on the side was to wind them. *He was an officer!* Then he wanted to give us a pile of Russian occupation money. I should have taken it but I didn't. A truck with a white flag full of people came along and, when it was about 200 yards from us, he gave orders to shoot. In that same village, a French first aid man came and told us to come with him into a house. We went in and saw a young girl of about fifteen, naked and screaming. She had been raped by seventeen Russian soldiers and was cut all over and covered with blood. This was revenge.

The next day, this officer told us where the front was. We told ourselves that we had walked enough so we went into a barn and swiped a horse and a wagon. On the way out of the village we were stopped by two Russian soldiers. They were young girls and they came with us. We were told that wherever we went, we had to report to the Russian in charge of the village and tell him where we were sleeping. That night, while we were sleeping, two Russian soldiers came in with rifles looking for the girls. If we had been sleeping with those two Russian girls, I wouldn't be here today. We kept going until we got to a big city and were told that this was the end of the Russian side. Our horse was stolen—probably for soup. We swiped bicycles and rode all night until we saw a bridge. The Russians (all drunk) were on one side and the Americans on the other. We crossed and a soldier told us to report to an officer. "Did you have breakfast? We said no. He told us to line up and the cook took two fresh eggs and asked, "How would you like your eggs?" FRESH EGGS! And then he showed us two slices of white bread. And this is on the front line! We ate the food they gave us but didn't ask for more. I wasn't in too bad shape but I was thin and weighed about ninety pounds. Then a jeep came and took us to our camp. On the way, we went into a big city that looked like there had been no war. We asked the American driver to let us off and we went into a pastry shop. There was nobody there so we went behind the counter and started to take some pastries. Then a woman came and started to shout at us. We knew all the bad words in German and started to call her every name we could think of. She called her husband and he came and told her to let us take them. We came out, stole a motorcycle which none of us knew how to drive, and drove the three kilometers to the camp in second gear.

At our camp we were told that the cafeteria was open twenty-four hours a day. We had a shower, but kept our old clothes. There were all kinds of meetings and movies. We flew to Brussels where we came under British command. We were deloused, given a new uniform, boots, and 800 francs to spend (worth about $20 at that time). Then we went to England, cup of tea and all that, and then I got a pass to go to Brighton. I spent about fifteen days there and then took the boat home. After the war, I wanted to get back to civilian life and earn my living honestly and forget about the army. I worked first in Dow Brewery and then bought myself a Veterans' Taxi. I sold my taxi after eight years and then worked as a private chauffeur for thirty-seven years. When I was working, my mind was on my work, but when I took my pension, all the memories of the war came back. At night I would have nightmares and I even slapped my wife in the face two or three times. So now we can't even sleep together.

Bernard Finestone

Bernard Finestone was a rarity in the pacifist and war-weary Depression years. To please his father, a World War I veteran, he enlisted in the McGill University COTC in 1937. His father's words, "I don't care what they say. There's a war coming." were prophetic. Before graduation, he joined the armoured corps and, after nine months of training, he joined the 9th Armoured Regiment (British Columbia Dragoons) as a lieutenant in September 1941 and left for overseas one month later. Soon promoted to captain, he served as senior liaison officer at 5th Canadian Armoured Brigade Headquarters and later at the 5th Canadian Armoured Division Headquarters. In November 1943, he embarked for Italy. He is the recipient of the Croix de Guerre (France). Still active in the insurance business, he also maintains his links with the military. He is the honorary colonel of the BCDs, serves on the council and executive of the Royal Canadian Armoured Corps Association and is the major and Montreal garrison commander of the 78th Fraser Highlanders. He is also the secretary of the executive of the honorary colonels of Canada.

THE FIRST PLACE we went to in England was Marlborough, a beautiful town about eighty miles west of London and not too far from Aldershot. We spent two years training and there was a vast amount of it. We were far from fully trained and had no equipment. We finally got tanks and were learning to fight as troops, as squadrons, as regiments, as brigades, as divisions, and even as corps. We had something very funny happen to us that we never understood and we thought the army was "out of their tree". About every four weeks, we were moved somewhere else and always at night. We'd be moved to Crowborough or Bournemouth or Brighton or Aldershot. I never understood it until I read Churchill's books. All the men who had come back from Dunkirk left their equipment in France and they were busy trying to re-equip them. We were the only division that was fully equipped with tanks and Churchill was moving us around so the German reconnaissance, when they came over, would discover an armoured division in Bournemouth and then, a few weeks later, would see one up near Aldershot or in Woking. He was trying to persuade them that he had lots of armoured divisions. So we were busy moving around and training for war and going on courses.

We went to Italy in October 1943 in a very large convoy which, unfortunately, was torpedo-bombed two nights before we arrived off Cape Bon in the Mediterranean. We had no casualties but we lost two ships and one of them was carrying all our medical people—the hospital, field dressing stations and the dentists. The other ships rallied around and we pulled everybody out but they lost all their equipment. That was exciting and so was landing in Naples. They were fighting at the far end of the town and we landed at the bottom end. We got re-equipped. We took all the obsolete equipment that had been ditched by the famous Desert Rats of the British 8th Army when they went back to England to get ready for the second front. It had gone all the way through Africa but at least it moved and we started to train to 8th Army standards getting ready for the breakthrough. We were training with British people who had seen a great deal of action. Some Canadian officers also had fought with the British so we had some war veterans with us. At that point, I was posted as a liaison officer to 5 Div. and was doing staff work which meant

(Above)
A group of Royal Rifles of Canada approaching Hong Kong.
For those who survived the battle, starvation, maltreatment,
and torture awaited in Japanese prison camps.
National Archives of Canada, PA-1666999

(Below)
Lt. Bernard Finestone (left) with Jack Cook on the firing
range in England. This picture was taken through the gunsight
of a Sherman tank.

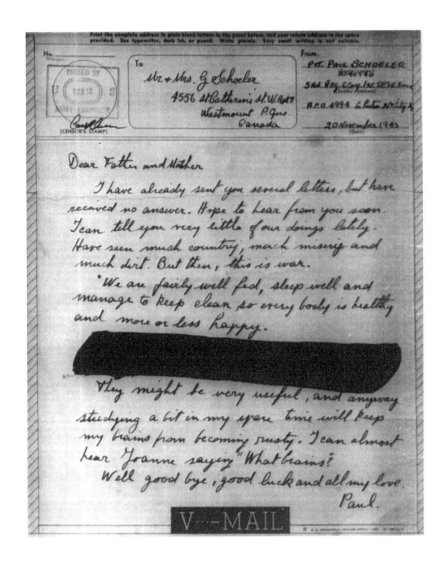

Letter (showing the heavy hand of the censor) written by Paul Schoeler to his parents, November 20, 1943, just before the assault on Mount La Difensa.

that I wasn't stuck in one place like the regiment was, but moving all over the place. On December 20, 1943 the G 1 said to me, "You're not really needed here. 1 Div. is going into a big battle up on the Adriatic north of the Melfi River. Why don't you go up there and see if you can give them some help and see what you can learn."

So I presented myself at 1 Div. Headquarters just in time for the Battle of Ortona which was quite an introduction to real war, I'll tell you. As a liaison officer, I wasn't actually fighting, but that famous Christmas I was assisting the people who were fighting. I was bringing men out of the fighting front lines where they were shooting at the enemy. I would take a troop or a platoon out for an hour and a half to give them Christmas dinner and bring them back again. The BCD's Christmas card that year was a picture of a wrecked tank and a pile of rubble with signs all around that said, *MINEN*. It was terrible. An awful battle—the first real battle that the Allies ever fought in a city. Normally, we went around the cities and cut the enemy off and tried to persuade them to surrender. This time there was no choice. Ortona was perched on a cliff overlooking the Adriatic and an inland valley. There was no way we could go beyond it. We had to take it. The 1st Canadian Division invented the techniques now famous, of going into buildings and blowing holes in the walls called "mouseholing" and advancing up the streets, one after another.

Ortona was taken on December 28 but that wasn't the end of it because the 1st Canadian Division—the Big Red Machine, as they called it—had suffered terrible casualties and they had to re-group and bring in and train new reinforcements to get ready again. They couldn't do that and hold the front so about January 15 we took the 11th Infantry Brigade, which was part of the 5th Division and lent it to the 1st Division. We went up to the front, just inland from Ortona and spent six weeks there while the re-grouping was going on and then we went back as infantry to the 5th Canadian Division about two weeks later.

I declined a posting to corps headquarters as a staff captain in March of 1944. I wanted to get back to my regiment and go into action in the Liri Valley and the Hitler Line, two very big battles. The first time I encountered German infantry in battle was when they opened fire on our tank. I laid my gunner on them and had him open fire. The co-driver also got his machine gun going and I saw them falling and I was actually so excited I jumped up and down in the turret. I was hammering my hand and saying, "My God, it really works!" I had been training for two years and finally, when my life was at stake, I did the things I had been trained to do and the damn thing worked. You'll understand—I was only twenty-three. I was a trained army officer but I was still a kid.

The Sherman tanks weren't the best but at least we had them and we didn't have them before. I went through the three-person Bristol Mark VI B, which was a tiny little tank armed with a machine gun. I then moved to the Valentine tank, which was again, a three-person tank with a 2-pounder gun. Then the Canadians developed the Ram tank which we hated because the first time we used it on a range, some guy made a mistake and, instead of firing at the target, fired at the tank and drilled a hole two inches wide right through it. We looked at that and said, "We're going into action in that damned thing!" But we liked it because it had a 6-pounder gun. Then they finally gave us the Sherman. Sure, the Sherman was called the Ronson and everything they said was true but the damn thing ran and it had a 75mm main gun and we could do something with that. It also had a coaxially mounted 30-calibre machine gun and the co-driver also had a machine gun. In the turret, I had a .50 calibre ack-ack machine gun. We were able to do some fighting but until you get into action and the enemy starts filling you full of holes, you don't realize how bad the equipment is. What we didn't like about the Sherman was its height. It was two to three feet higher than every other tank and hard to hide. We knew it had a terrible profile but against the PKIV, the standard German tank, it did a good job. When the Germans brought the Panthers in—that was another game. It had an 88mm high velocity AA gun.

There were five people in a Sherman tank: the driver; a co-driver with a machine gun; an operator/loader in the turret on the left who would load the big gun and operate the two wirelesses; the gunner on the right-hand side right under me and I was the fifth one, the troop commander, with my head sticking out of the turret. The only ones who can really see are the troop commander, the gunner who is looking through a gunsight, and the driver who has a periscope. The gunner's field of vision is very narrow and focussed and it's up to the troop commander to give him orders so he can get on to the piece of land that you want him to be engaging targets on. We had a whole jargon and procedure: "Driver: Right. Gunner: Bushy treetop. Thousand yards. Right twenty feet. Small house. Left. Enemy. FIRE!" It was a little-known fact that the Canadians never "buttoned up". The crew commander never closed the lid unless we were not in active combat and were being shelled. If we were waiting for movement orders, we would close the tops to avoid shrapnel and snipers and so on but the minute we went into action, we opened the lids. The

Shermans had a lid that opened half on each side and you could prop it up so at least you'd have some defence from snipers. We fought our battles with our heads sticking out because if we looked through the periscopes we were like the gunners with a limited field of vision and we wanted to see everything in front of us so we could detect a gun flash anywhere.

The last hour before you go into battle is awful. You're in the tanks ready to go and, if it's breakfast time you open a can of bully beef and wash it down with rum, believe it or not. I went into action as a battle captain, second in command of a tank squadron which had sixteen tanks and eighty men, one of whom was the major commanding the squadron. He was running the squadron and I was responsible for the men, particularly the men in my tank, and I had to keep their spirits up. I've often said, and I mean it very truthfully, that the stress was so terrible that I don't know if I personally could have stood up to it if I wasn't an officer. I had responsibility for all of these men and *couldn't* allow my fears to dominate. Once it started and they said GO and we were moving, all that disappeared and you were then a trained fighting machine doing your thing. You were looking for the enemy, trying to find targets and achieve objectives and pass messages. You were busier than a one-armed paperhanger! You were really, really busy and trying to be the best at everything. I had to do my rear link job so that my squadron commander would be in touch with the colonel and passing that information and simultaneously keeping my troop in order so it would be where it was supposed to be in the order of battle, going up the center line that you were supposed to follow and fighting my troop and most of all, fighting my tank because if I didn't spot something shooting at us and get them out, they would get us out. They say that the threat of hanging wonderfully concentrates the mind!

One problem that we had when we went into action was that there wasn't much room in the turret and everyone was cramped. Some couldn't stand it and just gave up. Shell shock, we used to call it. We did our best for them and I would speak to the adjutant and say, "Trooper so and so, can you put him in B Echelon?" We tried to find them a rear job in the regiment so they'd be out of the range of fire. This happened also to men who were driving trucks up to the front. Some people were just so shattered that there wasn't anything you could do, but we didn't want to have to put them through the indignity of going to the hospital with that kind of problem. We once had an officer who joined us, a big husky guy who was built like a wrestler. He didn't even last one day in action. You could take a trooper and tell him that he was now loading ammunition in B Echelon but you couldn't do that with an officer so he was gone and we never saw him again. On the other hand, we had a stereotypical hobo from the late 30s, who used to say that the first square meal he ever had in his life was when he joined the army. He was a goddamned nuisance and was so badly behaved that if he didn't have a pass, he'd be AWOL. If you gave him a job to do and didn't send a sergeant with him, he wouldn't do it. He was a bloody pain in the neck *until he got into action.* We put him in the recce troop because if we had put him in a regular squadron he'd destroy discipline. With the recce troop, he was up front and engaging the enemy in every which way. He was so brave and so courageous and fought so well that we all took our hats off to him. He survived the war and I hope he wasn't a bum back in British Columbia. He was a good guy. So that's the opposite side of the coin.

Italy was a terrible place for tanks. Every three kilometres there was another river and the Germans were superb at mounting rear defences. When there was a real battle, it was one thing when they stayed there and fought but they would set up a defence at a river—you'd come on and they'd fire at you. Standard procedure—you'd get out of your line of advance and deploy to engage the enemy. So you would break your formation and get into fighting formation and try to get a scissors bridge to get the tanks over or try to capture a bridge or whatever. Every battle was different but they always delayed you— two, four, six, eight, ten hours or two days. Eventually you'd get over and kill those you could and the rest would disappear and you'd be free to get back into a line of advance and three kilometres later there was another damn river and you had to do it all over again. When there was mud we would "belly down" and, in the winter, we didn't move. It was impossible. The Germans didn't move either. We just stayed where we were all that winter and sent out patrols to fight.

The Germans were *incredibly* good soldiers. I think that, constitutionally, as a nation, they are good soldiers but they had much practice as they had been fighting since '39. They did miraculous things. Whenever the Germans found out that the Canadians were there, they would move the 26th Panzer Grenadiers or the First Paratroopers—their two best divisions—and put them in front of us because, as we found out from their post-war diaries, they really respected and feared us more than anybody. We once moved to a different part of the front and broke a division that wasn't one of their good ones. They went away in pieces and we thought that division was finished. The German officers took all the bits and pieces of broken-up regiments, formed them into fighting units and they counterattacked within thirty minutes. Now that's military ability of a superior order. They knew how to lay down covering fire, analyze land and make killing fields, all the things that we had to learn. It takes a lot of learning and they knew all that cold.

Your training is never finished until you're in your first battle. That's when you know whether you're well trained or not. Once we had gone through that and had become blooded veterans, our guys were good, too. But the Germans were unbelievable. We were working with Canadian volunteers. They were working with German volunteers, and conscripts and captured enemy soldiers who had been swept up and forced to go into the army. They were working with the sweepings and they would get miracles out of them. If you capture half of a Czech regiment and treat them so badly that they're starving and afraid of dying and tell them that if they join your army they'll be fed properly, all of a sudden they're wearing field grey and they're German soldiers. You wonder what kind of soldiers they really are in their hearts, and yet they made these guys fight and fight well.

Everyone in my regiment was either Roman Catholic or Church of England. I was the only Jew and my identity discs had OD (other denomination) on them. One was a round green one and the other was a hexagonal red one. One was tied to the other and your information was on both. If you were killed, they cut one off for the casualty reports and the other one stayed on the body. I wore those until I went into action in early April when the quartermaster sergeant brought me a new set of discs that he had made which said CE (Church of England). I told him I had a set but he told me that I couldn't go into action with them because they would shoot me immediately if I were captured. (I brought both sets back with me and gave them to the museum in my synagogue, Shaar Hashomayim in Westmount.) The padre that we had was a very handsome priest from Toronto. The day before we went into the regiment's first battle he came to me and said, "Barny, I want you to know that I've been up to the 8th Army headquarters." I said, "What in the world were you doing up there?" He said, "There's only one rabbi and he's with the 8th Army. I want you to know that if something happens, I've got the Jewish burial service and will bury you properly." I said, "Why am I not too enthusiastic about that?" (laughs) You have to joke at times like that but it was very nice of him.

We didn't have too much to eat—mostly bully beef. In fact, it was so monotonous that if we got close to Americans and could swap for some of their infamous K rations which had Spam, we thought that was a great treat.

We had a lot of hardtack which was as hard as this desk in front of me. We learned to live with it and would soak it overnight in our mess tins with a little water until it was like dough. If we had an onion, we would chop it and add it to the hardtack and bully beef and then heat it or fry it and have something that was a little different. In 1944, all of a sudden, the hardtack came in and it was soft and delicious and we enjoyed it. I went to the supply depot and asked what the hell happened to the hardtack. They said, "You aren't going to believe it. We finally used up the World War I stuff." That's the God's honest truth!

The Italians? We said the Italians were great lovers. They weren't fighters. In early March, after the 11th Infantry Brigade came out of Ortona and the 1st Div. took over, we lent the Brigade to the 1st New Zealand Division which was holding the line in the mountains overlooking the valley at the famous Monte Casino and the Hitler Line where our major battles were later on. I was sent down as an extra liaison officer to help the 11th Brigade work with the New Zealand Division. I spent six weeks at Monte Cassino and, during that time, for political reasons, Italy wanted a regiment in the front line. The Italian Alpinieri Regiment they sent us was supposed to be the cream of the Italian Army but the New Zealanders were very unhappy because they thought that if the Germans attacked, they would just crumble. The Italians looked beautiful. They were clean and their uniforms were lovely while we wore dirty old coveralls. We had to do it so we put them in the front line and right behind them we put one of our regiments so that if they broke and ran, at least we would have a regiment there.

Did we trust the Italians? Justifiably, not one bit. Coming back to Altamura one day, I was going up a little road and looked across a field. About 250-300 feet away, there was a line of either telegraph or electric poles and all of our divisional signals had strung their wire on it because you don't like to use your wireless all the time. There were two guys; one at the bottom of the pole and one climbing up to cut the wires. The field was about twelve inches deep in mud and I didn't think too much of my chances of getting to them if I had to run through the mud. I had my usual weapon, a Thompson sub-machine gun, and I did the obvious thing, thereby preserving the wires and stopping interference with the division doing its job. That sort of thing was symptomatic. In any town, even those way back from the front, we never would walk at night down the sides of streets, but always down the middle with our weapons loaded and the flap undone because you could be killed and many who were careless were killed. We never took a bath without having a weapon right beside us. I still have the habit (which my wife makes fun of) of never sitting with my back to the door. I always like my back to the wall and this has not left me. I understand that some Italians were fighting on our side and some were neutral but enough of them were Fascists and rooting for the Germans. Our lives were at risk and we watched them.

We went to Afragola which is right north of Naples and then we went across to a town called Altamura which is near Bari, a big port on the Adriatic. We fought our way up to Rome which is very sore spot for Canadian soldiers. I was wounded at eleven o'clock on the 30 of May and Rome fell soon after. We had broken through the Liri Valley and through the Hitler Line which was a terrible battle and cost us a lot of men. The regiment was twenty-six miles from Rome and the Germans were running. The best thing to do when the Germans are running is to keep them running and not give them any time to settle down because they do that in a big hurry and you have to fight another battle to get them moving again. They were heading, as we later found out, north of the city and there was nothing to stop the Canadians from taking Rome. When the G1 came to visit me in the hospital, he told me that when the Canadians were an hour from Rome, we were told to stop dead. The order might have come from Eisenhower in London because they wanted the Americans to capture Rome. If they hadn't done that, by God, it would have been the Canadians that took Rome. When you fight so hard to get to an objective, you hate to be stopped twenty-six miles short of it.

I was wounded as we were heading up to Rome with our right flank on Highway 6, which, at the time, was the main north-south highway. To our front, on the right, there was a range of mountains with two towns called Pofi and Ripi. The Germans were on a hill overlooking the whole valley. They had a vast supply of 88mm guns and it was like a shooting gallery. It was a terrible place but we had to get across another bloody river and called for a scissors tank which is a tank with a scissors bridge on top. The damn tank was broken and there we were with lots of shellfire coming in. Our colonel was Fred Vokes, General Chris Vokes's kid brother. He was screaming and hollering, "GET MOVING. GET MOVING!" We were the forward squadron and I delivered the message to Major Kinlock. He said to tell the colonel that if he couldn't send a bridge we couldn't get over the river. This went on for over an hour until, finally, the pressure got too much and Kinlock wanted to know where our infantry were. We had the Westminster Regiment with us and I told him that they were where they should be—in slit trenches. Kinlock said to get the lieutenant and tell him to get down to the river and walk it to see if he could find a place where the water was only two or three feet deep and would allow our tanks to get through without a bridge. So I got out of my tank, which I didn't much like to do under shellfire, and went looking for the lieutenant. Oddly enough, en route, an ambulance jeep came up. They used to fix jeeps so they could put two stretchers on them because they didn't want to put an ambulance in the front line where it would be shelled. The Germans used to fire at the Red Cross all the time. So this fellow came up, saw me and saluted. He said, "Captain, you've been in action since five o'clock. It's now eleven o'clock and you haven't called for us. Is your radio broken?" I said, "No, the radio's fine. We haven't had any casualties yet but it can't go on for long, stick around."

I went and found the lieutenant. He wasn't very happy but I got him up with his ten men and, when they were on their way to the stream, I was headed back to my tank when the shell landed right beside me. How I survived, nobody knows. I was blown about forty feet through the air. I have major shell wounds on my right side where the shell landed and half my right leg is gone but, oddly enough, they also found wounds on my left side. The doctor said that while I was in the air, I was turning over and got some shrapnel on the left side. You don't feel anything when you're hit. It starts a little later. The ambulance jeep was right there and they stuck a rifle in the ground and started to transfuse me right there. I was badly wounded but I looked at them and said, "This looks like a bond poster." (laughs) They got me back and into a real ambulance for the ride to our hospital at Caserta. Ironically enough, one of the last jobs I had done at Div. Headquarters was to lay out the routes forward to this battle and back for the ambulances. The trail had been bulldozed and, boy, was it rough.

They spent six weeks trying to save the leg from being amputated. I also had a terrible infection that sulpha wouldn't control so they gave me the first Canadian-made penicillin—$100,000 worth, they told me. We hadn't yet learned how to make it and it wasn't properly purified. It did its job but every time I got a shot, it was like being kicked by a mule. They used to have to give me a shot of Novocaine and then the penicillin. They also hadn't yet got to where they could give you a 24-hour shot so it was 4-hour shots which I had six times a day for ten days. I don't know if my life was ever in question but they wanted to save the leg so they put me on a South African hospital ship and sent me to England where I spent about four or five weeks at the 23rd Canadian General Hospital at Watford, north of London. You could get on the tube at Watford and go right into downtown London. It was an interesting place because it meant that all the V1s that overshot London landed up there. The hospital wasn't hit but the bombs were blasting around us every night. You'd hear the engine and then hear it cut and know that it was coming down somewhere. The V1s were unlike the V2s which you never heard. At the hospital they told me that I would not fight again and they were waiting for a berth on the *Lady Nelson* to send me home. I was a stretcher case and couldn't walk but I talked the doctor into giving me a set of crutches and letting me go to London for a final weekend. I went to see some plays.

Back home, I spent about six months at St. Anne's Military Hospital where I had a couple of operations and then I went to the Montreal Military Hospital which later became the Queen Mary Veterans' Hospital. There were thirteen guys with my condition and we all had an experimental operation which was invented by the Russians, believe it or not. In this operation, they took the ends of the severed nerves in my leg, cut off the scarring and put the nerves together and wrapped it with tantalum foil. I was put in a bent cast with a turnbuckle which was turned a bit every day. It took five months to straighten the leg. The nerve regenerates one centimeter a month and it took thirty months to go down to the toes. In my case, it never got all the way down but enough so that I was in no danger of an amputation. I had seven operations in all and was in the hospital until October 1, 1947 although I would get out between operations and go home for a week or ten days. Here I am at eighty-one (in 2001) and still playing golf so they obviously did a good job. As a kid, I didn't want to be hobbling like a war veteran. I was on crutches for a while and then a cane. I wore out my spine forcing myself to stand erect for more than fifty years and more than half my friends don't even know that I have a crippled leg. Like all real tank veterans, I've also lost my hearing. We were firing those guns and we never put plugs in our ears—we didn't know about those things. I must have been in a turret while several thousand rounds were being fired but I have very little to complain about.

We were called the D-Day Dodgers. On June 6, 1944, I was in terrible shape in a hospital and I had been fighting for eight months. The whole campaign in northwest Europe had lasted from June till the following May— eleven months. I had done eight months before they even started and we left a lot of good boys dead in Italy, hundreds and thousands wounded. We thought that was pretty grim. The final insult was when I read in Churchill's books that the primary job of the soldiers in Italy (once the idea of going up Italy into Austria and attacking from behind was scrapped) was to bring the Germans out of northwest Europe and keep them busy. They kept about twenty or twenty-five divisions down there and they were firing ammunition and consuming supplies and so we were sucking material out of Europe to make it easier for Eisenhower and the boys over there. An important job but you like to think that you're right on the cutting edge. I wasn't with my regiment when it landed and fought terrible battles through Belgium all the way up to the North Sea in Holland. We freed city after city and fed the people but, militarily, our main job was to bottle up 250,000 Germans and keep them out of the war. We cut them off and they finally surrendered. They didn't like being cut off and it was a very expensive deal. We certainly weren't dodging D-Day. We fought and bled and died and if we kept twenty-five or thirty divisions busy in Italy, they weren't there to greet the boys in France.

The war shaped my character. I still run my office on the same systems I learned as a staff officer because they work well. I'm very good at handling people. I learned how to live with people and how to make them feel good about themselves and want to work and achieve things. In fact, I was the only officer in the regiment that always said please and thank you to his men. Living with five people in a tank, you're very intimate. The men treated me very well and I had a good relationship with them. They say you can't teach leadership but you can sure provide a means for a person to learn leadership and a sense of values. I'm a very moral man. I got that in part from my father but it certainly was reinforced by my military experience. You had *responsibility for lives.* If you were very tired and there were things that you could do that might make it safer for the men the next day, would you do it and lose badly needed sleep or would you sleep and let the men take their chances? Not everybody came up with the same answer. There are many ways of doing a better job for your men and for your country if you had a good set of moral values. Even small things like who should be on sentry duty, is it the guy you like or the guy you don't like? Soldiering is not fun and killing people is not fun. You also learned from older officers and I had fine role models like Colonel William Murphy, who later became a highly decorated brigadier and was a brilliant lawyer. He treated me like the son he never had and I learned a lot from him.

The armoured corps was special. You'd come out of action and would have to get new ammunition, petrol, food, and sometimes, new tanks if some had been blown up. It could take three or four hours to do this. If you came out of action at eight or nine o'clock at night, it would be 10:30 or eleven o'clock when you came back. If the men didn't like me, I'd have a slit trench to dig and food to cook. How long do you think an officer would last doing this—three days, four days? But if they liked you, when you came back, there was a slit trench all dug and they'd have a fire going with food for you to eat so you could go to bed and be ready to fight at five the next morning. You can't order that. They either do it or they don't, so if the men value you as an officer, they keep you going. The BCDs were a good bunch but they got rid of the odd officer who was too impressed with himself and didn't look after his men. All this I learned in the army.

The Germans are paying reparations and they have certainly been the most generous nation in the world to Israel. The youngsters in Germany today aren't the ones who did it, but I still have to make a value judgement and I have an instinctive feeling that whatever it was inside the Germans that allowed Hitler to do what he did—because he didn't do it by himself—is still inside them. The Germans are our allies and every couple of years when I go to NATO on a liaison trip, I see them there in their field grey, the same colour they used in World War II. The Canadians officers get along fine with them and sometimes they lecture to us, but in my heart, I don't trust them.

Paul Schoeler

The First Special Service Force was unusual in that it was a joint Canadian-American unit which operated from 1942 to 1944. Composed of an eclectic group of fighting men, it worked surprisingly well as a fearless assault unit skilled in specialized reconnaissance and raiding. Under the brilliant and charismatic leadership of Major General Robert Frederick, the Force fought its way from Mount la Difensa to Rome through the winter and spring of 1943-1944. The Germans called them the "Devil's Brigade", a name later used both for a book and a movie about this elite group of men. The Force was disbanded on December 5, 1944 at Villeneuve-Loubert in France when it was no longer useful for the huge final assaults that ended the war. Paul Schoeler has lived in Ottawa since 1954. His firm, Schoeler & Heaton Architects Inc. was a partner in the design of the Canadian Pavilion at Expo 67.

MY BROTHER had been killed in 1942 and the family were all very upset. My mother somehow got a scholarship for me to study civil engineering at the Polytechnique. All the guys were there to stay out of the army. You didn't have to go overseas but you had to do your service. Some guys were repeating their year three and four times. They said it was England's war and they weren't going to fight for the Limeys and for the King. I felt a little out of it although they were cordial to me. My family had spent five years in France and I felt differently because of the occupation. They couldn't have cared less because this connection with France is pretty tenuous. After trying unsuccessfully to enlist in the air force and the navy, I joined the army.

The plan was to make me a sergeant and send me to Petawawa to teach mathematics to the artillery. But one day, this American colonel, plastered with medals, came along. He was looking for men for a special service parachute group. It was very secret then and geez, I jumped on it and so did two of my friends. Within a week we were in Burlington, Vermont and joined the First Special Service Force. It was a highly trained, combined Canadian-American force. The original plan for them was to jump into Norway and blow up some heavy-water plants. It would have been suicide. By the time I joined, that plan was wiped out. They didn't know what the hell to do with us and finally, they sent us to Italy.

In Burlington we did jumps and spent about a month in manoeuvres throwing grenades at old buildings. My parents were very upset. They didn't know anything because I wasn't supposed to talk about it but eventually I told them. Then we went down to Newport News where we got on the *Empress of Scotland* and went off without escort. There were about 5,500 troops on board, all hemmed in. We were at the back of the ship on the third floor down. We slept on the floor, on the tables or in hammocks which were in three stacks. Our unit had about 2,000 men. There were 500 WACs who took half the ship— the upper decks, the promenade and all that. There were many attempts at fornication but I wasn't involved in that. I was too young and innocent. I couldn't stand the heat and the smell where I was sleeping so I volunteered for the job of spotting airplanes on these little flying bridges. I had binoculars (my eyes weren't very good but I didn't say anything) and I could sleep up there in my sleeping bag. The food on that ship was appalling and most of it was thrown away. The Limey crew sold us oranges which, I'm sure, were part of the rations. When we landed in Casablanca we were glad to get off. They loaded us into "forty and eights" (could hold forty men or eight horses). These were cattle cars with sliding doors and no springs. Just before we got into these boxcars, we saw right beside us on the siding, a flat car with wine barrels and the first thing you know, one guy goes out with his bayonet. You have to make two holes to get the wine out. Finally, we got the thing to piss out wine and we started filling our water bottles. Suddenly the train started to go and we had to run like hell to catch it. I can still see that barrel with the wine pouring out. We slept on the boards and it was a three-day trip from Casablanca to Oran in Algeria. Because it was so terribly hot the guys would climb up on ladders to the top of the cars and three were killed. The tunnels are very low and they couldn't get down fast enough.

When we got to the desert, outside of Oran, we rested and saw an outdoor movie called *Song of Norway.* Four or five guys got killed there because they tried to get laid. They went into the native quarters of Oran and we never saw them again even though we sent patrols in to find them. They were a wild bunch, some of the Americans. The Canadian recruits were pretty earnest and very good. Some of them were Indians from out West and it was a terrifically good mixture.

We then got onto an American troop ship where we had ice cream and steaks. We couldn't believe it! They had a stainless steel cafeteria and compared to the British ship, this was heaven. We landed in Naples and because the docks had been bombed we went in on little boats. Then we marched with all our gear to our base at Santa Maria which is just outside Naples. We had the best American equipment. Anything new, we had, including the first bazookas and packboards which are just wooden things with supplies that you carry on your back. The training that we had was very extensive because we worked in fighting patrols. There were three regiments, each had two battalions and each battalion had three companies so there was a total of about 2,000 which was usually undermanned, probably around 1,500 most of the time.

The 5th Army was blocked north of Naples at a mountain called la Difensa and that's where we were sent. The German positions were all set up with machine guns. The 5th Army tried to take it three times but then they ran out of ammunition and food and when they were counterattacked, it was pathetic. We'd find young dead soldiers as we went up. The mountain had an elevation of 4,500 feet and some of our scouts—guys from out West—went up the rocks right to the top and waited there at night. At dawn, they took the Germans by surprise. Since all their guns were fixed on the obvious and easiest way up the mountain, we went around to the other side where they had no defence.

There were some very heavy casualties there. Our battalion happened to be one of the suppliers so I wasn't involved in that combat although we had to deal with snipers left behind in the rocks. The Germans were shelling with mortars and they got a crew of British radio fellows. One had his head in the rocks and his legs blown off ... (emotional pause) Survival was the only thing. La Defensa was quite a victory for us because it opened the way for the 5th Army going up. Then we pulled back and rested. We had to get new recruits because we lost about a couple of hundred men, wounded or killed.

We were then sent out to Mount Majo, which was one of the highest mountains. We arrived at night so the Germans wouldn't see us. It was raining and just as I was jumping out of the truck, there was a heavy artillery blast and I landed in the mud on my hands and knees. This was Christmas night. We had to wait until dawn to start climbing and get into action and a couple of us found a nearby cemetery that had little crypts where they put coffins. We found one with empty niches and that's where we slept. We thought it was terrific, a little hard but it was protected from the rain. The next day, my buddy and I were sent out as lookouts in case a German patrol came in. It was snowing and colder than hell—the winds were incredible. We tucked ourselves in the rocks and fell asleep. When we woke up, our unit had left. (laughs) We thought we'd be court martialled but they were glad to see us because they thought we had been shot or were missing.

Once, we got an afternoon off and my buddy and I went into a village. It was full of little kids saying something about a "big sister" and to follow them. The price was rations or cigarettes. We rarely had any money because we never had a chance to spend it. My buddy's face lit up and this little kid took us to this house which had nice big rooms but was very poor. There must have been about half a dozen men sitting around a big table—Free French, Limeys, everybody waiting their turn. The grandmother was serving vino which was green and gave you the runs. There was this big stairway and everybody would drink and take their turn. This girl, who looked no more than fourteen, came down tugging her skirt, and the next guy went up. My buddy, who was married and a very nice guy—Christ, he shot up. When my turn came, I couldn't. (laughs) But I drank the wine. I had quite a bit of wine and we were drunk going back in this horse and buggy to the camp. We went right through the gates without even stopping to be checked by the guards.

We were in an olive grove in the bay of Naples on a beautiful, mild winter's day. As we were ready to march down to the landing craft to go up to Anzio by sea, this little old lady came along and from out of her skirt, she pulled a couple of bottles. We were standing around and somebody made a bet that I couldn't drink the bottle. It was a half litre and, like an idiot, I did and went berserk. My captain was being shaved and I went over and sent the Italian who was shaving him sprawling. The guys around thought I was going to kill the captain and suddenly there were four guys sitting on me. I was in trouble on that one. We marched, with our full packing load to the landing craft while the Italians in the little village all cheered. When we got to the landing, about four guys in our unit were lying down, foaming at the mouth because that liquor was just awful stuff. These landing crafts are small things; you pack about a hundred guys on them and you excrete in a hole in the deck. Well, the landing crafts rolls and sometimes the guys miss and my job, as punishment, was to spend the night cleaning the bloody deck. The glories of war! (laughs)

We landed at Anzio at dawn. The Germans were dug in but were slowly retreating. We just had time to get cleaned up before we took up our positions on the Mussolini Canal. The Germans started pouring in and from our fixed position we sent out fighting patrols. I was out almost every night patrolling no man's land checking out farms. We had a lot of casualties because of the mines. Then one day, there was a sort of an armistice with the Germans to clear out the farms in no man's land and we had to evacuate the Italian families. The men were mostly gone but there were a lot of kids. During the armistice, the bloody Germans started shelling and we had these kids and old women going crazy. They were trying to get under the bridge which was full of mines and they couldn't understand why we were pushing them down to the ground and stopping them from going under the bridge.

After four months at Anzio, there was a breakthrough and we advanced across the canal which was pretty tough. There were more patrols. One time the whole company went out. We had seen some American engineers laying mines and we didn't know where they were because we hadn't been informed. The blundering. It was full of things like that but it's pretty hectic at times. Somebody way back was informed that these mines were placed where we were walking. I was fourth in line and suddenly the guy in front of me steps on a mine and blows up. He was an Indian from Winnipeg who had very nice eyes—we called him "Dark Eyes." Just a hell of a nice guy. I said a Hail Mary … (emotional pause) The next day we were out patrolling and we found his boot with his foot in it. We buried it.

We were a few miles out of Rome, just ahead of the 5th Army checking out things. Off we go on another patrol at dusk. We had just occupied this farmhouse which had pigsties and outbuildings. We took up positions with machine guns. Three minutes later the Germans came along in a rear guard action. A young American was with me. I had an anti-tank gun and big pouches of ammunition and grenades. We opened fire and killed a bunch of Germans coming in led by an Italian. When he was hit, I remember him screaming *Gesù, Maria,*... One German, instead of running back which most of them did, ran forward and came around the pigsty behind us. Luckily, the fellow who was with me heard the noise and turned around in time and shot him. We started to crawl back to get some ammunition when the Germans started shelling. I lay face down and got hit with shrapnel. (This was as I was saying a Hail Mary.) I was hit in the base of the spine and it took out the coccyx and then chewed up the intestines. I was absolutely clearheaded. When you're wounded you're supposed to call out your number: "D140540. Wounded. I'm here! Pulling out!" There was a first-aid guy in the farmhouse so I crawled there with the other kid who had got some shrapnel in the shoulder. I crawled over the dead German, took the Luger out of his hand, and gave it to this young fellow. We had to cross a courtyard and by this time a full moon had come out.

I got to the door and knocked and I just went out after that. The next morning when I woke up, the Germans had pulled out but they were shelling the place with mortars. The guy with the first aid kit pumped me full of morphine every place he could. There were jeeps running back and forth to pick up the wounded which is a high-risk thing. My buddy and I were put on stretchers and were carried through the field—I was floating just above the wheat and the stretcher-bearers were standing waist-high in it. Suddenly the Germans spotted us and started shelling. We all flattened out and started crawling. The jeep came (the driver had a lot of guts because the Germans were shelling the road). They strapped me on the windshield, which was down and the kid with me was in the back seat. They took off and there were deep shell holes in the road. The first-aid guys were terrific. They were risking their lives. As I was lying there, I could see the shrapnel cutting the tops off the poplars and see them folding over. We got to the first-aid station at the base of this village. It took a long time to get to the field hospital back near Anzio because of the military traffic. I guess it was at night—I was pretty vague—and almost twenty-four hours later before I got on an operating table.

They operated several times and I was in a coma for the first week or ten days. I woke up on D-Day. Everybody was all excited and running around because the news had just come about the landing in Normandy. The nurse came and pulled back the sheet. My stomach was bare and there was this little "cherry" on it. I said, "What the hell is that?" They said it was a colostomy. I didn't know I had had one and was appalled. The flesh wounds weren't serious but they had taken out five feet of intestine. From there I was flown to an American field hospital in Caserta, near Naples. The Americans took hospital teams and this one had a team from Mount Sinai in New York—a Jewish doctor and his troop—terrific. I was there for four months in a stable with about forty-five wounded people. The smell—you'd smell the horse manure and there were rats running around and over the beds. We all had serious internal wounds and the orderlies were taking bets on who was going to die that night. The medical crew was terrific though and I was lucky. There were guys dying and I nearly got it.

It took a while and then, eventually, I could walk. Suddenly, I was transferred to the 14th General Canadian Hospital in Naples. I think half the patients were there for syphilis. I can remember chasing flies off my wounds when the nurses went for coffee and I don't remember seeing a doctor. I was then transferred to a beautiful Dutch hospital ship called the *Oranje*—real beds with sheets and good food. We landed at Liverpool and went by train to a Canadian hospital. I came back to Canada on the *Lady Helena*, a little ship made for cruises in the Bahamas. We had, I think, 500 shell-shocked people. They put nets on the decks so they couldn't jump overboard. I was on the bottom bunk (there were five) because I was having treatments and when the ones on top got seasick, it was a bloody nightmare. I could walk, thank God, and I'd try to stay out on deck as much as I could. We ended up in Halifax and got on board a hospital train which was beautiful. They had just finished it and the varnish was still tacky. I had a perfect bed by a window and it took about two days to get from Halifax to Bonaventure Station in Montreal.

I was a year at St. Anne's because I wasn't healing. Finally, they closed the colostomy which was a relief. I was studying architecture with this absolutely terrific plan for veterans and, one day I felt very uncomfortable in class and had to go to the Queen Mary Veterans' Hospital. They hadn't found all the shrapnel and I had to stay there for about six months. We used to give the janitor some money to go to the liquor store in Snowdon. We'd put Scotch in our Corn Flakes and be bombed by nine o'clock in the morning. (laughs) The nurses were NOT amused. You go crazy in a hospital, you know.

G.B. Okill Stuart

After attending Bishop's College School in Lennoxville, Okill Stuart was sent to Gordonstoun School in Scotland which has been described as a cross between a Victorian orphanage and a Scottish commando camp. While there, he was a classmate of Prince Philip, later the Duke of Edinburgh, with whom he still maintains contact. The war ended his plans to attend Oxford and, returning to Canada, he enlisted in the 14th Canadian Field Regiment. He was recommended for a commission but declined on the advice of his father. He fought through the European campaign to the end of the war as a bombardier and a gun position officer's assistant. He serves as a lieutenant colonel in the re-raised 78th Fraser Highlanders Regiment and is currently involved in the Canada Normandy Project/Juno Beach Centre which, when completed, will celebrate the achievements of Canadians who were willing to fight and die for freedom. This is his account of the D-Day landing.

THERE ARE CERTAIN EVENTS in life, though diluted with time, which stand paramount in one's mind even after more than half a century. One of the most important dates in military history occurred on the 6 of June, 1944, for it was the begin-ning of the end of Nazi Germany's domination of Europe. A combined operation of land, sea and air forces comprised the greatest armada ever assembled. Two artificial harbours know as "mulberries" had been designed. A pipeline, "Pluto", was ready to carry oil under the channel. Immense forces had been assembled: 1,200 fighting ships; 4,000 assault craft; 1,600 merchant vessels; 13,000 aircraft; and allied armies of more than 3.5 million men.

Two American divisions, two British divisions and the 3rd Canadian Infantry Division, of which I was a member, spearheaded the assault on the Normandy beaches. It is safe to say we Canadians from the generals down were well trained—but green. Nevertheless we were resolute.

We slipped out of the old docks at Southampton at noon on June 5. At two, when all the craft had cleared the boom between the Isle of Wight and the mainland, the signal was given to open sealed orders. It was not until then that it was truly known that the long awaited D-Day had arrived. While maps were studied, the seas began to swell. There was a special issue of Allied French franc invasion money which quickly came into play with dice and poker games during the crossing. This form of entertainment was interrupted with trips to the gunwales to relieve queasy stomachs. (When in France, it was quickly learned that the only accepted form of currency was in the way of cigarettes!)

(Above) Normandy, D-Day-Plus-3. 81st Battery, 14th Field Regiment, RCA command post (left to right) Capt. Gillespie, Bdr. Okill Stuart (and inset), Lt. J. Lacroix, Gnr. Emory, L/Bdr. Copeland.
National Archives of Canada.

(Below) Doris Taylor (right) and her friend Anne O'Brien just before leaving in convoy for the continent, March 1945.

Lt. Col. (then Captain) Pierre Sévigny, 4th Medium Regiment (RCA) being decorated by General Haller, commander-in-chief of the Polish Armies, with the Silver Cross of the Order Virtuti Militari, Poland's highest medal for valour. April 4, 1945, 22nd Canadian General Hospital, Surrey, England.

At about six o'clock on June 6, as dawn approached, I looked out and saw more ships of every imaginable shape and size than I ever thought existed. It seemed one could walk back across the channel hopping from vessel to vessel just like stones at low water in a salmon stream.

I was with the 14th Field Regiment, Royal Canadian Artillery, in the 3rd Canadian Infantry Division, approaching "Juno" Beach at Bernières-sur-Mer on the road to Caen in Normandy. As Canadians, we can be proud of the fact that we made the deepest penetration of any forces on that first day. The success of the day was made possible by the fact that neither the U-boats nor the German air force was able to offer anything other than minimum interference. Being a subordinate and barely out of my teens at the time, I knew little other than my own particular job, "like a goldfish in a jar", plotting guns and targets with a self-propelled field artillery regiment. For the first time I saw floating tanks, many of which capsized in the rough seas. There were barges with tiers of rockets going "swish, swish, swish" as they approached the coast. When you heard "chug, chug, chug" you found it to be the noise of the 16-inch shell from a battleship, so far to the rear that you could not see it. Something different was happening everywhere—all with a bang!

On the way in on our landing craft, we were given the task of firing a barrage in front of the infantry as they were assaulting the beaches, a somewhat tricky operation from a craft bobbing up and down in the rough seas. In anticipation of the possibility of a counter-attack after going ashore, all vehicles had a string of land mines tied around their perimeter. It did not take long to come to the conclusion that it was safer to take our chances with a counter-attack than to be blown to pieces with these mines being set off by stray shrapnel. So without authority, mines were dumped overboard while we were still in deep water. We had our anxious moments though. The forward engineers had cleared the beaches of mines, or so we believed. Our particular landing craft hit a mine and the ramp was blown off. It sank in about six feet of water. The first vehicle off was an infantry Bren gun carrier with temporary elevated sides for the possibility of landing in such deep water. It too met with the fate of being blown out of the water. I was in the following vehicle—a command tank, telling myself that lightning did not strike thrice. Recently there was an article in the press where a friend was being interviewed, bragging at how his company of engineers cleared the beaches of mines ahead of us. I must remember to have a word with him!

At 9:30 a.m. our guns touched down. By this time the beach was under heavy enemy shell and machine gun fire. As well, we had to contend with strafing from a few low-flying German aircraft. The one exit from the beaches was clogged with traffic, so it took a good hour to enter the town. The beach was just plain hell, with a host of dead and dying together with a multitude of enemy prisoners under the sea wall. One of the batteries, when entering its first gun position, was welcomed by a German 88mm gun over open sights. Lacking our vision, these self-propelled guns still had a string of mines around their perimeters. This resulted in several explosions and many casualties. By and large, the air was ours by day and the Germans' by night. For the first few days, as soon as darkness fell, German planes flew over and searchlights came on in the beach area. Tracer bullets from ack-ack guns lit up the sky followed by ammo dumps exploding—a better show than any 24 of May!

We all know that "all work and no play make Jack a dull boy." At about 10:30 on the morning of June 6, our tank sat in the traffic jam of Bernières-sur-Mer. We were approached by an adventurous elderly couple with bottle and glass in hand. Through obvious sign language a glass of Calvados was offered and accepted as I sat in the turret of a Sherman tank. Subsequent signs resulted in similar libations passed to the rest of the crew. The strength of the Calvados took our breath away and cancelled communication for quite a spell.

By the evening of June 6, 156,000 allied soldiers had been landed ashore. Two days later I finally had my first sleep, the only time in my life standing up in a hole in the ground. It was not until about six weeks after the initial landing that help in the way of spare parts arrived. In the interim, one had to just put up with things like a toothache and when the dentists finally showed up, they acted "as the veterans", announcing that this was war so instead of filling teeth, they yanked them out! Without cooks we tried to survive on K-rations, a do-it-yourself eating kit in a wooden box. The food was dehydrated and the cigarettes were known as "coffin coughers." As you can imagine, it was not just the Germans with which we had to contend. The good things we remember, the other side of war we have long since put out of our mind. And I might add, any soldier who claims he was not regularly frightened out of his wits is suffering from a half-century lapse of memory.

I must tell you a little story which occurred about five weeks after the invasion on the left of the main Caen-Falaise highway. A major attack was about to get underway. The initial softening up was a monstrous 600-bomber raid by the U.S. air force on the German front lines. The bombs landed on our infantry as well as the Polish Division. Not satisfied, the following day there came another raid—this time our own Canadians together with the British in Lancaster and Liberator bombers. They were a little less accurate than the Americans! In fact, they knocked out most of our wagon lines, which were located well to the rear of the gun position. This resulted in some slight disarray in the ranks! Then there was the story of the guy heading back to the beach in disgust where someone asked him if he was scared. He said, "Hell, no! But I passed quite a few guys who were!" At least this fellow knew what he was doing. I remember a reinforcement officer who wanted to know which of the two barrels the bullet came out of.

We came, we saw, and as proud Canadians, we did our job. Let us count our blessings here in Canada. We have few poisonous snakes, relatively minor springtime floods, only window-rattling earthquakes, relatively clean water and no plagues. There is still medicare, even welfare and by and large enough to eat. And above all, we have not known war on our soil for over a century. To every man who has ever felt the sting of steel, he will remember the name of the game, Kill or be killed—and for what? We may ask ourselves, what is being gained today in many countries, where we see only strife and civil war. No matter the cost, we must, however, never let down our guard. As Prince Philip remarked when inspecting the Bishop's College School Cadet Corps at Lennoxville in May 1989, "If you want peace—be prepared for war! If you do, that preparedness starts here." We answered the call and did our duty. And we must never forget those who did not come back.

Doris Taylor Rasberry

More than four thousand nurses helped care for Canada's wounded soldiers in the war. The majority (3,649) served in the Royal Canadian Army Medical Corps (RCAMC) while the others served in the RCAF and RCN. They were referred to as nursing sisters and were all commissioned officers with attendant authority within the forces. They had to be British subjects, between twenty-one and thirty-six years of age, nursing school graduates registered with the professional association in their province, and single or widowed without children. They also had to satisfy military requirements of health and knowledge of military law. Doris Taylor was working as a nurse at the Reddy Memorial Hospital when she decided to enlist in the RCAMC. Heading for Britain with the rank of lieutenant, she was on board the *Empress of Scotland* on June 6, 1944, totally unaware of the importance of the date. After the war, she worked until 1951 at the Queen Mary Veterans' Hospital, helping to care for the veterans of both world wars.

I WAS IN A CABIN with seven nurses and it took us six nights to cross the ocean. One of us had to sleep on the floor so we took turns in alphabetical order. Since my initial was T, I never got to sleep on the floor. (laughs) Not that it mattered. After we landed in Glasgow, we went right down to the 23rd Canadian General Hospital in Leavesden and started working. The hospital was near Watford and from there we could get on the underground and go into London very easily. We started receiving the troops from overseas right away. They'd fly them over as soon as they were stable. Each one would have cards and tags on them telling us what treatment they had had. Sometimes, I would recognize the name of a doctor on these tags because there were a couple I knew who were over on the continent by this time. We didn't see the worst cases because they didn't live, but the ones that we had, once they were fixed up, recovered quite quickly. When people are young, they can recover quickly. Penicillin had just come out at that time, too. From our hospital, a lot of them went home but many went back to the front. The ones returning to the front always wanted to go back. The air force fellows, especially, were always ready to return to duty. There were many amputees who came up from Italy and we prepared them to go to Canada. There was one very nice-looking chap that you could feel sorry for because he had had both arms amputated but even he was in good spirits. I guess he was making the best of it, but when he got home... You didn't want your patients to suffer and we could always give them something for pain, but they never seemed to ask for anything. You'll never meet nicer people in the world than Canadians. I never heard one complain or cry or make a big fuss about having things done.

Some of our patients had shrapnel wounds in their abdomens which were really bad and I saw one terribly burned patient. (The burn victims were in a special hospital and there was another hospital for neurological injuries which took care of the shell-shocked victims.) We didn't have time to shed tears over what we saw—we just worked and slept. We worked twelve-hour days or nights and we'd have time to go for a rest period or go for lunch. We'd be on duty by seven or 7:30 in the morning. We had to help the patients; bathe them, help them get up and help with the meals. We also had to give medicines and change dressings, what you would do in any hospital. Giving penicillin was hard then because you had to give injections every three hours. Once, on night duty, I had to go around all the wards starting at six or seven o'clock. I'd just get finished and it would be just about time to start again. I could have worked in the operating room but I decided I liked to work with patients more. The planes were going out every night from England and when the buzz bombs and the rockets started dropping, I think the patients were more scared than when they were out in the field because they couldn't get out of bed or do anything.

Sometimes on a Saturday night, we'd go to the Officers' Mess where it was mostly nurses and doctors. I wasn't too anxious to get involved because you didn't know if the men were married or not. We just had a good time. I met one fellow later on in Germany and we went out a few times. One night he got injured and since I was on duty, I saw his papers and found out he was married. We also had quite a bit of entertainment in the hospital auditorium. At first we had the ENSA shows which were British and not very good. Then we got the Navy Show and that spoiled us forever. It would last for about an hour and a half and the patients who were able to would watch it, of course. It was very important for morale to have a show like that and the entertainers would go and talk to the patients. They were very talented and the show was just wonderful. I saw it at least twice. One of the dancers was Blanche Lund but John Pratt was the hit of the show when he sang "You'll Get Used to It." Everybody loved it.

We used to like going into London on our days off. I can't remember doing much shopping but we would go to movies and plays or out for lunch. We'd always tour around a little bit and visit churches like Westminster Abbey. We wanted to see what the Savoy Hotel was like so five of us stayed overnight (I still have the bill) just so we could say that we stayed there. Once, another nurse and I went up to Edinburgh and then to Glasgow. When this man saw that we were Canadian, he wanted to invite us home and was very anxious to do something nice for us. The Scottish people were like that with Canadians. They would do anything for us, more than the English actually, but I think the English had had too much of the war by then. We also went to Belfast where they served us steaks and eggs. You never saw that kind of food in England.

In March of 1945, we left by convoy for the continent. We went to a hospital in Oldenburg, Germany. I remember the first night there because the Germans had just left and I was alone on the ward with just an orderly. I think there were about fifteen or sixteen patients who came in that night injured, but not from the war, they were all motorcycle accidents. None of them died but there were a lot of broken bones. We used to say, "Give a Canadian a motorbike ...."

The German women used to come in and take our laundry. If we gave them starch, they'd never give it back. I don't know what they did with it, maybe made bread! From Germany I went down to Holland and worked in a large hospital in Nijmegen where we treated all nationalities. I remember one Polish soldier who was really angry when he got a letter from his family telling him not to come home because of the Russians. Then it was down to Bruges in Belgium and back to England. I could have stayed for the army of occupation but decided to come back to Canada.

The boys were all *so young*. When I came back I said that if I were ever lucky enough to have a son, I wouldn't let him go to war. I'm sure I wouldn't really have stopped him, but wars are so terrible because the big shots who start them never get killed, do they? I think Canada was devastated by the war because we lost the best and when you look at pictures of these handsome fellows and know that they never had any children, that's the part that I find really sad. Imagine, too, how many women here had nobody to marry. There were many men who went away for three or four years and when they came back, they were not the same. It disrupted families all across the country. I think you could say that there wasn't a family that wasn't touched in some way. You learn a lot about humanity in a war, that's for sure.

Pierre Sévigny

One of Canada's most illustrious war heroes, Colonel, The Honourable Pierre Sévigny P.C., O.C. has also had distinguished careers in business, politics and education. He is the author of *Face à l'ennemi*, his war memoirs, and *This Game of Politics*. Belgium and France honoured him with their Croix de Guerre and he received Poland's highest military award, the Virtuti Militari, for his competence and heroism in saving the Polish position on Hill 262 (Maczuga) in Normandy from certain annihilation in the desperate days of August 1944. As forward observation officer (FOO) attached to the Polish Armoured, he saved the day by calling down an artillery barrage on advancing German forces in the pivotal Battle of Falaise. First elected to the House of Commons in 1958, he was appointed Associate Minister of National Defence in the Diefenbaker government in 1959 and was sworn to the Privy Council in the same year. Now in his eighties, he is a much-loved and award-winning professor in the Management Department at Concordia University and is truly, in the words of his son-in-law, Richard McConomy: "...still a vital force who has done his fallen comrades proud."

My FIRST EXPERIENCE with the military was during the Depression years. Everybody was broke, including my family, and I was informed, when I was about fifteen or sixteen, that if I joined the Canadian Officers' Training Corps, I would be receiving a few cents per hour. I made calculations with some of my friends and we realized that if we joined, we'd get $13.60 which would be our spare cash for the Christmas holidays. In any event, it seemed to be something interesting to do and, if we followed the training, we would have the opportunity to write an examination and obtain an officer's commission so a few of us said, Well, why not? I did not join because I wanted to fight a war but because I wanted to get $13 for my Christmas vacation. (laughs)

We volunteered in 1933 and I'll never forget it. We were given some World War I uniforms which were taken out of moth balls and smelled like you wouldn't believe. We were also given boots and puttees. (Making soldiers wear puttees in World War I is something I've never understood.) Because much of the training would be in November and December, we were given a greatcoat and a cap. The training took place in the drill hall, which is famous in Quebec City, and at some of the sporting facilities at Laval University. We were trained by professional, non-commissioned officers from World War I. The instruction was in French but the books and orders were all in English. Nobody complained about that and we all had a great deal of fun. This is when I met Paul Triquet who would win the Victoria Cross at Ortona during the Italian campaign in 1943. He was then a young NCO who, of course, would become very famous. I also met at that time another young lieutenant who had graduated from RMC and who would become a famous major general. His name was Paul Bernatchez and he also would become a friend of mine.

In those days there was a lot of drilling and courses in map reading which I knew something about. The reason I knew map reading was because when I was a child, my family would spend its summers in Murray Bay (La Malbaie). There was in La Malbaie, an old sailboat captain who had a little shop on the wharf with all kinds of maps on the walls. Because I had nothing else to do I used to go and see him. I was curious then, as I am now, and I would ask him what these maps were. He would tell me that they were maps of the Murray Bay region and he then taught me how to read and study these maps. I never realized, because I was only a child of ten, that eventually this would prove to be very helpful to me after I had volunteered.

During the summer we were, as trainees, given the opportunity to go to Valcartier, the military camp near Quebec, for a three-week training course and there again, I volunteered, the reason being that I would earn the few pennies I needed at the time. I must say that I found the training which we had to follow somewhat ridiculous. We had to do some interminable route marches and furthermore, we had to drill and fire rifles which dated back to World War I and which were totally inaccurate. I was not too keen on the army because of this form of training. I did not then suspect that a war would come when this basis of army life would be essential to do the job I would be asked to perform.

In the summer of 1939, I was with my family in La Malbaie. It looked as if war would come, which indeed it did in the early days of September. We were informed, like the rest of the world, that Mr. Hitler and his Nazis had invaded Poland, a move which would lead the British and the French to tell the Germans that enough was enough and to proceed with a declaration of war. The Americans, however, were determined at the time not to become involved. There was in La Malbaie, a Miss Boardman, a very old, very rich American lady who always gave a party once a year in the beautiful home she owned at the top of Le Boulevard de La Malbaie. That particular third of September, the American and Canadian residents were invited to this function and, to make it a big show, Miss Boardman had commandeered the orchestra of the Manoir Richelieu. This meant, of course, on that special occasion, that all the war songs of World War I were played and sung by those present— "Pack Up Your Troubles In Your Old Kit Bag," "Over There," and a few others. All the young Canadians who were present knew that Canada would be involved in some way or another in the action that was just starting. The Americans were a little embarrassed by their neutrality but they still wished us good luck and, of course, we accepted these good wishes. Then we all looked at each other and wondered, "What next?"

At this particular party there were such people as the Rowley boys from Ottawa, John and Roger. Both of them were to become senior infantry officers. Roger was decorated with the Distinguished Service Order (DSO) on two separate occasions. John, unfortunately, was killed in Germany one hundred yards from where I would myself be wounded ten minutes later. There were others who were there who also would be either wounded or killed in the years that followed. One was Charles Hill, a cousin of my wife-to-be, who joined the Queen's Own Regiment in Toronto and was killed in June 1944 in a small French village called Banville. There were also at the party, the two O'Brien brothers, Billy, who would serve in the air force and be cruelly wounded in a raid over Germany and Stuart, who became a fighter pilot and was killed in action. There were many others who were either killed or wounded as the war proceeded and who, like myself, did not know what their destiny would be for no one knew what the war would be like and there was nothing much that we could do about it.

Anyway, it was quite a party and when it ended I got into a car with a friend of mine to go back to Quebec City. It was a beautiful, moonlit September evening which I will never forget. This young friend, Jacques Parent, had some money which was something few of us had in those days, and drove a beautiful Packard convertible car. I was in that Packard with the top down, looking at the stars and the moon and I then made a decision to become a fighter pilot. One way or the other, I knew I was stuck and would have to enlist so I thought I might as well be a pilot. The next day, I went to the armed forces headquarters and there I met an old friend of mine, Joe Gignac, and told him that I wanted to become a fighter pilot. He said he thought I was crazy but let me sign up. By eleven o'clock that morning it was a foregone affair. Joe had told me that I might have some trouble with the medical examination because I suffered from migraine headaches which had been the plague of my life. The medical officer I saw was a chap who had treated me for my migraine headaches and my application was refused. That ended my flying career that very afternoon.

Another friend would later say, "Why don't you join the navy with me?" I spoke about that with one Dr. Giguère who was then courting my sister and who eventually became her husband. He reminded me that I got seasick in the bathtub. I decided that he was right and frankly I wasn't very tempted by the sea. This was at the very start of the war and the spirit then was not what it became later on. At that time, too, I was making quite a bit of money selling life insurance. A great many Canadians, particularly in Quebec, felt that we had no business to go and fight this war. Mackenzie King, our prime minister, had said that Canada would become the arsenal of democracy and that the British and French would thus get everything they needed from us. There would, of course, be men in the army, navy and air force but each one would be a volunteer.

Initially, mind you, there were a great many volunteers. Many, of course, joined up because they wanted to go and fight the war but it was a period of acute unemployment and others joined up because of the pay. Then in May of 1940, what had until then been a phoney war changed when the Germans attacked Holland and Belgium and then found a way to get around the Maginot

Line. Within less than a month, France had been forced to capitulate and it looked as if England would soon be invaded by the invulnerable forces of Nazi Germany. Until then, the reports had been that the Allies were sure to defeat the Germans because the French army was supposed to be the strongest and most well equipped army in the world and the British had a navy which was immensely powerful. It was felt that the Germans could not defeat such a coalition.

What saved the day was Winston Churchill when he said that England would never give up and would fight until victory was theirs. We realized that, unless we helped the British, it might be very difficult for them to defeat the Germans. By then, too, we were starting to realize that the Germans were performing in a most cruel manner wherever they occupied. Some of the Poles who had escaped were telling what the Nazis were doing in Poland and suddenly, we realized that we weren't fighting only a conquering nation—we were fighting an evil force—and people like myself who were doubtful about enlisting felt that we had no other choice but to do so.

A family friend told me that he had been given the job to train the conscripts who might volunteer for overseas service and he asked me to team up with him. So I became a soldier, something for which I was trained. I was told that if I passed the officers' exam, I would get two pips which would give me the great sum of five dollars a day. Furthermore, I was told that I would be free to volunteer and go to England or stay here and train conscripts. Because of the preliminary form of training I had acquired in map reading in my younger days at La Malbaie, I came first in the province in the exam and this gave me a little prestige in the city of Quebec.

By then I knew that I had to get overseas where the action was taking place and I accepted to go to Brockville where I got the necessary qualifications to become an infantry officer with the specialty of handling machine guns. I did not know which infantry unit I would have to join and, frankly, I felt that I would prefer to do something more interesting than the infantry like joining the armoured corps or the artillery but there were problems. Number one, there were no tanks in the Canadian army at the time and the artillery was still in the process of being organized. It was then that I met a friend who had received a mandate to mobilize an artillery battery and he asked me to join up with him. I found the suggestion interesting but it meant that I had to go back to Brockville to become qualified in the science of artillery. I accepted this move and I became an artillery officer and was all set to go overseas with this new battery, which was part of a regiment being formed. My friend then told me that there was a problem. It seemed that they needed gunners—as artillery soldiers were called—and it seemed that I had been designated to be in charge of a recruiting campaign.

I was told that I would have to circulate in the villages close to Quebec and try and meet the young men who might be interested in joining the army. This meant that I had to talk to these young men and find the words to convince them to volunteer for the Canadian Artillery. This was not precisely what I had been trained to do but if that was what was desired of me I agreed to do it. We were in the middle of winter and for the next three months—and I'll never forget those days—I had to go to the countryside and get to parish halls where the parish priest, upon orders from Cardinal Villeneuve, if you please, had been advised that the parishioners should be grouped and should listen to what I had to say. Sometimes I was successful and recruited a few men but very often others would say, "Why should we go overseas? We are not forced to do so and we are not particularly interested in making this move."

One day in Matapédia, I was making a speech in which I was saying, "Look, you're going to be dressed. You're going to be equipped. You're going to be treated medically and dentally. You're going to be fed and furthermore, you're going to be paid $1.30 a day, so why don't you come along?" It was cold like you wouldn't believe and everyone was shivering in the hall. A young man lifted his arm and said, "What about heating? Are you going to heat us?" I said, "Of course we will." He said, "Well, then, I'm in." This young man volunteered and he became my batman and was with me for the next four years. His name was Ovila Bernier. Unfortunately, my good friend Ovila got killed in France at a place called Jort the very first day that I was asked to join the Polish Forces. Much later, I was in France and I found the graveyard where he lies in Bretteville-sur-Laize in Normandy. I went to see my good friend Ovila and I cried when I saw his name on the grave.

We eventually had sufficient men to form a regiment. It was the first French-speaking artillery regiment of the Canadian army and it was called the 4th Medium Regiment of the RCA. I became a captain in that regiment and was made a troop commander. We went overseas in August 1942. We sailed from Halifax on a beautiful cruise ship called the *Capetown Castle* but there was a slight inconvenience. I had a lovely cabin—but there were twenty-two of us in it! We crossed during the month that there was the heaviest sinking of Allied ships by German U-boats. I remember a beautiful night when, because of a clear sky and the absence of clouds, we could see the other ships of the huge convoy of which we were a part. Suddenly in the distance, we heard an explosion and I could see the flash of this explosion. It meant that a merchant ship had been hit by a U-boat torpedo. No sooner was this explosion over than there was another one on the other side of the ship and then I was a witness of a phenomenal sight which I will never forget. First the sirens sounded and we could see destroyers, frigates and other warships going at full speed and seeking the presence of the U-boat which had caused the damage. I'm not sure of the fact but I believe that they destroyed that U-boat.

I landed in England on August 19, which was the day of the Dieppe raid, a colossal mistake and a disaster for the Canadian troops. We started our training in Bookham, a beautiful village in the garden-like county of Surrey. The training lasted a long time because it was still a time when it was felt that the Germans would try to invade. There were still some air raids, which I'll never forget, but they were not as gruesome as they had been during the Blitz. When we could get away, we used to go to London where we'd see Canadian, Australian and a few British troops. The Americans had not yet arrived and when they did, they took England by storm. They were the only ones you could see because they had more money than we did. (laughs)

The time came when it was realized that there would be an invasion of "Fortress Europe." The Germans were having their troubles in Russia and were more or less paralyzed in Italy. The only way to end the war was to invade. It was obvious for geographical reasons that it had to be in France. Our regiment was ready and we were ordered to cross in the early days of July 1944. My first experience with action happened two days later. I reported to the headquarters of a British brigade and I was told, "You are here because you speak French. We've decided to send recce troops into the city of Caen because we have to know if the Germans are getting ready to stage a battle. If they are occupying homes and we attack Caen, it will be the worst kind of battle that there is. The Germans are there and we have to govern ourselves accordingly. You will go with these troops and speak to the people you meet."

I had never been in action before and was very excited. There I was with my steel helmet and my gas mask. We were all told to wear a gas mask which we eventually threw away because there was never any gas used. I had my pistol, my radio set and my map. We were in little armoured cars which had two machine guns, one on the driver's side and one which could take care of aircraft if we were attacked. Then we went into Caen. One of the sad things about the war was that wherever we went, we saw the citizens come out from their homes in a state of excitement the likes of which we had never seen. They were greeting us and saying, "You're the liberators! You're the Allies!" Wherever we went, we realized that there were no Germans. The people were unanimous in saying that the Germans had left the day before. Mind you, we had not been through the complete city of Caen but we went quite far in and Caen is not such a big city. I remember having a cognac in a bar near Saint-Étienne, the church of William the Conqueror.

We ended our reconnaissance—there were twelve cars in our team—and we went back to the brigade and reported that we did not have to fear a street battle because we had learned that the Germans had left. It seems that this report of ours was accepted and we were told that we could go back to our respective units. I had not yet seen a German soldier and we were sure that the next move would be that the Allies would go into Caen, cross the city, and move forward towards where the Germans probably were, but this is not what was done. It was decided at a high level to bomb the city of Caen and the next night, a night I shall never forget, we saw hundreds of bombers flying at very low levels and coming towards the city. In my opinion, what followed was one of the biggest mistakes of the war because, mind you, there may have been pockets of resistance in parts of the city we had not seen, but this weak, minor defence did not justify the almost total destruction of such a beautiful city. What this disaster succeeded in doing was the killing or wounding of thousands of Frenchmen, and doing something which delayed the eventual assault by one week because all the houses had been destroyed and the rubble filled the streets and had to be cleared up before our troops could advance. The bombing was perhaps a safety measure taken by the high command but our report and two other similar reports made by other recce troops were totally ignored. Some of the people that we saw said, "Why? Why?" and that was a good question, but the French did not turn against us, which I considered somewhat surprising in view of the extent of the damage that had been caused.

It was after that that the war really started for my unit. The week that we lost gave the Germans a chance to bring back armoured troops from the east and south and form a defensive line south of Caen which could not be pierced for six solid weeks. One of the most gruesome parts of the war was the weeks that followed when we started attacking south of Caen. The Germans had built up these pillboxes where they had mounted their machine guns. They also had the deadliest weapons you could imagine. They didn't have much artillery but they had these mortars that were extremely precise which they manipulated with a great deal of ability. They had one mortar in particular that we called the "Moaning Minnie." It fired six shells in a sort of butterfly fashion and wherever one fell, it fell with precision and caused a great many casualties. Their tanks were better than anything we had. They had the Mark III, the Mark IV (which is what they had the most of), the Panther and the Tiger. Fortunately, they didn't have too many Tigers. They were equipped with a gun that was much stronger than the one we had and which could not be destroyed by our own tanks. The only way you could destroy these tanks was to hit them in the tracks, slow them down and destroy them. We had more armour than the enemy did and if we threw enough shells at them eventually, we could stop them. Why we persisted in sending into action these Sherman tanks is something I've never understood. The tragedy was that the moment the Sherman was hit, it was set on fire and was useless. I was knocked out three times myself and was lucky to survive because, believe me, it was pretty rough when you got hit by these German shells.

To show you how bad it was; in the middle days of July I was asked to support a British tank regiment with my guns. We were given orders to follow a dirt road for about a mile to get to a wood which was our objective. They didn't want us to go through the field which might be mined—the Germans were good at mining—so as we were proceeding on that road we suddenly saw a moving mass come out from a bush and we immediately realized that it was a German tank. Suddenly, there was a flash and we saw one of our tanks get hit and start flaming. A few seconds later there was another shot and the same thing happened. The tanks that were left started aiming at this thing with these luminous shells. We could see them hit the German tank and bounce off but they couldn't stop it. That tank knocked out sixteen British tanks, including mine, but I was lucky. It hit the front portion and one of the tracks but I couldn't move any more. If the Germans had had more tanks and been able to support them with aircraft, I wonder what would have happened. They would have lost the war eventually but they could have resisted much more than they did and heaven knows, they resisted strongly enough as it was.

We attacked night and day during these weeks in July. The Germans kept resisting and counterattacking and we were getting nowhere. The Americans were stuck in the northern part of Normandy. They wanted to open up a seaport at either Le Havre or Cherbourg but were stopped in the St. Lô region. The only way that was found to resist these German tanks was via a plane called the Typhoon. It was a plane that could dive and throw rockets that were strong enough to stop these tanks. If not for the Typhoons, it would have been disastrous. The Germans were losing a lot of men and their generals told Hitler that it was madness and that they couldn't defeat the Allied forces. Hitler was the boss and gave the order that they had to try to attack all the way toward the cities of Avranches and Argentan. The attack started and for about eight days the weather was bad which prevented the Allied planes from flying. During this time, the German tanks succeeded in pushing through and, if the weather had persisted, it is very probable that they would have succeeded in getting farther than they did. Fortunately, the skies cleared up and then the Typhoons came along and that was the end of that particular assault.

It was then that the Germans realized they were defeated—that the strength of the Allies was such that they could not win. Still, they decided to retreat and establish another line of defence which could be reinforced by troops that would come from Germany. Mind you, it was a dream but it was attempted. It was more easily said than done because by then the Allies had succeeded in penetrating from the north, the south and the west, forming a pocket with the Germans inside. Their only avenue of escape was through a very narrow corridor which led to the roads that went towards the Seine River via the city of Vimoutiers. That was the pocket of Falaise.

The Poles who had succeeded in escaping from Europe and had come to England had been formed into two armoured divisions; one under the leadership of General Anders (who was perhaps one of the finest generals that the Polish pre-war army had), and the other one was commanded by General Maczek, another prominent general. One division, with General Anders, was sent to Italy where they suffered terrible losses but nevertheless succeeded in winning control of Monte Cassino. The other one, the 1st Polish Armoured Division under General Maczek, was sent to Normandy in the early days of August along with the 4th Canadian Division—these were the reinforcements that we had been asking for. The Polish senior officers were all well trained but their second language was French, not English, and they wanted a French–speaking artillery regiment. They thought they could get one from the Free French but they were not available. The only available French-speaking regiment was ours so we were ordered to support them. I received orders to join the 10th brigade, which was the reconnaissance brigade, and proceed with them in such assaults as they were ordered to perform. The poor Poles had had the misfortune of being bombed through a mistake of the

Allies on August 8 and they lost a great many men. The Canadians also suffered quite a few losses and that, of course, was not a good start to the action.

These Polish officers and men all had a score to settle with the Germans. There wasn't a single one of them who didn't have a tragedy in their lives. Either they had lost their loved ones or their homes had been bombed and they wanted revenge at all costs. That made them very dangerous soldiers. At one point they had orders to reach a certain objective and wait until the Canadians and others came. Once they got to this objective, they saw a hill and, on each side, there were two escape routes for the Germans. The commanding general wanted to get control of this hill and prevent the Germans from escaping. The Germans were so disorganized that capturing the hill was not too difficult but when they realized that we occupied the hill, they started attacking us from the left, from the right and also from the west so we were being attacked on three sides. The Germans know how to fight, you've got to give them that. They also used the forces which were outside the pocket so they could keep the doors open for escape.

We started being attacked from the east also. We realized then that we were completely surrounded. We were attacked for three solid days and nights and I tell you it was not a picnic. Eventually, it reached a point where there were no more machine gun bullets and no more shells. The wounded could not be treated because there was a lack of medical supplies and there were many dead in my sector. There were only about 104 men left capable of fighting and only two officers and I was one of them. Mind you, a great many of the regular German troops were surrendering and when they did, we had to try and protect them from these Poles who wanted to kill them and some did, you know. When I had a chance to do so, I told the German prisoners to go to a wood which was in the center of the hill, and lie down and not move. If they didn't get to the wood, they were in trouble. We had to feed them too, and that was no joke.

On our hill, the men had next to no ammunition still available. This is why I was asked to use my guns, which were the only weapons we had left, and I had to fire with precision. I succeeded in this task and then I had quite a spectacle. In fact, I never saw anything like it. I could see the guns I was directing when they fired in the distance and I could see their shells hitting the Germans. It was an unbelievable battle, the likes of which can hardly be described. There were so many dead, so many wounded and so much suffering. While I'm talking to you now, I have the smell of the battle in my nose. Whenever I think about it I can now describe that battle as being perhaps as grim and gruesome as Stalingrad in Russia probably was. Eventually, the Canadians succeeded in coming close enough to us so we could join forces and that was the end of the battle of Normandy. The hill where I was is called Hill 262 (Maczuga). It's in the commune of Mont Ormel and the French and the Poles have erected a beautiful monument on the site to commemorate the Polish and other Allied soldiers who died in the immediate vicinity.

If the assault had been continued against the Germans, the end of the war would have come much earlier but the orders were given to halt and wait until supplies could be sent. The Germans were very good at reorganizing and it is estimated that out of an army of 300,000 at least 65,000 escaped and joined the remaining forces. The regular soldiers wanted to surrender but Hitler would not do it. There was an attempt on his life on July 20 which failed, but he was strong enough to arrest 5,000 people and have them executed, just to show his power. He also knew that the fate that awaited him was not the best because of the horrors they had committed. It's a tragedy that the war did not end sooner because, if it had, the people who were in concentration camps would have been liberated. But the Germans—I have to give the devil his due—they're terrific soldiers and they had the weapons. They had these tanks and machine guns. I mention machine guns because it was one of their main weapons and they had, of course, the mortars. I tasted their mortars.

I was wounded on February 24, 1945 during an assault which led to the crossing of the Rhine. During the night preceding this assault, the Germans had penetrated the Allied forces and concealed some of their mortars and some 88mm guns and tanks. The Allies were ready to cross the river but were stuck in a traffic jam, so to speak. They opened up with these weapons and caused terrific damage. At ten o'clock I was moving forward and suddenly, I saw a 6'4" fellow. It was John Rowley and I said, "John, do you recognize me?" He said, "Pierre, let's have a drink!" We had a drink and then I told him that I had to move forward. I went back to my jeep and was trying to direct the men. Suddenly, I heard an explosion of shells and the cry, "TAKE COVER!" I turned around to move away and then I saw that a shell had hit the spot where I had been with John Rowley. He got killed, the poor fellow, and I was wounded minutes after.

I lay in that field for about an hour and then they picked me up and gave me first aid treatment. I had so many shell splinters inside me that the doctor said I had to be treated in a hospital. The orders were to take me to a Canadian hospital but there was so much traffic on the road that the ambulance I was in was proceeding at a snail's pace. I had so many holes in me that I was bleeding from everywhere. I felt that I was getting weaker and was sure I was going to die. I know that I never could have reached that hospital but I knew of a British hospital which had been established in a convent. When I saw it, I asked the driver to stop but he told me that his orders were to go forward. Using what strength I had, I opened the door and threw myself out of the ambulance. People saw me and came to pick me up. I was unconscious and they saw that I was in a dreadful condition. They operated on me and three days later I was feverish and smelled this weird smell. I had gangrene and the doctor came and said, "We've got to take your leg off. You're going to die if we don't." I said, "Do what you have to do." What can you say?

Today, I think my leg might have been saved, but in those days it was a bit different. I was also having trouble with my left arm and I had difficulty seeing from my right eye because of shell splinters which had hit me. I was told that the doctors wanted to take my arm off and also that I was probably going to die. "Well," I said, "if I'm going to die, let me die with my arm on, if you don't mind." (laughs) The doctor, whose name was Harrington, wanted to operate and claimed that he could perhaps clear the infection. He operated one last time and when I woke up from this operation (forty-eight hours later, I was told), everything was clear, the fever was gone and it looked as if I was out of danger, the danger of dying, anyway.

My convalescence was very long but I'll tell you what saved my life really. I was taken to this hospital in England and seemed to be recuperating but I got sick again and started feeling sorry for myself. It was inevitable. I was saying, "Here I am, twenty-seven years old, minus a leg. They want to take my arm off. I'll never be able to walk again. I'll never be able to do what I want to do. I'm wounded in my eye (which still gives me trouble today) and may lose it." I felt sorry for myself and had these crying fits which I just couldn't stop. There was a very handsome guy in a wheelchair who every day would come into the room where I was. He was dressed in an air force uniform and would go to the end of the hall where he would play chess with somebody. He'd look at me when I was having these crying fits, but he never spoke to me. One day, he rolled himself towards me and said in his beautiful British accent, "I don't know you but I've been watching you. You have nothing to gain by feeling sorry for yourself. Look at me. I was a fighter pilot and was shot down. I'm a paraplegic and will never walk again. But I've decided that as long as I can play chess and think and read and write, there must be a life for me. Are you going to cry for the rest of your life? You've lost a leg. You've still got your arm. You can't see with your right eye. Can you play chess? Yes, well, you can play chess with your left eye. Stop feeling sorry for yourself. Say to yourself that you are going to live today and get better and then tomorrow, do the same thing. Eventually, you'll be able to rebuild a life. This is war. I didn't want to get shot down. You didn't want to be hit. But I got shot down and you got hit so try and do what I'm doing. You're young and I suppose you're saying that the girls won't look at you. You're wrong. I've got the girls and you'll get them too." He finished by saying, "I'll come tomorrow and I want to see you smile."

He made me think. I liked what he said but the next day when he came along, I still wasn't smiling. About three or four days later he gave me hell. He said, "I don't like your attitude. You're much better off than me. You'll be able to walk but I'm paralyzed for life. When you go home and meet your parents, you've got to learn to encourage them to accept you the way you are and the only way to do that is by smiling and pretending that you don't mind anymore." That guy really saved me. On the ship on the way home, all I could think about was what he had said. He gave me a way of thinking which gave me a chance to face my parents, my friends and life. Everybody looked at me and said, "You're terrific. You're not complaining and you seem to be taking what happened to you with a smile." Sometimes, at night, I'd cry, I assure you. When friends would ask me if I had any pain, I'd say no but I was filled with drugs and was in pain like you wouldn't believe. It wasn't much fun but I'd remember this guy and tell myself that I had to smile.

Eventually, I was fitted for an artificial leg and knew that I was going to keep my arm. That's what terrified me really, losing my arm. I realized that I was not going to lose my eye and that had terrified me perhaps more than my arm. Things got better, but it was a long, long time. My parents didn't understand my attitude because I was putting on an act wherever I went. At one point I got discouraged and then I did foolish things like drink too much and nobody gets too bright when they have too much to drink. I'd then ask myself what this guy would say and I remembered that he told me to be careful about drinking.

I met this lady whom I married and she's taken care of me for fifty-five years (in 2001). We've been a good couple although we've had our problems. Very few people don't have problems. I had a period in my life when I had very grave business and moral difficulties which led to a nervous depression.

The biggest threat for war veterans is depression and when it hits, you can't fight it. There's no remedy against it. But I remembered this fellow's philosophy, and it saved me again and I came back to a normal life.

There are a few doctors who know my story and sometimes when they have patients who have lost a limb or who have had an accident, they call me and ask me if I would be kind enough to go and talk to them. I sometimes do it, at times with success, but I can't succeed all the time. Nobody can succeed all the time. I sometimes go to the Veterans' Hospital and twice I have met veterans who were in an advanced state of depression. I succeeded with one but not with the other, but what I tell them is to accept the things they cannot change and try to change the things that they can. I also tell them to try and live one day at a time which is the best that sometimes they can do. As one gets older, the pain often is worse, but the secret I have learned is to be patient and realize that to be alive is better than the alternative.

Paul Champagne

Perfectly bilingual, Paul Champagne graduated from Lachine High School and was planning to become an engineer. He interrupted his studies at the Polytechnique at the age of nineteen to enlist. Like many other Canadian servicemen, he was to spend years in England preparing for D-Day. He fought his way through Normandy with the rank of sergeant, was wounded, treated and then sent back to continue the battle in Holland. He was in Germany when the war ended and spent two months as part of the army of occupation, only arriving home in September 1945. Although he expresses some bitterness at the way veterans were treated after the war, he has even less respect for those who evaded military service. After the war he had a long career as a police officer, first with the RCMP and later with the Sûreté de Québec. While in England during the war, he had some good times. His friend, Barny Rapin, was with him for those good times and then later in Normandy when he was injured. The two men are now (in 2002) living on the same floor at the St. Anne's Military Hospital.

The reason I joined the Black Watch was because my friends were joining. On a Saturday morning, December 6, 1939, a group of us from Lachine got together and said, "What do you say we join as volunteers?" There were the two MacPherson brothers, the two MacDonald brothers, Gavin More, Tommy Gemmel, myself, and a few others. We arrived at the armoury, gave our names and signed papers. They sent the whole gang of us for a medical. We were nineteen or twenty years old and in very good physical condition in those days—no dope, no smoking, no drinking, no nothing so we passed the physical. We went back and they gave us First War uniforms because Canada was not ready to go to war—no way. We were issued with a kilt which is quite a funny feeling from being used to wearing pants. None of us were patriotic. We thought we'd go to England, have a good time and then go and help out the French behind their Maginot Line which was impregnable. We figured that the war would not last very long and we would be safe. We also did it because we were young and nobody could get a job. The government had given orders to the big shops in Lachine not to hire anyone from the age of eighteen to twenty-five. Oh yeah! This I learned after the war. Nobody could get a job. That's how they forced the young generation to go to war. We wanted adventure, too, because none of us came from rich families so we didn't have a chance to travel too much.

When I first joined the army (wearing a kilt and everything), I decided not to go home because I figured my father and mother would not like the idea of me joining up so I stayed at a friend's place. About a week later, I decided to call home. My father answered and I said, "Dad, I joined the army." He said, "Which regiment did you join?" I told him the Black Watch and he said, "That's a good regiment. Come and see us." He worked at Dominion Bridge and they had quite a few First War vets and the Black Watch had a good reputation. So I went home and they made me welcome. My sister, who was ten years younger than me, was just a little girl when I left and when I came back from overseas after so many years, she was a grown-up woman.

We first took our training at the Champ de Mars in Montreal and then at Mount Bruno. At the end of December 1939, we were moved to Toronto and we stayed at the Canadian National Exhibition grounds in Toronto. They just took the horses out of the stables and put us in the stalls. There were four of us in each stall in two double bunks. Every time we went out someone told us we stank of horse urine—and we did! Another thing too, the cement of the horses' stalls was soft and we had hobnailed boots so we got a lot of dust in our lungs. I believe that 25 percent of the regiment had to go to the Christie Street Hospital and I was one of them. Then we came back to Montreal, had a week's leave, and went to Valcartier where we trained for three weeks. I was in A Company and we went to Newfoundland and spent three months guarding the airport in case of German attacks. Then we moved from Newfoundland to Nova Scotia and were there for a short time before we went overseas in August 1940.

In barracks at Aldershot, the Black Watch used to wake up half an hour before the infantry to the sound of a piper. The poor piper used to get boots thrown at him by the Régiment de Maisonneuve who didn't like that noise. We did a lot of training because we were the only troops to guard the southern coast of England; all the British army was down fighting in Africa and Greece. We didn't have too much ammunition and used old rifles from the First War but we were good in bayoneting. The Canadians as a whole had a lot of guts and we proved it eventually. They tried to make us as comfortable as they could but we were living in bell tents and, in England, it rained most of the time and we were always wet. We were seven per tent and we all slept with our feet in the middle. We went on different schemes and then the army decided to make a motorcycle reconnaissance outfit with the 5th Brigade which included the Black Watch, the Régiment de Maisonneuve and the Calgary Highlanders. They asked for volunteers: you, you and you. That's how I joined the 5th Reconnaissance. Major Charlie Petch of the Black Watch became commanding officer of the 5th Recce. When the 14th Hussars came overseas in 1941, they joined us and we became one unit, called the 8th Reconnaissance Regiment.

We were about two miles from the town of Petworth and, one day, the Germans decided to bomb a building which they thought was an ammunition factory but they bombed a school instead. A truck went by and told us to get in so we got in and helped the civilians take the debris away and saved quite a few children. Some were killed but I took one child out of the building myself. All my life, I wanted to go back to Petworth and try to find this survivor, or *any* survivor, but I never had the chance. I went to England a few times but I didn't have the time to get to Petworth.

When I got leave, I went to Scotland a few times. I went to Inverness and Glasgow and even took the train and went to St. Andrew's and played golf. Barny Rapin and I were friends and one day we decided that we had both been to Scotland and wanted to go somewhere else. There was a map of England on one of the walls so we each decided to throw a dart. We agreed that we would go to the place between the two darts. We went back about ten feet and threw. The closest city was Sheffield in Yorkshire and we were very fortunate because, coming off the train in Sheffield, we saw a kiosk with a sign, FLEUR DE LYS, WELCOME CANADIANS. So we went across the road and spoke to the beautiful young woman at the kiosk. She asked us if we wanted to stay with a family instead of going to a hotel. We said yes and she told us to take a certain bus and go to Mr. and Mrs. Gould's house on Thorsett Road. So we got on the bus with our packsacks, respirators, steel helmets and ration coupons. We knocked on the door and a man came out. He said, "Welcome Canadians. You're welcome in our house." Mrs. Gould kissed us. We made a big hit with Mr. and Mrs. Gould and they were such good people. He had been a captain in the First War and was an engineer with the Yorkshire Collieries. Mrs. Gould was like a mother to us. We used to go shopping with her and we gave her our coupons but no way would she let us pay for our meals even though we tried. We slept in a beautiful bedroom with two beautiful beds and a fireplace. Every night the maid would light a fire and Mrs. Gould would bring us hot Ovaltine because it was cold and damp in England. Mrs. Gould liked to play ping-pong and I was a pretty good player when I was a kid. She would put a net on the great big dining table and we used to play and sometimes she'd win!

Barny and I went back to see the lady at the Fleur de Lys kiosk and thanked her for sending us to such a nice place. I mentioned that I played golf and she told me that her father played golf. Her name was Dorothy Denton and she told us to go to her place and she would introduce us to her parents. Since Barny didn't play golf, I took the bus and went to her place. When I met her father I said, "Very glad to meet you, Mr. Denton." He said, "Call me Charlie." Wow! Him being a millionaire and me being from a poor family! His name was Charles Denton and he owned the CRD Steel Company which is now Wilkinson. He said, "I understand you like to play golf. Come back tomorrow afternoon and we'll play." So, the next day I was ready and played golf at the Dore and Totley Golf Club. The club is still there but I don't recognize it in pictures because Sheffield had to be rebuilt after the war. (On Sundays we used to go to church and I remember the first time we went the roof was missing and somebody had to hold an umbrella over the priest saying mass.) At the club they gave me full equipment and a locker with a key so every time I had a chance (we used to get leave every three months) I'd go to the club and if Mr. Denton was there, I'd play with him. I kept in touch with Dorothy Denton for quite a few years. Barny even wanted me to marry her. But there were too many differences. We were a poor family and I couldn't afford to bring a lady like that to my parents' place in Lachine.

The English and the Scotch people—they were wonderful. They treated us well, because, like I said, we were the only troops to protect the south of England. When we were on schemes, the NAAFI (Navy, Army and Air Force Institute) would come and give us coffee but then some ladies would call us over to have a cup of tea. We were very, very well treated. The only problem was we had to eat a lot of mutton, sometimes three times a day. Mutton chops, mutton stew and sometimes a mixture of the two. It was the only food they could get because the transport ships were being sunk. We never had oranges or bananas because these were kept for the civilians who needed them.

In June 1944, we went to France. Don't ask me about the trip over. I was so seasick I would have gotten off the ship even if 10,000 Germans with machine guns were waiting for me. I was so sick I wanted to die. I was section NCO of a group of armoured cars and I was in the lead car. You go because you're ordered to go and trained to go so you try to leave the fear behind but you still have a little fear inside that you're going to get hurt or killed. It's painful when you see your own men being shot, but when you see civilian deaths it's worse. If you see a soldier dead, well, he's a soldier but imagine seeing women and children and farmers machine-gunned. Those are the ones that hurt you more.

In Normandy some of the people were surprised that I spoke French because to them, we were all British. During the war they were friendly enough but a bit cool, but when I went back after the war they were very friendly because we had saved them. What we really liked was the Calvados. It was made with apple cider, aged five years in big vats and it was about 95 percent proof! So it was a joke with us—our water bottle was always filled with Calvados and, when somebody got hurt, WE took a shot. We had a lot of help from the underground. They told us where the Germans were and one time when we were on patrol, a civilian stopped us in the middle of the road. I got out and he told me where the Germans had put some land mines. He showed us a short cut we could take to avoid them so if it hadn't been for him it would have been POW!

I got hurt at Orbec on August 22. We knew that there were Germans hiding in the town. We had the armoured cars all lined up to be ready to shoot if any Germans came out. I was in the first car that went in. We could hear tanks at a distance so my troop officer, Lieutenant Owens (a very, very good officer with a lot of guts), told me to take a volunteer and see where the tanks were. I told Sgt. Kenneth Smith to come with me and we both went off carrying machine guns to where we could hear the noise of the German tanks moving around. We went around a corner and came face to face with two SS so we exchanged shots. One SS got hurt and fell. The other one was hurt, too, but took off. I got hit with a bullet in my upper left leg, which went right through and cut the nerves, and again in my left arm which broke the bone. I was hurt all right. I'll tell you how it feels to be hit by a bullet because not too many guys can tell you. When you get hit by a bullet—and I got hit by two that day—it's just like being hit with a sledgehammer and it burns. Shortly afterwards you don't feel a thing but it hits so hard.

Smith got shot, too, and had passed out. I was so darn mad that I chased the guy. He was hiding behind a bush and shooting at me. I could hear the bullets flying and shot him. I went around where he was and shot him again to make sure he was dead. You know, you're wounded and you want to survive. Smith was badly hurt and bleeding but not dead so I patched him up. The first thing I did was give him a shot of morphine in the arm (sergeants and up, we carried morphine) and I gave myself one too. Then I put a tourniquet around his arm which was all broken up. I grabbed him by the belt and pulled him into a doorway where he could hide. I put two hand grenades and his machine gun next to him and said, "Look after yourself. I'll go get help." I figured that if anybody got too close, he could throw a hand grenade. I left him there and walked back on one leg. When Barny Rapin saw me, he took me behind a house and gave me another shot of morphine and a big shot of Calvados (laughs) and patched up my wounds with sulpha drugs and bandages. Barny saved my life. I told him where Smith was and they sent a Bren gun carrier to pick him up. They took us both on stretchers to the South Saskatchewan field hospital. I remember the name even if I was half doped. At the hospital they gave me another dose of morphine and another shot of Calvados. Then I passed out.

When I woke up the next afternoon, I was lying in the sun wrapped in a blanket at a big hospital at Bayeux. I could see Polish, British and even German guys going by and nobody was paying any attention to me. I was so mad I said, "I'M A CANADIAN!" so somebody picked me up and the next time I woke up I was in a bed with white sheets. I tried moving my legs but the left one wasn't moving and that's when I got scared, not scared of dying but of losing my leg. I was in Bayeux for two days and then they put me in an old DC-3 and flew me to England with about thirty others. I was at the hospital in Leavesden for three months and was well treated. When I woke up from my operation, who was there in the bed next to me but my old school friend, Guy

Leduc, who was with the FMR (Fusiliers Mont-Royal). I hadn't seen him since 1936 or '37. Then a guy in a wheel chair came in to see me. He had two legs cut off and he came over and said, "Hello, Frenchy." This was the only guy who could beat me in long distance races—he used to be a professional long-distance racer before the war. This guy always knew how to take a third breath. We'd have a mile to go in a 22-mile race and he'd be behind me. Then, all of a sudden, he'd gain, one inch, two inches, and the first thing you'd know he'd beat me by a hundred yards. I never raced after the war. The operation was a success but I had no feeling in the middle part of my leg and it always felt cold. I went back to Holland after that and was there when the war ended. Holland was rough all right but I had the experience of France so that was good. I did some occupation work in Germany until we were relieved by the Zombies in July 1945, I think it was.

Did I have nightmares after the war? Oh yeah! My mother and later my wife used to find me under the bed quite a few times. I was trying to hide. Crazy. I used to dream that bombs were falling on me but they would stop. Then I'd wake up. Or sometimes I'd dream that I was on top of a tall building that was coming down and I'd wake up before it hit the ground. I'm eighty-two (in 2002) and I still have them the odd time.

If I had known then what I know now, I would never have joined the army. I would have taken off for the bush and lived with an Indian woman. (laughs) It's because of the way we were treated after the war. We had to look for a job ourselves and the married men had to look for their own housing. Personally, I can't complain. They wanted to send me to Windsor, Ontario to study engineering and were going to give me $60 a month to spend but I'd been away from home for too long so I said no.

Maxine Llewellyn Bredt

In January 1944, Maxine Bredt enlisted in the medical corps of the Canadian armed forces and served as a nursing sister in Italy and England. A woman of tremendous fun, energy and caring, she must have been a welcome sight to the many wounded soldiers she treated. After the war, she worked as a stewardess for three years for TCA (Air Canada) before her marriage to a pilot, Bill Bredt, whom she met while based in Moncton. She is still doing volunteer work at the St. Anne's Military Hospital that she began in 1974. She takes the patients out for rides in her car, plays golf and cards with them and, in one case, was the only visitor one forgotten veteran had for the last thirteen years of his life.

I LEFT CANADA on about the 29 of May 1944 and arrived in England six days after D-Day. My first posting was at the No.18 Canadian General Hospital in Colchester. It is near the east coast and we received very heavy casualties in the month that I was there. Then we staged at No. 22 in Bramshott for two to three weeks so we could learn to be soldiers—marching and things like that. I think the sergeant just gave up on us on the marching. (laughs) Then we were all given battle dress, which they didn't wear in England. We sailed on a Dutch ship and were, can you believe it, almost two weeks going from England to Naples. We had to zigzag to miss the U-boats.

Miss Herman, who was matron of all the hospitals in Italy said to me, "Miss Llewellyn, how did *you* get here?" I wanted to say "by boat" but I thought I'd better not because I was a second lieutenant. You had to be a full lieutenant before you left Canada and I had to take my exam later in Perugia. We were attached to the British 8th Army and wore their patches on our uniforms. For a short time at first we lived in tents with dust up to our knees and when the rains came, I can remember a river running through our tent. There were about eight of us who nursed in Rome for about five weeks and then the 14th Canadian General Hospital took over a tobacco factory in Perugia when it moved up from Caserta as the action changed. We took buses from the nurses' residence which had been a convent. The hospital had no windows and, on the surgical floor where I was, there were 250 beds. There were about twenty patients on the DI (dangerously ill) list and about twenty on the SI (seriously ill) list and then the others. I had 117 patients and only one orderly. I could never do that in civilian life. One night the rains came and flooded this whole floor and we had no time to look after patients because we spent most of the night picking up their gear which was under their beds.

The wounded boys would first go to a CCS (Casualty Clearing Station) and then be sent to us. As soon as the patients were brought in, you looked in their eyes and could tell how much pain they had when you did their dressings. The amputations were done in the OR. I was nursing on the floor and did not work in the OR. Post-operative nursing is interesting and the patients are just glad to be alive. The really bad cases were all sent to England as soon as there was space for them to be evacuated. I was on nights most of the time in Perugia because I was younger. We wore big boots and battledress and got about an hour to an hour-and-a-half rest in our twelve-hour shift.

I have to tell you about the boy who wrote me a letter. We took British patients at our hospital because their nurses had gone on to Europe. There were two young boys about eighteen and twenty. One had lost his left arm, the other one his right arm. They would go around the ward trying to learn how to tie their shoelaces which we thought was great. They had so much stamina and courage and wanted to live. (emotional pause) One of those boys wrote me a letter which is one of my greatest rewards of the whole war. It says: "As a British boy to one of the best and kindest nurses, I want to thank you for all you did for me while I was ill. If it wasn't for Sisters like you, a lot of us boys would not be here today. Therefore, we British boys thank you with all our hearts for the great work you are doing and wish you all the very best and good luck in the future. Thank you, Harry."

Another patient was Sgt. Daniel MacDonald of the Cape Breton Highlanders. He was from Prince Edward Island. He was a big, tall fellow who filled the bed. He had already lost his left leg at a CCS and when he came to No. 14 Dr. Petrie, a Montreal doctor, had to amputate his left arm. Here is this giant of a man, a great athlete, twenty-seven years old and they had to..... We cried that day. He was evacuated immediately but that was one of my saddest days, I think. He was a very ardent Catholic who never even got to visit the Vatican because when his regiment went behind the lines for two days' rest he took part in the sports' days. I saw him after the war when he had become the Minister of Veterans' Affairs. He was invited to a sod-turning ceremony in Hudson and the Honourable Dan said he wanted his favourite nurse to be there. He invited my late husband Bill and me to visit his farm in Souris, P.E.I. but we never did go, although when he died we went to his large funeral in Charlottetown.

Once when I was on days, another nurse got a parcel from Montreal. She opened it up and it was a large girdle (she was a big girl). This was during the siesta hour when the patients had to be very quiet. She held the girdle over her head and exclaimed, "FELLOWS, LOOK WHAT MISS LLEWELLYN GOT!" You should have heard the uproar, the laughs! But the sad part of that is that the patients said it was (emotional pause) the first time in four months that they had laughed. *The first time in four months!* Going around doing treatments, the patients would say, "Sister, does it fit?" "Sister, could I help you put it on?" The occasional one would put out his hand and try to pinch my backside. (laughs) We had some fun with the patients, too. We would "french" their beds when they went to X-ray. One day they got me, though. One of them got a package from home and in it was some Dentyne gum. I should have known better but I hadn't seen gum in a long time. I told them I couldn't chew it but they told me to take it because I was about to go off duty. They had put a Mepacrine tablet in it which is a tiny, bitter, yellow pill to prevent malaria. Oh, it was bitter, and the snickers! So we did have some good times and the patients were so grateful. They *appreciated* us like you wouldn't believe and we were like family and *cared* about them.

Since I was on night duty most of the time, every day I would go to the British Officers' Club and dance with this British officer who had his own big band in London. The two of us would dance for more than an hour, only two of us with a twelve piece Italian orchestra. And oh, it was wonderful! The only problem was that I took a double A shoe width and had to dance in D-width Oxfords. On one of the few nights off that I had, my friends played a trick on me. They told me that Major Walt Disney was there and that the Americans had hired him to teach the Gurkhas manoeuvres by cartoons. I was just so proud to meet this man. I introduced "Major Walt Disney" (who was drunk) to all the senior nursing sisters. I can still see him today with his head almost on my shoulders as we danced. He was a Disney, all right, but not *the* Walt Disney. Two days later, Richard Llewellyn, the one who wrote *How Green Was My Valley,* came in but I refused to believe it and I missed meeting him. There was also a darling Scottish officer—oh, he was adorable—who took me on a day trip to Capri. I had another good friend who was killed. The nicest friend of all was one who was in the First Special Service Force, but we parted when I went home.

One day I felt I needed some exercise and, on seeing a hill near Perugia, I decided to go skiing. By using sign language, I borrowed skis, climbed a chicken-wire fence and skied. I was cheered on by three young Italian boys saying, "Bravo, signorina!" For this episode, I was supremely reprimanded as it was a former minefield and a woman had previously lost a foot on a Schü-mine. Another time I went to get a haircut at dusk at a little place in town when a ferocious-looking Gurkha soldier peered in the window. Both hair-dressers fled, so, with dripping wet hair, I ran down the hill to the nurses' residence—the first person ever to do the four-minute mile—in the dark! One memorable experience was getting to Assisi. At the church of St. Francis of Assisi there was a wonderful, peaceful feeling which came over me and I absolutely had the feeling that I was close to God. It's hard to explain but the feeling was there.

At the end of the Italian Campaign in March 1945, I transferred back to England. I remember we spent five days anchored in Gibraltar and were not allowed to go ashore. Oh, that was disappointing! When we got to England I went to the No.1 Canadian General Hospital in Basingstoke and worked on the burn ward. That was the most traumatic nursing I ever did. The patients were either tank burn victims or air force boys that had crashed and I often had to fight back the tears. I was looking after this one patient who begged us to let him die. His face, ears and hands were burned. They had grafted his left hand to his abdomen to try to grow skin between the fingers and when I first did his dressing, I saw this big mound of white. I took a look and it was maggots which were put there to eat the infection. I said, "Excuse me. I have to go and get some other dressing." I dashed back to the nurses' station and said, "help!" I had never seen maggots and wasn't told about them. I saw this boy later at the Shaughnessy Hospital in Vancouver where he was the life of the ward. He had had more than one hundred operations and I thought he looked quite well. I've seen far worse, oh yes. There was another patient at Basingstoke walking around with a pedicle of skin that had been grafted from his back to his chin. I saw this little thin line of skin pulsating and thought, "Well, this is progress."

I wasn't at Basingstoke very long. When they closed it, I went to the No. 4 Canadian General Hospital at Farnborough. After the war all the POWs went through this hospital when they were liberated and before they went back to Canada. The dieticians asked all the patients what they would like to eat and, if possible, they could have it. One story we loved was when these two young boys asked for—you'd never believe it—rice pudding with raisins! (laughs) That was their comfort food at home and they never got that in the prison camps. There was a POW camp right next to our hospital and we had two German patients. They weren't there for too long but we had to subdue one boy who was so angry he wanted to kill them. There were also two French Canadians who lost their eyesight when whoever served them Calvados in France put some V2 rocket fluid in it. This is what we were told and this was after the war. Another time I couldn't believe my ears when a soldier bragged that when his English girlfriend had to go to work, he crawled into bed with her mother!

I love people and I loved my nursing. In training the others thought I was weird because I couldn't wait for the two-hour break to be up so I could get

Paul Champagne (right) and Barny Rapin standing beside a Bren gun
carrier, England 1941. Together for the good times, the bad times,
and now together at the St. Anne's Military Hospital.

(Above) Maxine Llewellyn Bredt (front) in Bramshott, England
prior to embarking for Italy.

(Below) Three young Italian boys with Maxine Llewellyn Bredt
after she skied down a former minefield in Perugia.
"Bravo signorina!"

back on the floor. My career in the army was short but very rewarding. To quote my good friend, June Plummer Newton, "We nurses owe a debt of gratitude to the patients for their bravery and how they appreciated us."

Stan Matulis

Born in Lithuania, he came to Canada at the age of two and spent his early years in Goose Village, an area of Montreal shared by many ethnic groups. He remembers in the pre-war years the Italian Fascists celebrating in the neighbourhood with flags and bunting. He was sent in as a reinforcement to the Black Watch after their calamitous losses in Normandy in July 1944.

WORLD WAR II BREAKS OUT and some soldiers, wearing World War I uniforms—the jackets, breaches with puttees up to their knees—were sent to guard the Lachine Canal which was a sensitive area because if you sabotaged the locks, you couldn't use the canal. I used to see them whenever I went to the Atwater Market. I was at the Montreal Technical School heading for a career in the tool and dye makers trade and, when I finished in 1942 I worked for about six or seven months. Now we come to 1943. I'm seventeen-and-a-half years old. I had seen the older guys from Goose Village jump into the war as soon as it started. I was now living in Ville La Salle where I made a completely new circle of friends. All my buddies were enlisting but you had to be at least eighteen before you could join the army. The Canadian government put out all kinds of displays: LET'S GO, CANADA and, LET'S SHOW THEM HOW CANADA CAN FIGHT. I may not have been sophisticated enough to appreciate the international politics but I had to get in. Now what was I to do? There must be a way of getting in.

I told my dad that I had a chance to get into the Royal Canadian Electrical and Mechanical Engineers Corps of the army that had nothing to do with fighting and with my trade I would be able to get in very easily, but it had to be done immediately because they were recruiting. My dad said, "You're sure now?" So he and I went to the Verdun City Hall where my dad told the justice of the peace (who was a friend of his) that I was born in 1925 instead of 1926 and that made me eighteen-and-a-half. The very next day, I went to the recruiting depot on University Street. I was accepted, Zippo, no birth certificate required. These guys don't look a gift horse in the mouth, you know, when you're big and brawny. Hell, I'd go for twenty-plus anytime.

After basic and advanced training, the draft was picked to go overseas. I'm now nineteen years old minus two weeks. Nobody went overseas unless they had reached their nineteenth birthday. This was a terrible blow to me. All the guys I trained with went directly to Italy. So two weeks later, I got on the *Ile de France* and went to Scotland. I caught bronchial pneumonia and since it was a critical case I spent four weeks in a British military hospital in York. After recuperating I was put on draft and was told that I was going to the Black Watch, which was okay with me. While I was at school I had trained for one year with the Black Watch reserves so I had a good background.

On July 25, 1944 the Black Watch took horrendous casualties at a place called St. André-sur-Orne in the Verrières Ridge area. The battalion was just virtually cut to pieces. On the 26th, I came in with two other guys to the Fleury-sur-Orne area where the Black Watch had pulled in to lick their wounds and get re-equipped and reinforced. Sgt. Tommy Garvin of D Company told me I was going to be a lance corporal. I told him I had never had an NCO course and knew nothing. He said, "We have nobody here. They're either dead or wounded. You're going to be 2 IC and Charlie Blackburn will be the corporal." We were there for about a week and a half and got a new company commander whose name was Ron Bennett. He was related to R.B. Bennett, the pre-war Conservative prime minister and I liked him very much. He was the kind of guy, "You lead sir, and I'll follow." We had pickup games of softball and what not to keep morale up. We were about three kilometers from the front lines and there were no barns or houses so we lived in the slit trenches that we dug and covered over with anything we were able to scrounge to protect ourselves from the rain.

On the night of August 4, we went up to St. André-sur-Orne where we were to take over from the Fusiliers Mont-Royal who were holding the line. At noon the next day we were told that we were going in to May-sur-Orne to capture it or *try* to capture it. We had to walk about a kilometer or a kilometer-and-a-half to reach it. The day was hot and sunny and, as we looked around, we saw bodies still lying there—Canadians unfortunately. They had been there for quite a while unburied and it was a disturbing sight. You had to look away and not ponder too much over these guys. I can't take a guess over whether they were Black Watch or somebody else but it was a disturbing sight, no question about it. We were walking in single file and, when the guys in front of you stop, you stop. So we lay down and, boy, the stuff was coming over. The

Germans had mortars which made a demonical sound as they flew over. They were geared to make different sounds and it was a wail that was nerve wracking. They were called Moaning Minnies and they either had a six-bomb mortar or a twelve-bomb mortar. Or maybe they had two in tandem. You could count them and, if they stopped at six, you knew you had a bit of a respite but if they went to 7-8-9, you could expect the twelfth one sooner or later. They were pounding all over us and hitting the houses on all sides. The place was a complete fog with all the cement dust that arose. I saw a buddy of mine holding his head and walking back on his own. We were just lying there waiting for a command. We knew that the mortars would sooner or later hit our area so three of us went into a house to wait. House, ha! A *quarter* of a demolished house, but nevertheless some sort of shelter.

I walked in front of the window and felt something very funny. I was swirling and turning. No pain but the room was going around and around. I was on the ground and couldn't breathe. I said to myself, "This is it. It's only a matter of seconds before I go. Have I been friends with God?" I thought about Him and about my mother. I thought, "That poor woman is going to cry. I know the way she cried when she got the news that her two brothers died in Lithuania. I don't want her to cry like that." Then somebody asked me where I had been hit. I thought that he knew I was cut in half but was just making me feel good. He told me I was hit in the neck and patched me up with a field dressing. Then Cpl. Johnny Forsythe came in and said we were pulling back. He yanked a door off the hinges to make a makeshift stretcher and said, "Let's get him out." My weight was too heavy for this rickety door and the damn thing broke and I crashed right through. So Forsythe took my arms and Johnny Fiezo took my legs and out of the house and down the road we went. They'd carry me about twenty feet and then have to fall down because the mortars kept pounding and pounding. Forsythe finally said, "If you can walk, we'll support you but we can't carry you anymore. Sorry. We just can't." There was a Bren gun carrier that was just ready to drive away. Cpl. Forsythe yelled, "If you drive that carrier away, I'll shoot you." It felt very comforting to hear that. They put me in the carrier with about four or five other wounded guys and away it went. We were lying atop one another like sacks of potatoes. Maj. Ron Bennett was killed the same day.

I got a bullet right through the back of my neck. It went in one side and came out the other. (I found out years later that the bullet took a chip out of one of the vertebrae.) After being treated at the first aid station, they put me in a proper ambulance and took me to the Canadian hospital in Bayeux. I stayed there for a couple of days before I was put into a DC-3 and sent to No. 17 Canadian General Hospital in England. I was there for about four or five weeks and then I went to a convalescence depot where we did physiotherapy and PT and that kind of stuff. I was going to be sent back to my unit which didn't bother me at all but I noticed that I didn't have good finger control and couldn't locate the right size coins in my pocket. I thought that if I was going to go back, I had to have good control of my fingers to use a rifle or a grenade. I complained about this and they sent me to another Canadian hospital in Basingstoke which was where they sent neurological cases. While there I saw Marcel Lamarre whom I knew from basic training in Farnham. He joined the Régiment de la Chaudière and when I saw him lying in the bed, I could hardly recognize him because his face was so horribly mutilated. Marcel was nineteen and an up-and-coming boxer.

They gave me a few tests but could never find anything. They asked me if I wanted to go back to the depot for more convalescence. I told them that I wanted to be sent back to the reinforcement depot at Aldershot. I figured the sooner I rejoined my unit, the better. I got an eleven-day leave which was mandatory after hospitalization and I went to London. Had a grand time! When my money ran out I got a job in Watney's Brewery. They needed help either down below in the brewery rolling the barrels or assisting the guys in the lorries delivering kegs to pubs. The best thing was that they paid you twenty shillings a day, paid off every night. After eleven days I said, "I'm not going to go back to camp now, the hell with it. I'm going AWOL. It's nice to be in London." I did want to go back, but on my own time. They always looked at a pass to see if it was legit so I doctored mine up but made a hell of a mess of it. I rubbed out the original date and inked in another one but the ink spread and it looked terrible. I was staying at the Maple Leaf Club on Vauxhall Rd. near Victoria Station. It was a beautiful hostel and, as the days went by, I never knew why they didn't question me. By then, I was promoted from rolling the barrels in the basement at Watney's to being the third helper in the lorry. One day, as we were driving along, I could see the Provost Corps, the Canadian military police, on the sidewalk walking in my direction. I always wore my uniform so I ducked below the window. One of the guys saw this and said, in his Cockney accent, "Don't worry, Canada. You just come for the ride. We'll do the work."

I spent Christmas Day at the Maple Leaf Club and had a wonderful time—

I've still got a copy of the menu. Then I decided I had enough so I took the train back to Aldershot. It was about midnight when I arrived and the sergeant on duty said he would have to lock me up because I was so many days AWOL but he wouldn't if I promised to be on parade the next morning. The next day the colonel asked me what my excuse was for staying AWOL twenty days, twenty-three hours and one minute. Fifty-nine more minutes and I would have been a deserter. I told the colonel that I wanted to stay over for Christmas with my relatives. He said, "You expect me to believe that? TWENTY-EIGHT AND TWENTY-EIGHT. MARCH HIM OUT!" I lost twenty-eight days' pay and had twenty-eight days of field punishment which automatically meant a total of fifty-six days' pay lost. Field punishment means you could do your training with the guys and eat regularly but they piled on extra work after supper until ten o'clock at night. Then you were locked in and couldn't go into town or anything.

So then that period was over for me and I rejoined the regiment at the end of February and went back to the front lines. When I got back and they saw that I was a lance corporal, they told me that they needed a corporal in the worst way and I became a corporal. We did operations in the Hochwald Forest and Xanten. The Rhine had not yet been crossed and the entire 2nd Division pulled back into Holland for a two-week rest period. When that was over we crossed the Rhine at Emmerich. We were fighting back and forth in the area of the Dutch-German border. Maybe we'd be in Germany for two days and then we'd pull back and fight in Holland.

It was Easter Sunday, 17 Platoon was giving us covering fire. I was point man leading a section and as I walked past Cpl. Johnny Pierson, a boyhood friend from Goose Village, he said, "Good luck, Stan." We came to a rise in the ground. I raised my head and saw, just over the crest, about fifteen feet away, three Germans who were crouched and talking. As I aimed, one of them looked up and gave a hell of a shout to his comrades. I squeezed the trigger. Three rounds came out and then I ran out of ammunition. They scooted behind a shed so I took out a grenade and lobbed it. I never threw a grenade so beautifully in my life. WHAM! The minute that happens you have to move and not give them a chance to recuperate. Two gave themselves up and one didn't survive. We went on. Since they were giving up so easily, I thought they were demoralized. About one hundred yards away, I went around the corner of a house and saw another German. I yelled, *"Hände Hoch!"* and he whipped around as fast as lightning, took me by surprise and let me have it but I had the presence of mind to duck. It is a learning experience to be battle wise. I had him dead to rights and thought I would spare his life. He was shot by someone else advancing in the next platoon.

Now we came to the end of April and things started to move very quickly. The Germans were surrendering. We were now in Germany. D Company (my company) had a rendezvous with the Germans to surrender. A German vehicle, equivalent to our famous jeep, came down the road fluttering a white flag and our major negotiated with them. I remember the German officer saluting but our major wouldn't return his salute. I've always remembered that. You know, chivalry and military tradition, you return a salute whether it's your enemy or not. We mounted RCASC 3-tonners and away we drove in the direction of Oldenburg. There were many, many German soldiers along the roadside. They knew the war was over and looked at us glumly. We never jeered or mocked them.

I can never knock history. As bad and as bloody as things were how can I knock history? If it wasn't for those bad times, I wouldn't be doing the things I'm doing now. It would never have happened. You think too about the force of history. You may moan and say that if Chamberlain had stuck to his guns and stopped Hitler then the war wouldn't have started. But it happened. If I hadn't joined up, my parents wouldn't have been able to send me to university. Never. I didn't have the scratch but the DVA paid my tuition and gave me $60 a month. I only had one year of high school but I worked hard and I did it. The day that Loyola accepted me, I walked out the door of the college and wanted to hop, skip and jump with joy. I went to McGill after that and graduated in 1957 as a metallurgical engineer. All I can say is that history has been good to me.

Jean-Charles (Charly) Forbes

A "soldier's soldier" and a born leader, Charly Forbes has the heart of a warrior and the soul of an artist. A musician, painter and author of his autobiography, *Fantassin, pour mon pays, la gloire et ... des prunes*, he was also the recipient, in 1945, of Holland's highest military award, the RMWO (Military Knight of the Order of William) for his continuous bravery while fighting in the Scheldt campaign. This award is equivalent to but predates the Victoria Cross. A francophone from Matane, he is a descendent of one of the privates in Capt. Nairn's 78th Fraser Highlanders who fought at the Battle of the Plains of Abraham. He studied English for two years at Collège du Sacré-Coeur in Victoriaville but only perfected it later at the Royal Military College in Kingston. He served with the Régiment de Maisonneuve as a lieutenant in northwest Europe during the war and, in 1985, was appointed its honorary lieutenant colonel. Anyone visiting the armoury of the regiment on Cathcart Street in Montreal can see his large and evocative oil painting which shows soldiers making their tortured way across the Walcheren Causeway in Holland in November 1944. A career soldier, he also fought in Korea with the 1st Canadian Contingent, serving with the 2nd Battalion Royal 22nd Regiment. He received a citation during the Battle of Hill 355 on November 22, 1951.

WHAT I CALL "THE MONTREAL CLUB," was very influential and powerful. This "club" of officers included French and English Canadians with names like Ostiguy, Molson and Morgan and was made up of "la noblesse" of Montreal. If you came from outside Montreal, you weren't a member of the club. These men could pick up a phone and give orders. When I arrived in Liverpool, I wanted to join my buddy, Philippe Rousseau, who was running a French-speaking company of the 1st Canadian Parachute Battalion, so I submitted my application to Canadian Military Headquarters in London. Then Col. Morgan, who was commanding the 6th CIRU (Canadian Infantry Reinforcement Unit) in Whitney called me and said that my idea was crazy. I told him I wanted to join my friend and become a paratrooper—part of the elite. He said, "Never mind the elite. Wars are won on the ground. I'll send you to a good battalion." He grabbed the phone and called Col. Bisaillon in Brighton who said that he had more officers than he needed. Morgan said, "Take one out and put this one in. He's a good one." Then he told me that I was taking the train the next day to join the Régiment de Maisonneuve. So I arrived at the Maisonneuves. Hmm, they thought—"Forbes (Scotch name) from Gaspé whose mother language is French (in fact, he speaks it better than many French Canadians from Montreal)." But anyway, I joined and did the job.

We landed at Courselle-sur-Mer on the 18th of July 1944 and went into action at Faubourg de Vaucelles, a suburb of Caen. I was commanding 18 Platoon of D Company. My first battle was fought at St. André-sur-Orne where we faced the 12th Panzer Division. We finally captured it after losing it twice. What do I remember of St. André-sur-Orne? As we moved at night, we came under a terrible mortar bombardment. We managed to hold on but had many casualties. One of my men was bleeding very badly and yelling because a shell had blown his leg off above the knee. I went over to him and could see that his leg was completely open and he was going to die but I took a shoelace off my boot and made a tourniquet while I was sitting on his other leg. The next day when I woke up, my battledress was covered with blood. It was in my pockets and everywhere. It was disgusting but, deep down in my heart, something popped up. I said to myself, "My boy, this is war. You'd better get used to it. *Look at it. Smell it. That's what you wanted. You got it!*" It comforted me, somehow or other, to be able to talk to my excited mind. I wasn't the kind of boy who liked to look at blood (all my wars as a child playing with lead soldiers, had been bloodless). The next day, we went into the village and there were German bodies lying all around. I looked at one corpse, kicked it, and said to myself, "This is the enemy." I picked up his beautiful pistol and walked back to my position, feeling sure of myself.

The night of the 7 of August, we began Operation Totalize. The road to Falaise—that was a horrible battle. (There was an old saying with the soldiers in Normandy, If you last three days, you're good for three months. After three months, count your hours.) We had over 1,000 planes and hundreds of guns supporting us, as well as artificial moonlight. The next day, my platoon was mounted on three tanks to protect them because they were vulnerable as they moved into the infantry lines. Suddenly, I saw some Germans in the field and threw a grenade. It killed one and wounded another. Perhaps some of them escaped but one came out with his hands up. I jumped off my tank with my pistol and put it in his face and said, "You're lucky. Your war is over. Mine is not." I spoke French to him and he understood—they all speak two or three languages. He was very haggard looking and spat in my face. I told one of my men to take him away because I had things to do and the tank commander was telling me to get back on the tank. Then I heard a bang and saw the German soldier fall. The soldier who shot him said, "He's not going to spit anymore." The German was about seventeen and a fanatic, a member of the 12th Panzer SS. I told the soldier that what he did wasn't cricket and not to do that anymore. He told me that the German was moving around, gesticulating and refused to keep his hands up. So he was shot. That was it and we moved on.

We went through a zone that had been bombed the night before which was full of craters. The Germans had all kinds of anti-tank and anti-aircraft guns and the famous 88mm guns. Kurt Meyer ordered his tanks of the 12th SS to line up. We were in a crater taking cover as the shells were coming over. Our tanks were being shot like ducks and, I would say, without exaggeration, that there were more than fifty of them burning. It was an ugly sight because, contrary to the Germans who used diesel fuel, the Shermans used high-octane gasoline which, when hit, caught fire. When a tank was hit you could see the boys who couldn't get out in flames. The advance was halted and my next objective was the village of Quilly on the extreme left flank of Bretteville-sur-Laize. When we reached it we stopped there. We were all tired and beat and hadn't slept in I don't know how many days. We had twenty-four hours to remain there and to rest and recuperate. We found a piggery which stank but any place that protects you from gunfire is good. I told my sergeant to wake me up if anything happened.

About three hours later, someone came and knocked at the door. It was Louis. He said, "Sir, can I speak to you?" I said yes. He said, "I just received mail, a letter from my girlfriend in Quebec." I said, "That's nice." He told me to read it. I did and then said, "What are you going to do, write her?" He said, "That's the problem. I can't write and my buddy who used to answer my letters was killed yesterday." He couldn't read or write. We did that very often—write for our soldiers. (said very softly) He said, "I would be most obliged, sir, if you would answer it." I told him I would but that he wasn't going to get it that night. So the next morning when I woke up, I said, "What do I write?" I was engaged at the time and decided to write as if I were talking to my fiancée. That was the only way. "Dear Agnès, I was so pleased to receive your letter. I'd like to tell you what we are going through but I cannot. All I can say is that I am in France. I think of you very often....I love you. I love you. Louis." When he came back, I read it to him. He said, "Tabar....Lieutenant, it's nice. I never thought you could write like that." Then he said, "At the end of the letter, could you ask her to kiss her mother for me. I never knew mine." To me, this is one of the most beautiful human stories of my life and of war, where human beings remain human beings. He went away and showed his letter to everybody. Then three other boys (who could write) came to me. "Lieutenant, we thought your letter was damn good. Could you write us one too? We'll copy it and send it to all the girls we know and get some mail back." I don't think until that particular moment that I realized what a letter means to a soldier. It's a link with the family and with the country. It's the umbilical cord between hell, beauty and comfort.

We fought through northern France and liberated Bourbourg, Bergues, Broukerke and Spyker. We moved along and then fought at the Albert Canal in Belgium. A group of eight Belgian men came to the regiment before we crossed into Holland. They were dressed up in old coats and helmets from the

First World War and wanted to fight with us. We had no French-Canadian reinforcements and platoons were down to about 50 percent of their normal strength. We put them to work in the kitchen but they weren't happy. One of them, Jacques Cantiniaux came to see me. He was the son of a doctor, very tall and noble-looking. "Monsieur," he said, "when we decided to join the Régiment de Maisonneuve in the Canadian forces, it was to fight under your flag for our country. We don't like to peel potatoes. Unless we are capable of lining up with your men, we will have to return to Brussels." We needed men and they had the languages. They spoke Flemish, English and French. I went to see Frank Robert, my company commander, and told him that we needed these guys and would manage them. We'd put Canadian uniforms on them but they would have no badges, no identification, no pay and no benefits. Lt. Guy de Merlis took four of them and I took the other four. They were so proud and the services they rendered to us.... First of all, it was their country and they had suffered. They were young and eager to fight. It was a bad note in the eyes of the British that King Leopold had surrendered to the Germans. The country was divided but these men *hated* the Germans. They were fantastic— brave and obedient and carried out military duties the same as we did until they disbanded in January 1945 and returned to Brussels. I am in contact with the two that are still alive, Roger Mathen and Jacques Cantiniaux and they came to visit me here in Quebec—brothers-in-arms.

It became very evident at higher headquarters that the port of Antwerp would have to be liberated so the Allied armies could be re-supplied before crossing the Rhine. Supplies had to be brought all the way from Normandy and we were in a critical situation—our guns were down to seven shells a day. We had reached Antwerp but, by the 1 of November, it was still impossible to enter the harbour. Antwerp was sixty miles from the sea and the only way you could get to this port was through the Scheldt Estuary. Because of the Allied failure to go forward and block the 15th Army, which had been kicked out of the Beveland by the Dutch, this army came back and reinforced its positions at Breskens, Walcheren and Beveland. German higher headquarters realized that as long as they had big, heavy naval guns on Walcheren and in Breskens, we couldn't enter the port, so it was a very complex sort of operation. The Germans reorganized very, very rapidly with two of their best brains, General Eberding and Baron von der Heydte with his famous 6th Flagger (Parachute Regiment). After the SS, they were the toughest boys the Germans had at the time. They had more than 25,000 troops to defend this area and they fought like hell. Their idea was also to defend Woensdrecht, which was at the entrance to South Beveland, at all costs. Their reasons were very simple. As the pressure was building from the south in the Breskens area, they wanted to retain the peninsula open for the escape of the 15th Army. So we can say this operation was divided into three parts, the Breskens Pocket, Walcheren Island and the Beveland peninsula.

General Simonds decided on a two-prong attack: one in a westerly direction from Woensdrecht and the other from the south in the direction of Breskens. The 3rd Division and the 4th Armoured Division were ordered to capture Breskens with a view to eventually cross to Vlissingen (Flushing) to support the operation on Walcheren. The 2nd Division would go around Antwerp and capture Hoogerheide and Woensdrecht and close the peninsula. Once the Beveland had been cleaned up we could enter Walcheren Island which had been 90 percent flooded by an Allied bombardment planned by Simonds. This was supposed to silence the German guns but they were on the dikes and still firing. I was with the 2nd Division and we crossed the frontier into Holland at Putte. Most of the area where we were fighting was polder country and had been flooded. This was really where the dirty part of the war took place for the Canadians as we were fighting in water and mud. It was October and the wind was blowing from the North Sea. Because of the water, the tanks could not support us and the artillery had difficulty finding places for their gun positions. We were tired and had no reinforcements. These are some details that one has to mention.

As the Royal Hamilton Light Infantry was attacking Woensdrecht, my regiment was attacking Hoogerheide. I was commanding the leading patrol and we got pinned down behind an anti-tank ditch and had to withdraw. I told my commanding officer that if we made a left flanking movement around the village with an attack by the tanks on the right side, we could manage to take it. We did and captured twenty-four German parachutists who were hiding in a hospital. These were the same ones who had been defending the anti-tank ditch. I got mad, lined them all up and told them that the Geneva Convention forbade them to hide in a Red Cross hospital and that they were going to be executed *in situ*. I said, "Where's the officer?" A very nice German gentleman with a hat, gloves, a greatcoat and beautiful boots came to me and said in French, "*Je suis l'officier. Je veux parler avec un officier.*" I told him I was an officer and he looked at me with disgust because I was covered with mud.

He turned around and spoke to his sergeant, "Yavasoltibihabsoitdiehow

OFFIZIER." Saying, possibly, "*This* is one of their officers?" The other one also looked at me in disgust. I said to my machine gunners, "LINE UP ON THE BANK THERE. WE'RE GOING TO EXECUTE THEM!" He heard that and, very arrogantly said, "I think I have the privilege of being examined by a court martial. Is this the way Canadians do it?" I told him that he was hiding under a Red Cross which was against the Geneva Convention and they were judged *de facto*. He was so arrogant that I made him take his boots off and my batman, Greg, put them on and was goose-stepping around. It was a farce but a sad farce because the machine guns were lined up and the Germans knew that I meant every word. He started speaking German to his sergeant and looked pretty much in despair. I then had a moment of hesitation and said, "I admit the fact that you may have been hiding under a Red Cross for protection but, if I find any weapons, that's it." He said, "You will notice that nobody here carries any weapons." I lifted a soldier's cap and he had a clip of five rounds of ammunition under it. I said, "You say you are not prepared to keep on fighting. What's this?" I showed him the clip of bullets and hit the soldier in the face with it, scraping the whole side of his face. The officer didn't say a word. He knew there was no argument this time. I told my boys to search the hospital (which was an orphanage with a Red Cross on the roof). They came back and said that there were no weapons there. All they found was a little valise. They opened it and there was a chalice, hosts and a priest's vestments. I said, " Those are priest's vestments. Are you a priest?" He said, "Yes, a Catholic priest. If you can't respect the Geneva Convention, at least respect my holy vestments." (I found out later that, in the German army, a padre had two roles. He was first and foremost an officer but, as a secondary job, he was a chaplain.) Now, as a Catholic, am I going to kill him? Our chaplains weren't fighters and I was completely disorganized. Then he told me that they had planned to surrender and had hidden their weapons in a well about fifty yards away. I sent the boys to the well and they found a .50 caliber machine gun, three or four mg .42s, machine guns, rifles and grenades. I told them they were prisoners and told my men to get them out.

The reason I mention this is simply because if war is ugly on one side, it was also ugly on the other side. We were dehumanized. We were soldiers. I got a bullet through my backpack that morning and the only thing that came out alive was a crucifix which I still have. My table knife was cut in half and planted in my back and I never knew until I came back and they told me that blood was coming out from under my pack. The tension in battle gets to be such that you lose your senses. You lose your human dimensions, your feelings. You get to rev at such a speed, your mind, your body, your muscles and everything, that you lose your sense of reality.

Sometimes we have a tendency to consider war as a continuous ugly show where we are always submitting to horrible sorts of things but there are some happy things that happen. We had found a violin in France which my men cherished. The company blankets were carried in the back of a carrier and the violin was wrapped in the blankets. The company commander went to check something out and came back under a hail of fire so the blankets got hit with German machine guns. When he got back, we looked at all the holes in the roll of blankets. The boys were more worried about the violin than they were about their lives and said to the major, "Look, you've destroyed the lieutenant's violin." So they started to unwrap the blankets and the bullets were falling one by one like drops of water. The violin wasn't hit and the great conclusion was that German bullets do not pierce through nine inches of Canadian wool blankets.

Following fierce battles fought by the three brigades of the 2nd Division in the area of Woensdrecht, Ossendrecht and Hoogerheide, we captured Goes on South Beveland and took about seventy-five prisoners. I liberated Bastiaan Berkunk and a few other resistance fighters at a small village called Arendskerke where they had been hiding. They were all completely delirious and jumped in my arms. Bastiaan felt that he owed his soul to me because he was wanted by the Gestapo and, when we arrived, he had about three or four hours left to go before he was to be picked up. From then on it was a race to the causeway. The macabre race (as they called it) because Brig. Keefler told the 4th, 5th and 6th Brigades that the first ones to make it to the causeway wouldn't have to cross it. The brigade that lost was the 5th, the Calgaries (the Calgary Highlanders), Black Watch and Maisonneuves. We had to cross it. The causeway was approximately 1,200 yards long and about ninety feet wide. There was a railroad on the right hand side, a road and a bicycle path on the left. It married up the island of Walcheren to the western part of South Beveland and the attack was to be on three fronts: British commandos were to attack at Westkapelle and Flushing and the Canadians were to go across the causeway, with the objective being to capture the two dikes on the other side. The Maisonneuves were the reserve battalion and we were going on leave for seven days in Lierre, Belgium. It was the first time that the 2nd Division was to be hauled out of the front lines since France and we needed it badly.

We're washing our clothes, shaving and eating and everything is hunky-dory. We are happy as hell. It's seven o'clock on the night of the 1 of November. We know there's a terrific battle taking place from the noise. We hear the guns and know the fighting is intense but, at platoon level, we don't know what the hell is going on. We were burning stairs, windows and everything else in the fireplace where we were so we could dry up to be prepared to go on holiday and meet the girls. I heard a motorcycle outside. "Lieutenant Forbes here?" "Yes." "The commanding officer wants to see you." When I got there, Col. Julien Bibeau told me to get ready, that I was going to be the leading platoon of D Company and the plan was to attack at four o'clock in the morning behind a concentrated artillery barrage. Our objective was to capture the right side of the dike on the island while Guy de Merlis was to follow and capture the left side. At six o'clock we were to be relieved by the Glasgow Highlanders. When I came back, my face was as long as a dehydrated sock and the boys looked at me. They asked what was going on. I said, "We're attacking tomorrow morning. The Black Watch and the Calgaries haven't been able to make it across so the brigadier has asked the Maisonneuves to try and establish a bridgehead so that the 52nd Lowland Division can get through."

It was a very sad moment. We all looked at each other. Then, a terrible incident in my life as a platoon commander occurred. I was telling my men what was going to happen and how we were going to advance. At about 3:15, half an hour before we were to start, one of my men said, "I'm not going. Sir, when you have enough, you have enough. Do you understand?" In front of all my men! I told him that I understood but that this was going to be our last effort and we would be back in two hours and go to Lierre. He said, "No." We had received orders (verbal and written) that anyone who refused to fight or abandoned a position could be shot *in situ*. We were beginning to get deserters. People refuse to say that, but it's true. I told this soldier, "You know what my orders are. I have to shoot you." He said, "Shoot me." And he was one good soldier who had already been wounded twice. It was tough. I was completely thrown off my horse. It was to be our last effort and then we were out—that was it. It nearly killed me. Then one thought came to my mind. I said, "I'm not going to be your judge. If the men in the platoon say you're not going forward, I'll get you out and send you back. If they say to kill you, I'll kill you." Terrible! These are stories that are not told but they happened. So I asked the men what to do with him. The argument started: "YOU GODDAMNED GREENHORN YELLOW BASTARD! WE DON'T WANT YOU HERE! GET

OUT! WE ALWAYS THOUGHT YOU WERE A SON OF A BITCH ANYWAY."
This fellow answered, "I WAS HERE BEFORE YOU. I STARTED TO FIGHT
IN FRANCE AND YOU'VE ONLY BEEN HERE TWO MONTHS." I told him
it was his decision and he said, "Jesus Christ, Lieutenant. I'll show these young
bastards who I am." None of them were old fighters like he was. So that was
settled. I said, "I need you. Stay by my side." And away we went.

On the causeway, we had to advance 1,000 yards practically in single file
which made us what we called an enfilated target by withering fire from
machine guns and an anti-tank gun which was coming from the right, left
and center of Walcheren Island. Aerial photographs revealed that midway
across the causeway there was a large crater with a smaller one in front of it
but the maps showed only one crater. I had gone about 300 yards and told my
men to take cover in a crater, which I thought was the only one, and wait for
the artillery barrage before advancing. We were tense as bloody hell. It was
pitch dark, the sleet was coming from the north and I could hear click-click-
click as the men worked their rifle breeches so they wouldn't freeze. I was
watching the clock and then the whole sky lit up and an artillery barrage came
close to my position. Then, through the flash and the explosions, we saw troops
coming toward us and thought they were Germans. I yelled FIRE and then I
saw that we were firing on the Calgaries who were pulling back from the second
crater. This is how the battle started and is war in its ugliest form. I jumped on
my machine gunners and stopped them from firing. The Calgaries managed
to get through and I had to remuster my troops. We continued along and saw
the other big crater which we had to practically swim through because the
water was up to our necks. At this stage, the bombardment was intense. I got
hit in the left wrist and fell into a pit. I thought about my violin because my
wrist was cut right across the inside and I could see all the nerves. I wrapped it
up and, since it was my left wrist, I managed to keep control. One of the
Belgians with me was also hit. Then Guy de Merlis came up and told me he
was going to drive forward and I said I would try to follow him. Guy got all
the way to the end and I managed to pull all the men I could behind me and
followed.

We did not capture our objective but bypassed it by 500 yards which meant
that the Germans were still holding the approaches to the causeway and we
were caught inland on Walcheren. We didn't realize it because there was water
everywhere. Guy went to the left with his men and captured a farmhouse. I
went to the right and was covering a crossroads about 200 yards from where

Guy was. We had no radio and couldn't speak to each other. We were about halfway to the town of Middleburg but nobody who followed was able to get through because the German guns were still firing on the causeway. Now it's six in the morning and we're in water like ducks with only our heads sticking out. I had twenty-one men when I started and by this time I had about eleven men left and one machine gun. Guy had about the same. There was so much pressure put on the Germans by the British that they decided to abandon the dikes at seven o'clock and they passed by my position. I can still see them with their greatcoats, frozen stiff and covered with blood, mud and ice. They were straggling in the water and looked miserable. We shot at them and captured seven prisoners. What was left of them pulled back into their positions and called for reinforcements. Some of the wounded were lying in water and drowning as the tide was rising and it was another ugly scene of war. It hurt my heart as I tried to pull one out but I couldn't as he was stuck in the mud. These soldiers were all forty to forty-five years of age and were what was called, a "white bread" division. We asked one of them some questions but he refused to answer, saying that his duty as a soldier was to give his name and rank. He said, "I cannot tell you any more. I don't know any more. I am forty-two years of age and have four children and a wife in Germany. Please, please, save me."

Then the situation deteriorated. I heard a bullet shot and then another which hit the concrete right next to my head. Then one of the Belgians, a runner, came from Guy's position and told us we had to withdraw. I told him I was staying there. Then, suddenly, Guy de Merlis ran to my position and said that we were pulling back. Then we had to go through hell again to get past the Germans on the dikes. I saw the Glasgow Highlanders all lined up at the end of the causeway. I had about six or seven men with me—the others had gone through—and we were being fired upon by the Germans. I asked an artillery lieutenant by the name of Innes to put up a smokescreen so I could pull my men back. He did and got the Military Cross for that. One of the smoke canisters fell on one of the British and opened his head right in front of me. I told my men to get out and we started to run. A German shell exploded about a third of the way across the causeway. Talbot, one of my men, got hit by shrapnel and was paralyzed from the waist down. He couldn't walk so I dragged him into one of the slit trenches on the side. I lifted his battledress and there was a sharp piece of shrapnel planted in his spine. Apparently, I never should have done it, but I pulled it out and he got the feeling back into his legs. He managed to stand up and I put him on my back. By the time we reached the other end it was about eleven o'clock on the night of the second of November.

When we arrived, there was only an ambulance at the end of the causeway. I put Talbot in it and the Dutch people, the resistance, were waiting for me. Bastiaan knew I was on the bridge and they were all there. They carried me to a house and gave me a shot of gin. They realized that I was out of my mind. I could hear bullets and was ducking bullets and was going through hell. I started to shake. I was cold. I was hungry. There were about ten of them around me. The women placed hot water bottles next to me, fed me milk with eggs and Dutch gin, and called a doctor in the village. They kept me for two days and I recuperated. When I saw a brigade vehicle going by the house, I stopped the driver and he told me the brigade was in Lierre and he was going back there. When I got to Lierre, everybody said that they thought I was dead because I was left on the causeway. I told them that I wasn't left on the causeway but *abandoned* on the causeway. They told me to report to the adjutant because I had been reported missing. When my mother got the news that I was missing she said, "He's not missing. They're going to find him. If he was dead, I would know."

Down deep in my heart, I wanted to be evacuated. I had had my time. In my company we had a medical corporal. He took the wrapping off my wrist and told me that it didn't look too bad and, if he evacuated me, I would be kept for about five days to have a good rest and then be put back in the reinforcement stream and would end up in another battalion. He said, "We'll lose you and wind up with a new lieutenant who doesn't know anything. Stay here." There are not too many testimonials of affection from your soldiers and it was fantastic to hear that.

In December 1944, I went on a reconnaissance patrol on the Maas River, near Groesbeek. My driver got killed and I was hit over my right eye. The skin was falling over my eye and I could only see with the left one. I was carried to a British tank battalion medical room. I sat in a barber's chair biting on a stick which they put in my mouth. The doctor wasn't there and a corporal told me he would sew it up before it got infected but I would need an operation because it was a very bad cut. He put in seven stitches and it looked bloody horrible. It was also bleeding every day so I went to see the CO because I knew I couldn't carry on. Col. Bibeau told me that the Dutch government had decided to decorate me. He gave me a letter from the corps commander and I was driven to Amsterdam dressed in boots, tin hat and everything. I didn't have a proper greatcoat and had to wear a woman's coat that buttoned up the wrong way. I arrived at the palace and was stopped by a corporal who said, "Where are you going?" I showed him my letter and he said, "Just a moment, sir." There were more police there than you could think of. I waited for about fifteen minutes and then I heard, "Forbes, Forbes, looking for Forbes." An officer said, "The Queen is waiting for you." Son of a gun, I said, "*the* Queen?" I was escorted to Queen Wilhelmina and she embraced me. She put a sword on my shoulder and said, "I make you a knight of the Order of Willem, my ancestor." There were five Canadians who got this medal and now there are only two of us left. Every five years, my wife and I get a ticket to go to Holland for fifteen days. There is a driver at the airport waiting for us and we're treated like royalty.

[*Author's note*: Having always admired the professionalism of the German soldier, Col. Forbes promised himself that, after the war was over, he would try to meet one of their officers. In 1994, on a visit to France, he met the mayor of Caen, Georges Denizot who, along with his wife, Anne-Marie, was working on a reconciliation project. Together they visited Baron Friederich von der Heydte (his former antagonist at the Scheldt) and made a recording of that visit. Von der Heydte spoke about his respect for the Canadian soldier and the fact that Canadian officers, unlike some others, fought alongside their men. "Canadian soldiers, the best in the world. The Canadian officers, they fought with their men." High words of praise, indeed, from this respected brigadier-general. Then they found Karl Walter Becker, a former officer in the 12th Panzer "Hitlerjugend" SS, who wrote a letter to Forbes and in it, he mentioned that he had captured two French-Canadian officers in Normandy. Forbes thought they might have been Lt.-Col. Julien Bibeau and his intelligence officer, Marcel Dusseault, who were captured but managed to escape on August 24, 1944. In fact, Becker himself was captured a few days later and spent four years as a POW in Scotland. The reason for his incarceration until 1948 was the ongoing investigation into the mass murder of at least eighteen Canadian POWs at the Abbaye d'Ardenne, the brigade headquarters of Standartenführer (SS Colonel) Kurt Meyer. It has been proven with certainty that 134 Canadian POWs were murdered by the 12th SS during the Battle of Normandy and it goes without saying that there was some understandable retaliation by Canadian soldiers. The following year, in Europe, Forbes met Becker and invited him to Quebec. In June 1996, Walter Hoffmann, a former corporal of the 21st Panzer Division, Becker, Bastiaan Berkunk, the former Dutch resistance fighter, along with their wives, visited Charly Forbes and his wife Nicole. Becker wanted to meet Marcel Dusseault who, having lost a brother in Italy, wanted nothing to do with the meeting until Forbes managed to change his mind. Interestingly enough, it was Dusseault's field notebook which saved Becker from execution after the war. For fifteen days, the group met and it was a very moving experience as they talked about the war and came to some kind of personal understanding of this most horrible event.]

Ivan D. Burch

Born in Victoria, British Columbia, Ivan Burch has lived in the Montreal area since 1953. His combat participation during World War II was relatively short but not uneventful. He had a liking for military life at an early age as a member of both the army and sea cadets. While attending Victoria College in 1942, he was a member of the Reserve Army (3rd Battalion, The Canadian Scottish Regiment) and in June 1943, joined the active force. By June 1944, he had completed his infantry training and was employed as a corporal instructor at the Infantry Training Center in Calgary, Alberta. As the Canadian army, by this time, was fighting in northwest Europe, it seemed like there was a strong possibility of an early end to hostilities. Champing at the bit to see some action before the war ended, he relinquished his rank and requested overseas service. As a private soldier, he arrived in England in mid-October 1944 and was quickly moved on to Belgium, landing at Ostend on November 6.

As a reinforcement infantry soldier moving up to the front, I had no guarantee as to where I would be sent. There were, in fact, twenty-five different Canadian infantry regiments in northwest Europe at the time, all in desperate need of trained soldier reinforcements. I, nevertheless, made it known at every opportunity that I wished to join the 1st Battalion, The Canadian Scottish Regiment (sister battalion of my former reserve army unit in Victoria). Nothing ventured, nothing gained. I was very fortunate in that my regimental destination was changed several times as a result of my persistent requests, and on November 16, I finally arrived at the rear echelon of the Canadian Scottish. As I was waiting with other new reinforcements, somebody called my name and I recognized a friend, Gordon McIntosh. He shouted to me, "Try for C Company, 15 Platoon." When the regimental sergeant major began assigning new personnel to various companies, I spoke up and requested C Company. He stared hard at me with a "how dare you" look, but finally pointed to the C Company group. When I arrived at the company area and asked for 15 Platoon to be with my friend, I was told that Corporal McIntosh had just been transferred to another company. I was disappointed but, as a reinforcement soldier, I had succeeded in getting to the smallest formation of my choice in the Canadian army operating in northwest Europe. I don't think any other reinforcement private soldier could have made that claim!

At that time, the regiment was located in the Nijmegan, Holland area where we spent most of the winter in a static warfare role. This involved mostly training, manning defensive positions and patrolling activities. The only real excitement came from incoming German artillery and rocket fire and patrolling. I was a member of one patrol when the guys in front ran into a minefield and one was killed and another died of wounds while a prisoner of war. It's scary and upsetting losing men. Even though you had only been with them a limited period of maybe a few weeks, you quickly melded and became part of the group. We're talking about a platoon, twenty-five to thirty-five persons, depending on the situation. There was also the occasional V1 flying bomb which was launched by the Germans on a course towards Antwerp and other coastal ports. The rocket engines were noisy and the exhaust flames made a spectacular show at night as they passed over our positions. I also remember watching a tremendous dogfight between Allied and German fighter planes on a clear and sunny New Year's Day in 1945. As they climbed and dived close to the ground, the spent bullets were landing around our slit trenches. These incidents certainly broke the monotony of our situation.

In early February, along with the rest of the Allied forces, we started to push towards the Rhine River. There were many small battles as we moved, in many cases, in amphibian vehicles, from Nijmegan, through flat polder country which the Germans had flooded. We passed through Cleve and, on the 15th the battalion took up a position at Heseler Feld with C Company in a reserve role. The enemy counter-attacked and pounded the unit with heavy artillery, rocket and mortar fire almost continuously for two nights and a day. The forward companies took many casualties but held on. On the morning of the 19th, C Company was ordered to attack and clear out enemy positions on the edge of the Moyland Wood to our front. The plan involved an advance up a hill, over open ground, without cover and only limited artillery and mortar support. The boggy ground ruled out close support by tanks. As the Regina Rifle Regiment on our left had been battling for three days to clear the same area without success, I think we all sensed that it was a difficult mission. Events later proved it to be "mission impossible". Turned out that we were facing elite German paratroopers who were heavily dug into Moyland Wood, apparently unbeknown to Allied intelligence sources.

As we moved over the ridge under intense enemy fire with mortars and machine guns, I looked back to find that I was the only one standing and one of my friends was yelling, "BURCH, GET DOWN!" I was almost what could be described as "bomb happy" at this stage but I did lie down in a shallow trench. I pulled my helmet over my face and was trying to keep my mind focussed. I suddenly remembered John 3:16 from my Sunday School days: "For God so loved the world that He gave His only begotten Son and whoever believeth in Him shall not perish but have everlasting life." I kept saying that over and over until I glanced up and there's a German paratrooper with a Schmeisser machine gun pointed at me about six feet away saying "*RAUS!*" I had no alternative but to put up my arms in surrender and be escorted off the field. Someone asked if we could pick up our wounded and they allowed us to do so. I helped to carry one of our guys into the German lines.

I was still very upset, as one can imagine, after going through this tremendous pounding of artillery, mortars and machine guns and then to see so many of my friends shot down. At one stage at least thirty-two of us were herded by the Germans and lined up against a wall. They made like a firing squad and started cocking their weapons in a little bit of intimidation. I'll always remember (laughs) one individual in the back saying in a very whiney voice to Sergeant Smith, "Smitty, what are they going to do?" The sergeant said, "SHADDUP!" so we all shut up. These German soldiers were very young but first-class soldiers. They were the elite 6th Parachute Division. They looked after our wounded and offered us cigarettes. They didn't try to take any souvenirs from us and I can't speak highly enough about their behaviour toward us. It was also the first time I saw an interesting way of bandaging an arm. They had these plastic things which they shaped to the arm to hold it in place. Then they put us in a truck and started to move us back to the rear echelons. We'd go so far and the road would be bombed out so we'd get out and walk. Overnight, we would stay in some building or other in a town and they would try to give us some food, a little bit of bread or soup, whatever they had. We did start to get kicked around in the sense that the rear echelon troops were more inclined to make fun of us as prisoners of war. They ridiculed us and took our watches, that sort of thing. We were looking pretty beat up after having been in dirty slit trenches and going through the battle. They thought this was great, the vaunted Allied soldiers, look at them, ha-ha-ha.

In a matter of two or three days, we arrived at Wesel on the Rhine River and walked across a railway bridge which was still intact. As we were crossing it, Royal Air Force Typhoons attacked with rockets so we were under tremendous fire from our own aircraft. As we got further back, the long-range artillery made it more dangerous as we moved towards the rear. You could almost say we considered ourselves lucky to get through the German rear area because the Allies were putting on a tremendous battle to get to the Rhine. We were walked and trucked to an interrogation center for prisoners of war located in a town called Bocholt. Then we were taken one at a time into a room where there was a German officer who spoke English fluently. He said, "You're a member of the 1st Battalion, Canadian Scottish Regiment, 3rd Canadian Division." I said, "I'm only entitled to give you my name, rank and number." He said, "Oh, come on. It says in your pay book that you're a university student. You're an intelligent individual." I said, "I'm sorry. I'm not entitled to give you any information and I'm only a private." I repeated again, "My name is Burch, Private Burch. My number is K51637." He passed across a package of cigarettes and said, "Have a cigarette." You know, this buttering up thing. I was being polite to him so I said, "Thank you, sir." I took this Ronson lighter which I still had and I lit my cigarette. He said, "Oh, could I have a light, please?" So I passed him my Ronson across the table. He lit his cigarette, continued to chat and put the lighter in his pocket. I said, "Excuse me, sir. Could I have my lighter back?" He said, "Oh, no. I always wanted one of these." This was a German officer of captain rank which really upset me. (laughs) We were not abused but they used all the various interrogation techniques, but they didn't say that they were going to put us out against the wall and shoot us or anything of this nature. I certainly was unnerved and quite frankly afraid because I didn't know what to expect.

After we were all interrogated, we moved on to a Stalag which is a prisoner of war camp. Again, by train and by truck, but with a lot of walking in between. We got to Hanover and had to walk through the city to get to another train station because the train line had been knocked out by an American daylight air raid. Fire engines were rushing around and civilians came out to throw rocks at us. We had Volkssturm guards. These were older or wounded soldiers and they protected us by fighting off the people. I can well understand their anger because the place was just in shambles after this bombing. The next thing you know, we're on a train to Fallingbostel (between Hanover and Hamburg), the nearest town to Stalag XIB which was an older camp that had originally been built for civilian political activists in the thirties.

S. B. BOUMAN Jr.

AMSTERDAM W., December 17th 1945.
GEUZENSTRAAT 85¹

Dear Stan,

We were very glad to learn from your postcard that you still remember us and we thank you very much for your kind wishes. Indeed, it was a great surprise !

You can hardly realize what this Christmas means for us without that terrible German occupation. This Christmas will really be for us a symbol of Peace. Therefore we shall never forget our brave Canadian friends who delivered our country from those Nazi-devils.

It is a pitty that you cannot get back to Canada before Christmas. If you might come back to Holland for one or other reason we should be very honoured if you would like to pay us a visit and pass a day in our home. For we can very well understand what a young fellow needs, especially when he is from home for such a long time already. You will always be wellcome!

We all wish you a Merry Christmas and a very Happy New Year too. Best wishes also from my sister in law and her parents.

Sincerely yours,

(Sjabbe Bouman)

A letter from grateful Dutchman, Sjabbe Bouman, to Stan Matulis,
December 17, 1945.
"You will always be welcome!"

(Above) Lt. Charlie Forbes (right) with some of the Régiment de Maisonneuve, Holland, October 1944. The soldier beside him is Belgian volunteer Henri Vermeer.

(Below)Ivan Burch (arrow) at a royal garden party for British Commonwealth ex-POWs, Buckingham Palace, June 1945.

Stalag XIB was like all the war camps you've seen on television. It was a fantastically large place with thousands of prisoners. We had Russians, French, Yugoslavs, Serbs, Dutch, Belgians, Poles, you name it, not only ABCs (American, British and Canadian). There were even tents on the sports field. We were in a series of buildings with central ablution facilities and very little else. There were triple deck bunks and we had a piece of carpet right on the bed boards and one blanket. This was in February, March and April so it was still cool. What we used to do when we needed firewood was to burn the individual bed boards so you'd end up with about four boards supporting you. As we got closer to the end of the war and the Allies were approaching, we started to dismantle the walls and then the washbasins and toilets were all in the open because we'd used all the wood. We had a little stove for one wing, which didn't heat much, and we were cold at night and in the daytime too. Damn cold.

We had our own clothing that we got captured in and, along the way, we managed to get some kind of a coat. We received Red Cross parcels very sparingly. I'm sure some of them were stolen by the guards. Normally it would be a small box about twenty inches by twenty inches and was shared by four, sometimes six of us. They contained a variety of canned food products, cigarettes and candy. The American food packs were better, of course. We'd get things like tuna, salmon or beef stew, that type of thing. It's a funny thing—all you think about is food. You never talk about sex. Sex is the last thing. The guys weren't talking about going out with a girlfriend and getting laid and that sort of stuff. English soldiers would talk about fish and chips and the Canadians would talk about steaks and roast beef. My buddy, Charlie Watts, was particularly great at cooking on little stoves we made out of tin cans. He'd make little canapés by sautéing and slicing sardines and putting them on thin black bread. We did all kinds of crazy things just to keep ourselves sane. We didn't always get three meals a day and you never knew what you were going to get. Breakfast was ersatz coffee. For lunch we each got an eighth of a loaf of German black bread with, occasionally, some kind of margarine. We got skilly turnip soup which was just turnips and water. One day a guy found a horse's tooth in his soup! Sometimes each person would get a couple of boiled potatoes. Remember, it was the end of the war and the Germans didn't have too much food themselves. I lost about thirty pounds during my period of incarceration.

Canadian prisoners were not abused physically, aside from a shortage of food, but the Russians certainly were. The Russians seemed to be all over the camp. I don't think they got any proper food at all and they went around stealing. You'd see a horse-drawn cart coming into the camp for the kitchen and then you'd see a Russian run out and jump up on the back and start filling his tunic with potatoes or apples or whatever it was. The German guards would come and drag him off and beat him almost to death. I'm sure some were killed. I clearly understood the Russian attitude to the Germans at the end of the war.

We had a regular routine among the Canadians. We were divided into groups and we would have to clean out our barracks and the outside of our hut. Our leader was a company sergeant major from the Algonquin Regiment and he had everything very well organized. You ate on the basis of rank in reverse order. Privates were first, then lance corporals, corporals, sergeants and very often our camp leader went without anything because he allowed the others to be fed. He established that strict protocol which was good. As prisoners of war, the Germans insisted that we go on work parties outside of the camp and, since they thought all Canadians were lumberjacks, we went on what we called "wood commandos." We would be led out and we might have to walk out two miles or more and, at the end, walk back. We had guards with us all the time. All we had was maybe a few picks and shovels and we were lucky if we had an axe. We had to do everything by hand: cut down trees, dig out roots and clear land for agricultural purposes. We'd work all day like that on our limited rations so we were very fatigued.

Every soldier's effort is to escape. That's what you're supposed to do. One of the ways we were proposing to escape was those "wood commandos." Several of my buddies did manage to escape because we would make diversions so one or two could get away but they were always captured within a few days and brought back. They were walked barefooted from the railway station back to the camp. Their belts were taken so they had to hold their pants up. They weren't beaten but the villagers used to come out and abuse them by throwing stones and that kind of thing. Most of our guards were almost psychiatric cases. They were from the Russian front and had been wounded or maimed. They used to like to wave their pistols around and, to keep control, they used to have parades three and four times a day. They'd have us all out on the parade square, line us up and then the count would begin. We used to have fun and games with them. The guys in the rear ranks would shuffle around and cover off spaces. The Germans would go down the line, "*Eins, zwei, drei, vier, fünf, sechs, sieben*…. They'd total it all up and then say, "*Ein Mann. Ein Mann.* Somebody'd say, "*Ein Mann scheissen*" and the guards would run off to the washrooms to see if they could find anybody. We suffered for that because they would make us stand out there for maybe four or five hours because we had given them a lot of trouble. There was no camaraderie. They were our enemy and we hated them and ridiculed them. That's why we used to play these tricks on them. We used to trade with them, though. When we had our Red Cross parcels, I would trade my cigarettes for bread or eggs. There was a scale of value—a loaf of bread was worth so many cigarettes so we had to bargain with them.

We got along very well with the Brits but the one thing we had against the Americans was that they didn't have the discipline we did. During the night, instead of going to the ablution facilities to relieve themselves, they would come out and literally pee right outside their huts. In the morning, there was a sea of urine around their barracks. Getting along with your fellow soldiers is sometimes hard but we had a strict system. If two guys had a conflict, we'd take them out, make them put on boxing gloves (there were some recreational things), form a ring and let them go to it. They'd eventually run out of steam and be falling over.

At Easter, the ABCs had a church service. We had two padres who had been captured with the 1st British Airborne at Arnhem. After the nice little service, we were all milling around outside the recreational hall (if you could call it that) and the German commandant approached with an escort of guards. He spoke perfect English and began speaking to various prisoners. As he came near me, there was a big roar of aircraft coming over. As you looked up, the sky was filled with American bombers. We were on a direct flight pattern to Berlin and they were doing daylight raids at this stage of the war. The commandant looked up and said, "Silver planes, American Air Force—Black planes, Royal Air Force (because they flew at night)—No planes, Luftwaffe." This was his effort at humour and, of course, we didn't know whether we should laugh or what. Finally, he started to laugh, turned and walked away and we all broke into laughter.

On April 16, British tanks roared up to our gates. As a matter of fact, the Germans had turned over the camp, weapons and everything, to us two days before as they retreated. When the guards left, the ABCs took over the guard duty. One warehouse had canteen supplies like combs and toothbrushes and we got these diaries and passed them around. In my book, RSM Lord, the senior non-commissioned officer wrote: "Stalag XIB relieved 08:50 hours, Monday, 16th of April by the 8th Hussars, 7th Armoured Division, the Desert Rats. Good Luck! John C. Lord RSM, The Parachute Regiment." We had a heck of a time trying to control the Russians and we actually shot some of them because they were breaking out and looting. There were big food depots near our camp which we had to guard. The food was for what we called AMGOT, Allied Military Government, and had to be kept for distribution to feed refugees. The biggest thing in a war is what you do with all these starving people flooding the place.

When our own forces arrived, we turned over our weapons to them. Bath units came in and we had showers and got a change of uniform. We had to be careful with the food. A lot of guys started eating white bread which was brought in and were sick. We were warned to be very careful in what we ate and they gave us canned juice, that sort of thing. We went by truck to a place called Dephalt to be repatriated. Then we flew in RAF C-47 transport planes to Brussels and from there we flew in RAF Lancaster bombers to an RAF airport outside London. In my case, I went to a Canadian Army General Hospital where I stayed for approximately five days. They checked us out, put us on a proper diet and then sent us on leave. During this leave, I was picked up and sent to Buckingham Palace for tea. (laughs) Actually, the occasion was a royal garden party for British Commonwealth ex-prisoners of war. They needed a group to represent Canadians and we were told to be ready to leave in half an hour dressed in the best uniform we had. We thought they were out of their minds. We were bussed to the palace and were milling around the gardens and then the royal family came out. I didn't talk to Elizabeth or Margaret Rose but the Queen was very nice and said a couple of words as she came by. You just say: I'm so and so, Yes ma'am, No ma'am, three bags full! You just answer them the easiest way you can.

A couple of weeks after I was captured, my mother and dad received a telegram saying I was missing. It was upwards of six to eight weeks before they knew what had happened to me. I was an only child and, of course, mother's little darling. She never really recovered from the fact that I was missing in action and was never the same in her whole behaviour pattern. She became sort of dead even toward me and didn't show that much joy when I came back. My father showed me a clipping of the *Victoria Daily Times* "Missing in Action" notice and told me that he was just so elated when he found out I was a prisoner of war.

I felt that volunteering to go overseas was the right thing to do. I knew it was risky but I also thought it was an adventure. The hard part of it was when you got close to buddies and then took part in a conflict where there were casualties, either wounded or more particularly, killed. That part of it sticks with you for a long time and, I guess, until the day you die. On my first and last day of combat, my company had sixteen killed outright, many wounded and forty-one of us became prisoners of war. I did have some shrapnel cuts in my back but they were superficial. I consider myself extremely fortunate that I did go through all the various experiences that I have related and am here today at seventy-seven years of age. (in 2001)

William Ludlow

Bill Ludlow spent six years and three months in the army. His father, Thomas, an out-of-work shipwright, joined the Royal Canadian Engineers and they served together for a time. As unusual as it seems, they were not the only father and son combination in the 16th Field Company, RCE. There were two others (Dunster and Smith) as well as six brother combinations, including a pair of identical twins (Skidmore, Dumbell, Walker, Clegg, Clouatre and Foster). An uncle and nephew also served overseas with the Company at the same time. It is thought that this must be a record for any Canadian army unit of this size (220 men) in World War II. After the war Ludlow organized yearly reunions of the former members of 16 Fd. Coy. RCE. Two of these reunions took place in Normandy, France at the official D-Day Memorial services on June 6. The reunions occur infrequently now that most members have passed away.

CANADA DECLARED WAR on the tenth of September and I joined the Black Watch on the 12th, the first day that they recruited. Two days later I turned nineteen. I went overseas to Britain around September 1940, in the same convoy as one of my uncles who was in the air force. I contacted him in the harbour at Halifax just before we sailed away and didn't see him again until after the war. My father joined the Royal Canadian Engineers in 1940 and came overseas in 1941. I transferred to his unit, 16th Field Company RCE, and we served together until just before D-Day.

We trained to build bridges and blow up bridges, lift mines and lay mines, and when push comes to shove the engineers are trained to fight as infantry. We were specialists but we worked right in close with the infantry and supported them. It was okay being with my father. I outranked him. (laughs) I made corporal and he stayed a sapper, which is the basic rank, like private in the infantry. That didn't worry us. Did I ever have to give him orders? Yeah, I told him to get his hair cut once. (laughs) We had two other father and son combinations, too, and they got on in the same way. I never called him Tommy. (emotional pause) I called him Father. We'd go to pubs together and once we managed to get leave at the same time. We went to Belfast where we had relatives and stayed with an aunt. We were both born in Scotland, but my mother was from Belfast.

Sometime around the end of 1943 they started weeding the older men out and my father was transferred to a base unit where I sometimes managed to see him. He was sent back to Canada and arrived on the 6 of June, the day that I landed in France for the invasion. I was glad for him. I was an only child and my mother was all alone in Montreal.

D-Day? Well, it was a busy day. (laughs) Very busy. The trouble is that when you see anything on TV or in the movies it's all American. According to the Americans, they don't even know that Canadians were in this thing. It's a fact that the Canadian 3rd Division with an armoured brigade in support penetrated further into France on D-Day than the British or the Americans but we were so few and so far out that we couldn't hold our position and had to fall back. The Americans couldn't even get off one of their beaches. I've often said that on D-Day, the Germans knew where they were but didn't know what was going on. We knew what was going on but didn't know where we were. That's about it.

Going over, I thought: This is it. It's coming on. All I remember is looking up above us and seeing hordes and hordes of airplanes going over and nothing but confusion up ahead. Before we got to the beach, all hell broke loose and it was just a mass of black smoke. I was in a landing ship tank (LST) and we were supposed to go into Bernières but we ended up at Courseulles because the beach was so jammed that we couldn't get in there. They let down the ramp and I was hanging on the back of a lorry. In all the invasion training we had in England we were usually up to our necks in water. Now the day I landed on the Normandy beach I didn't even get my feet wet! You haven't got time to think. You see dead men and you say, "It's not my time yet." We got off the beaches and inland as fast as we could. Some of our fellows went in with the assault at Bernières-sur-Mer. They went in with the infantry carrying packs on their backs with explosive charges. Their job was to get up the beach, hit the sea wall, put these explosives on the sea wall and then blow a hole through it. At one particular place they couldn't get through and they sent an armoured bulldozer up and the operator hammered and hammered at the sea wall until he broke it enough so that two men could get through and then 4,6,8,10 and they were all in. This was all done under fire, of course. He got a medal for that because he was all alone.

The bocage country, they call it. That was bad fighting. Very, very, bad fighting because there were sunken roads and hedgerows and there was no room for tanks to manoeuvre so it was real tough going. We just kept plugging along, day by day, day by day. Sometimes we'd be in front of the infantry sweeping for mines to clear a minefield or laying mines as defensive positions. Sometimes, we didn't have mine detectors and had to go out and probe for mines. Then we had to make a path through the minefield and put down white tape. Usually, that was done at night or otherwise we'd be getting blown to bits. If you're held up by some obstruction, you get covering fire from the infantry and go forward and try to blow up a pillbox or something. If we came to a river we had to build an assault bridge. It was a bit tougher if we had to build a heavy bridge for tanks. The Bailey bridge was the main bridge we used and it was a wonderful invention. It's only gone out of use in the last few years in the army.

The infantry had to lift a lot of their own mines too, mind you. We couldn't lift everything. I was an old infantryman and, to give them their due, they had their pioneer platoon and they could lift mines and do a certain amount of engineering but they didn't build bridges. Everybody does his job, you know. I've had fellows from the infantry say, "Oh, you were in the engineers. We used to be lying there giving you guys covering fire and you were out there exposed and couldn't fight back." And yet, I wouldn't be in the infantry for anything. Or a tank man will say that he wouldn't be in the infantry and the infantryman says that he wouldn't be in a tank because tanks brew. The Shermans brewed up like nothing. But the infantry had the dirtiest end of the stick, there's no doubt about it, the infantry is the "Queen of Battles".

Sweeping for mines is accomplished by one sapper using a mine detector, which is something like a carpet sweeper with earphones, attached to a backpack. When a mine is detected it gives off a faint pinging sound in the earphones. Another sapper then probes carefully with his bayonet to find the mine, gently digs it up making sure that it is not booby trapped then, very, very, carefully removes the detonator thus disarming it. There are many different types of mines, some with time delay fuses and some that actually jump out of the ground when activated.

The Americans have sometimes accused the Canadians and the Brits of not moving very fast, but Caen was the pivot. Once the Americans got inland they were just swinging around and acting like a big hinge. I'm sure the British and the Canadians held all the German armour at Caen. If that armour had been loose on the Americans it would have been a different story for Patton. He was running wild. Okay, good for him, but he wasn't fighting in bocage country. The German troops were very, very tough soldiers, especially these young SS fanatics. Oh yeah, some of my fellows were found massacred, shot in the back of the head. It was about the same time as the mass murder of captured Canadian soldiers at the Abbaye d'Ardenne.

In the army, rum rations are only allowed when your unit is in action. The 3rd Division went in on D-Day, June 6 and no rum ration was forthcoming for some time. (Maybe someone mislaid it on the beaches.) You were entitled to one ration at night so we fought all the way through the bloody thing, all through France, without it. We got one bottle of warm British beer a month or every two weeks, which we had to buy. Our general eventually got wounded and another general took over. The day he took over, we had a rum ration the same night and whenever possible after that. You got one shot, which hit the bottom, and if it was a real dirty, cold, miserable, wet night, that rum really went BOING. I wasn't used to it. I never drank, you know. Didn't even drink beer. You couldn't save it up. You were supposed to drink it in front of the officer on the spot (we saved it up). My mother used to send me little cans of concentrated orange juice; we would water it down and then put rum in it.

There was a big battle at Falaise where the Germans had been caught in a pocket. As part of the battle there was to be close support bombing by the U.S. Air Force just ahead of our assault troops. Most of the bombs were dropped short and landed on us with lots of casualties. A few days later they tried it again with the RAF with the same results. I was bombed in England but that was the first time I could look up and see the bomb bays open and the bombs starting to fall down. We just kept going and slogging along. When I went back to Belgium and Holland after the war, civilians asked me what I remembered when I first went into these countries. I said that it was just another field, another barn, another town, another river. We didn't have the overall picture; we just had the little picture. My war was just going on and on and on and on—banging around and ducking and weaving and just carrying on.

198

It was very warm around Falaise and you could see the clouds of dust for miles. If we ever got a chance to have a bath, they'd take us in the back of an open truck, or lorry, as we called them. They'd take us back where they had all these showers. You'd have a shower and maybe get some clean underwear or a clean shirt. You're back in the truck again hotter than blazes and by the time you got back to your own lines you were just as dirty as when you left. If we were back a bit we could have a sponge bath in cold water. We had these big tins with hardtack biscuits, which are like hard soda biscuits. We used them also for boiling water to make tea because we were like the British—we had to have tea. We wore our woollen battle dress, there was no winter or summer battledress. I used to change my socks. I'd wear my socks one day this side, turn them inside out the next day and try to wash them as best I could. There was nowhere to wash. You were out in a field.

Now we were in Belgium and then the next battle was up in the Scheldt Estuary. All I knew was what was ahead of me. It was only when I came home and heard someone like Terry Copp, the historian, or saw something on TV that I saw the big picture. In September 1944, I got my sergeant's stripes and I did have access to maps and could see more of a picture of what was going on. Because of all the water, the 3rd Division was known unofficially as the "Water Rats". We were building bridges and putting up signs like: COMPLIMENTS OF THE 3RD DIVISION, WATER RATS. Montgomery got word of this and put the brakes on it. He didn't like that because it interfered with his Desert Rats. Montgomery was a real showman. He'd get everyone all gathered around. You've seen pictures. I guess he was a good general but he was very impatient with the Canadian generals, except Simonds. He thought Simonds was his boy. He didn't like Crerar at all and always blamed the Canadians for being too slow and yet, geez, on D-Day, we were way in before he even got to France.

We didn't have too much contact with civilians but in Holland when we were going through towns, they're throwing flowers at us and we're throwing back cans of bully beef at them. We had so much bully beef we were tired of it. If we met some kids, we'd give them some chocolate or chewing gum. We saw a lot of starvation there. People were coming to our mess tents and eating out of the garbage. It wasn't very good food anyway. It was army food. (laughs) When we saw that, we couldn't eat. Here were these people digging in the garbage. They airdropped some food in but the Dutch had a pretty rough time and they were eating tulip bulbs. Then when I came home to Canada and saw the waste here....

The next thing you know, we went from Nijmegen to Germany and we were told that if there was anything in the way—knock it down. Don't try to go around anything. The first place in Germany I saw was Emmerich and it was flat as a pancake. The only thing standing was a chimneystack with a shell hole right through it. They used "artificial moonlight"(huge searchlights on the ground so it's like day) and apparently that was a failure because instead of letting us see what was going on we were being silhouetted by the damn things. The white flags were out but we weren't allowed contact with civilians at all. They were knocked out of their homes and were starving like anybody else. I suppose I thought, "Well, you asked for it."

The Germans were getting older men and young fanatics now. Young kids, really young kids, but they broke eventually and it was all over. We had to be careful because some of the Germans were isolated and didn't know. I was in Leer near Emden in Germany when the war officially ended. I still have the document from army H.Q. which notified all units of the German surrender. We got it a couple of days before the news was released to the press. Everything just stopped and there was silence. The continual sounds of warfare had ceased. There was no singing and cheering and young girls to kiss or bands playing as apparently there was in the big cities. We were up at the sharp end of the action and we were just tired and wanted to get home. On V-E Day we were issued a bottle of beer—which we had to pay for—and no bands played for us.

There was a marine barracks near Emden with a lot of German soldiers. They all surrendered, of course, and handed in their rifles. We used to cut each other's hair so they found a prisoner who was a barber in civilian life and sent him around to all the units to give the guys haircuts. We used them to cook and clean up and things like that—give them jobs rather than sit there. I saw a Canadian soldier and a German soldier both standing guard together and the German probably had a shot up the spout of his rifle, the same as the Canadian did. If you just put Canadian troops there they wouldn't have liked it. You never knew what was going to happen. They could descend on you. You say, "The war's over." And they say, "It's not over."(laughs) You have to respect some of these Germans as they were doing it for their country—we were doing it for our country. At least we had a choice to be in the army or not. They didn't. They were just drafted in like the Brits.

Back in England there weren't enough ships to take us back. I didn't get back to Canada until December 1945. We had nothing to do. What do you do with an army? They kept sending us on leave and you'd no sooner get back to Aldershot and they'd ask if you wanted another leave and how long do you want? (laughs) I was offered a promotion to sergeant major as part of the occupation troops. I thought about it and then I thought, "Geez, I've been away too long and my mother and father are waiting for me to come home." I came back on the *Queen Elizabeth*. There were so many men on the ship that we only had two meals a day and you could be eating supper at three o'clock in the morning. All the way over they kept telling us to get rid of German pistols and other German things because when we went through customs they were going to clobber us. They said we were going to be fined and would go to jail. Nobody even looked in my bags. I just had my fighting knife. That was all. I carried a Smith and Wesson .38 pistol but I left it in Holland with another sergeant. I said, "Some day I may get married and have children and somebody's going to get shot with that damn thing so I'll leave it." Somebody in one of our field companies had a Schmeisser machine gun which he dismantled and sent home. He still has it in a cupboard. When we landed at Halifax there was all kinds of cheering and shouting and what not.

We got on the train right away and the next morning we were back in Montreal—Bonaventure Station—and that was it. You couldn't get through and people were shoving you. I got separated from my parents and went outside the station where they eventually joined me. Then I went and tried to find my friends. Of course, I went away early. I had enlisted in the army in '39. I thought, "Where the heck have they disappeared to?" I had been in the Boy Scouts at Lorne School in the Point. We had a big troop with a bugle band. I was in the band which was comprised of the older boys in the Scout troop. Most of us joined up right away and many were killed overseas. Some of those who made it home did not stay very long in Montreal and moved to other parts of Canada. Sometimes I think back and wonder, "Where did all my old friends go?"

Edward Purcell

In 1939, Edward Purcell joined the reserve corps of the Victoria Rifles of Canada. Deciding to join "active" on January 13, 1942, he enlisted at Longueuil and did basic training at Huntingdon. For the first year, he helped build the obstacle course used in training soldiers. Then it was off to Borden for advanced training. It was there that he joined the Royal Canadian Army Service Corps.

I GOT THE OKAY to get married in 1943. The date was set for May 1 but, because of sickness, we didn't get married until May 15. I reported back to Borden after my leave and then in July the same year we were going to be shipped out to Debert, Nova Scotia and I was supposed to get another leave to go home. They put us on the train and shipped us right past Debert, on to Halifax and onto the *Queen Elizabeth* and shipped us right over. We didn't know at all that we were going. We weren't allowed to communicate with our family until we got over to England. My brother-in-law was stationed in Halifax at that time. When he saw my regiment getting on the boat, he sent a letter back to my wife saying, "Our friend Ed met Elizabeth," and that was a sign to her that he had seen me get on board.

We were not allowed to go in convoy because they were too slow. We had planes going out so far observing to see that there were no U-boats and we changed course many times so they couldn't get a bead on us. When we got part way over the planes came from the other side to meet us. There were about 20,000 on board—army, air force, women—and all the nice rooms were broken up. They had put in bunk beds so we were piled one on top of the other. There were four big dining rooms and it was well organized. We had regular times to go to eat and the rest of the time we'd just sit around. We played cards to pass the time and I made friends with people on board. We didn't feel any fear. I guess we were too young. After landing in Scotland we took a train down to Aldershot in England. On the way down we stopped at different stations and the people came to feed us sandwiches and welcome us. Aldershot was a regrouping center and that's when I was assigned to the 4th Canadian Armoured Division. My job was driving a truck. We got training in running convoys—delivering food, supplies, ammunition and petrol. It was tough driving the trucks (they called them lorries over there) on the wrong side of the road. That didn't help. Over there they had what they called the Bedford trucks, which were British made. They were taller than the American ones and not quite as wide because the roads over there are very narrow—get two of them together and they'd have to scrape by each other.

We were training for the invasion of Normandy and we had to waterproof our trucks because we were told that we were going to have a wet landing. We left the east end of London during the night in the third week of July and the next morning we landed in Normandy. We went aboard the LST which has a door that opens in the front and you just drive right on. We had a rough crossing. At that time, the Germans were sending out little torpedo boats and two of them were sunk on our way over. Everyone was quiet. We didn't know what we were getting into, you know. We all stayed with our vehicles. I felt a little nervous because I can't swim. (laughs) When we heard the alarms, I just grabbed a lifejacket and put it on—as a matter of fact, I got two lifejackets!

I suppose it was about nine o'clock when we landed. This was the time when they were preparing a ten-mile area radius. There were so many tanks, trucks and infantry all within ten miles. If the Germans had more planes available they could have done a lot of damage but the British had control of the skies then so we were a little safer. We were still bombed and shelled before we could get going. We were waiting for the big push to Falaise and they had hundreds of American bombers coming over to lambaste the Germans and soften them up. We could see the bombers up above us and a few of them started unloading bombs ahead of time and we were right in line and had to find cover right away. Once one started, you know, a few others followed suit until some of our planes came flying around swerving their wings to warn them. We were also throwing up orange smoke signals to tell them they were in the wrong place. They hit the ammunition dump of the Polish regiment that was right behind us and a lot of them were killed. Some of ours were killed but not too many, like the Polish. It was a rough time then because Rommel had brought in his SS troops. There was a lot of controversy about the fact that they were getting our soldiers and weren't taking them back but just shooting them. That made us mad, you know. You hear about them doing that and you say, "Why should we take them prisoners and have to bring them back to England?" The SS didn't give a darn for anybody. They were just there to kill.

The people of Normandy came out and brought us wine and cider (they were great cider and wine drinkers). They'd bring us eggs and we used to supply them with cigarettes. My wife used to send cigarettes over. For the soldiers they cost $1 for 300. The French were happy to see the end of it. They'd been in it so long and were happy to see the Germans gone. We had hot weather then and every time we went on a convoy in our lorries we'd send up dust storms and the German planes would come over and start strafing us. Sometimes we didn't have time to get out of our lorries and just had to hope for the best. (laughs) We stayed in our uniforms for weeks. There was no place to have a shower and you felt pretty mucky. Not only that; our uniforms were treated with some kind of disinfectant that smelled and when they got wet they smelled even more. I don't know what it was but you could see some sort of whitish stuff coming out. That wasn't very comfortable.

We kept going further and further and went right up into Belgium. We got stalled for a while and then went into Holland. Until they opened the port of Antwerp it was tougher for us because we had to get all our supplies through Normandy and we were on call twenty-four hours a day, going back and forth, to get supplies up to the troops. We slept in our lorries and were always a target. The Germans made it very hard as we went toward Nijmegen. As they were retreating, they changed all the road signs so the Canadians had a system. They had signs saying, MAPLE LEAF UP, which meant you were going towards the front and MAPLE LEAF DOWN was going towards the rear. We were advancing so fast, at one point, that our group went past the front line and we were surrounded. We didn't know until we got wind of it that they were all around us. We just stayed put until our own troops fought their way through to rescue us.

For fun we'd play cards and whenever we got a chance we went into towns and went to pubs. They'd bring us in the morning and pick us up at night when most of us were plastered! Every time we went out they gave us safes and when we got back they checked us for VD. At that time they didn't have the right stuff to cure syphilis. In the beginning it was a long drawn-out process and anyone with VD would have to go into the hospital for treatment. Some of them over there—they didn't know when they were going to get back or *if* they were ever going to get back and it was pretty grim.

The Dutch people figured they were going to be liberated in December. Things didn't go right and they weren't liberated until months later. In the meantime, the Germans knew they were being pushed back and they busted some of the dams to flood the area. The people were starving and eating tulip bulbs. That's when the Canadians came in and supplied them with food. When the Germans were retreating, they were very short of petrol and used anything they could—bicycles, carriages, horses, anything at all.

Once we were taking troops up for another push and we were travelling in the middle of the night. With no lights, you follow the truck in front of you which has a number painted on the differential and a light shining on it. That's all you could see so you followed that. I did that and ended up in a ditch. An officer took the men out and stopped the next truck behind and left me there. You never leave your lorry so I was left with a rifle to fend for myself. The next morning they sent another truck to pull me out.

We were truck drivers but we had also been trained for combat and once they called us in to replace the infantry. They had been there on a dike in Holland for two weeks and needed a rest. You couldn't walk around during the day or you'd be shot at. During the night we had to go into a building and fire tracer bullets mostly to let them know that we were there. Every two hours we'd be relieved and we had to say the password fast or we'd be shot at. They'd say "Sweet" and we'd say "Caporal". Another one was "Oh" and "Henry". Once, some of the infantry went out on a patrol. They blackened their faces, got a good shot of rum and went over to infiltrate the German side to see how strong they were. They had to walk through a minefield and pick up prisoners if they could. You'd hear them coming back, singing away, glad it was over. I give all credit to the infantrymen. They were the ones who came in contact with the enemy and, in some places, it was hand-to-hand fighting. They had to go through water and mud. We went through water and mud too, but in lorries. I think wars are won by the infantry.

We continued on and drove quite a few miles into Germany. We were on the way to Essen when the war ended. We were scared to fraternize with any of the people there but many of them had gone into hiding or gone east. Even in some parts of Holland we couldn't fraternize because some of them near the border were more German, I think, than Dutch. Once we were back in Amsterdam, we could celebrate. We were just glad the war was over. You couldn't beat the Dutch. They'd take us into their homes and try to tell us what had happened. You'd speak with your hands and with a few words you learned from a book they gave us.

They had a rotating system to come back to Canada, first over-first out, and we had to wait our turn. We weren't allowed to take any souvenirs. Military rules. I had a German rifle with a bayonet. I had a Dutchman reshape it and put it into a scabbard as a souvenir. We came back on the *Queen Elizabeth*. Halifax was too crowded with all the boats coming in so we went to New York. We got the train back to Bonaventure Station on December 8. I hadn't seen my wife in two and a half years. It was such a joy getting back alive! We went right back to the house and had a big party. All the neighbours came in. It was out of this world. Later on I never talked about the war and had some bad experiences with nightmares. I'd go to sleep at night and hear German planes going over. After a while, that stopped.

I went back to Holland in 1995 for the fiftieth anniversary of the liberation. My wife couldn't come so I went with my son, Norman. Fourteen thousand veterans from all over Canada went and we had a great time. We were met by a group of people who took us to different places. Some were going to Amsterdam, Apeldoorn, Nijmegen, Arnhem, all over the place. We stayed with a family in Groesbeek. They took us to different happenings like banquets and parades. The first parade was in Nijmegen. The people were shaking your hand and ... it just swells up in your throat, you know. They couldn't do enough for us. The big parade was in Apeldoorn. They bussed us in from all over and there were about 300,000 people watching the parade. They were lined up all over the place. I was marching and shaking hands. One person would give you flowers; another one would give you a glass of beer. It was just fabulous. They even stopped the parade because they wanted to get closer to us. My son was up in the stands taking pictures. It was funny when a few people shouted out, "Are you my father?" After the parade, they all gathered to ask questions and ask us to sign up if we thought we had a child there. I believe that a few of them found their fathers that way.

You wouldn't get the same patriotism now as you had in those days. It's not the same. It's more political with no national pride, just who's making money out of a war. The war against the Germans had to be done. They could have won the war and wouldn't have stopped at England. Hitler was out for the world and they would have come here afterwards.

Michael Delisle

More than 3,000 Native Canadians served in the World War II. Sergeant Tom Prince, the great-grandson of the legendary Chief Peguis became the most highly decorated Canadian Native of World War II. Kahnawake, a small Mohawk community near Montreal sent many of its sons into battle, some enlisting with the Canadian forces and many choosing to fight under the American flag. Michael Delisle fought with the U.S. 1st Army in northwest Europe and was awarded the Bronze Star, a decoration given to those who distinguish themselves by heroism or meritorious achievement.

To my way of thinking, the Mohawks didn't have to go to Europe to fight a war but our tradition is that the women stay home and the men go fight the wars, no matter where. North America is our country and we were fighting for our people and our country. I was living and working in New York City in high structural steelwork when I enlisted. As Indians we were allowed to work anywhere in North America. That was our right. Still is today! Those were hard times and most of the Mohawks were working there because there was

(Above) Sappers William Ludlow (left) and his father, Thomas Ludlow, 16th Field Company, on leave in Belfast, Northern Ireland, 1942.

(Below) Edward Purcell (with striped pole behind him) in Nijmegan, May 4, 1995. Fifty years after a hard-won victory, Canadian veterans return to Holland, a country that has never forgotten its liberators.

(Above)
Michael Delisle after finishing basic training at
Fort Jackson, South Carolina, 1943.

(Below)
The 79th Light Artillery in front of Molson Brewery, Montreal, May 7, 1942.
Frank Monroe is in the first row, fourth from left.
"When I saw all my friends leave, I enlisted."

no work here. I wasn't married then. I only had a mother and two sisters and we were all living in New York. I joined the 39th Infantry of the 9th Division of the U.S. 1st Army on December 15, 1942. My mother never told me how she felt about me joining up, but I guess she didn't feel very good about it because, after I went over, she didn't know where I was for quite a while. Many Mohawks joined the Canadian army but not as many as joined the American army because most of us were over there. We were all fighting for the same cause so why come back to Canada? I had no idea what I was getting into. If I knew I would never have gone, believe me. That's the honest truth. A man of twenty-two who never saw any part of the world but New York City—I felt it was an experience like the kids today backpacking through Europe. That was my idea of seeing Europe. Little did I know what I was in for, but I didn't turn back.

My initiation of fire was on Omaha Beach in Normandy. I landed on June 10, 1944, D-Day-plus-4. You could never, ever in your life imagine what we saw. I can't repeat all of what we saw. NOTHING was removed. There was no time. We saw bodies and bodies and bodies. The beach was still red. There was no stopping. They weren't even a mile in after four days and we were replacements, replacing old combat crews from the Italian campaign. They were already seasoned warriors at that time. So, in that sense, we were lucky that we joined an experienced outfit. That might be the reason I'm here today.

I was in heavy weapons, mortars and machine guns, and we'd go on observation duty every three days. Observation is not fun. You're directing fire in no man's land. We'd usually do that at night. We'd have to watch for any movement or fire coming out of the dark and we'd throw a phosphorous smoke shell which you could see at night. We would fire for effect, not really knowing what we were hitting. I was with a lieutenant and carried the radio and related back the firing orders. I was a private, first class. Never went any higher and never wanted to. Never volunteered for anything. Did my job and that was it. The only break we'd get would be to be sent a thousand yards back for a day at the most. There's one incident I remember that was funny. Me and my buddy were in a foxhole in Normandy. So many things were flying around that I said, "Hey, Alphonse, come out and see the fireworks. It looks like Mardi Gras and Coney Island." He says, "You can go to hell. I ain't gettin' out of this hole." That's what it looked like to me, Mardi Gras and Coney Island.

I can't remember all the cities and towns I was in because we weren't counting cities. We were just trying to get where we were going. It was all hedgerows—hedgerow-to-hedgerow, very close fighting. I remember the nice feeling when we would liberate a place in France. We couldn't speak French but there was a common language. The people would climb on the jeep and hug you and give you flowers. Whatever they had, they would give you. We were headed straight for Paris which we were all anxious to see. It was declared an open city. We got to about twenty miles from it but they wouldn't allow us in because they said we were too wild. We were combat troops and we weren't very good citizens at the time. I did get to see Paris later on, when we got a two-day pass after the hostilities ended.

At Thanksgiving a runner came up to our hole. He told us that they had a hot meal for us down at headquarters, turkey, dressing and everything. So we got there and you know what it was? (laughs) Canned corned beef with crackers! You can imagine what we said to the guy. On the way back we got a barrage and almost got killed on account of that damned corn beef. I didn't eat corned beef for a long time after that, but today corned beef hash with poached eggs is my favourite breakfast.

At the Battle of the Bulge, we thought we were finished but we survived. We were supporting General Patton but he was moving too fast and the supplies couldn't keep up with us. We were doing forty miles a day. How do you move an army forty miles a day and keep supplied? There was a series of battles all the way through right up into Germany and there it got even worse because the Germans were being backed up—Do or die. There were eight major battles in the European theatre and I was in five of them. After the war I got a Bronze Star. There was no specific reason but I guess it went by how many major battles you had been in.

When we got to the bridge at Remagen, our officer was leery about going over because he thought it was unusual that it was intact. He sent scouts over to check it out and then we got the wave to come. There were two Germans there with detonators who were supposed to blow it up, but they were drunk. There was a distillery the size of Seagram's on the other side so you can imagine what happened when we got there. The Germans were gone and we were shooting each other with champagne corks all night. Some of us had never drunk alcohol before in our lives. (laughs) We were all drunk that night and if there had been an attack, that would have been the end of our outfit, I'm sure.

The German soldier? Let me start with the SS troops. That was the German elite. They were Hitler's children and we were told never to take them prisoner. That's what we were up against and that's what was done.

When we got to the end of our drive we were in Dessau, Germany, 40 miles out of Berlin. We weren't allowed to cross the Elbe because that was ground the Russians were going to take. Then we saw the ovens. I don't remember the name of the camp but you could get the stench for miles away and we couldn't figure out what it was because we had no intelligence with us. You couldn't picture what we saw. It was one big camp with Hungarians and people from the Baltic countries. Women, children and older people—those they couldn't use for work. I guess many were Jewish. When they saw us, my God, we were their saviours! We gave them what we had. What gets you is the little kids who are prisoners. How can that be in this world?

When hostilities ceased, we were assigned different towns as occupation troops until we could get a ship and go to Japan. My outfit had been in combat for one year but we were still slated to go to Japan to finish it off. It felt good that everything was over in Europe but we still felt sorry for the German people who had nothing left. We gave them whatever we had in rations and it wasn't a hell of a lot either, but we gave them what we could spare. They weren't the ones we were fighting. They were the innocent ones. The regular German people to me were more hospitable than some of the French were. Some of their soldiers, though, had been brainwashed and they'd kill you for nothing. We were told not to fraternize but I had confiscated a motorcycle—I always loved motorcycles. A German mechanic (they're all good mechanics) tuned it up for me and I'd ride around in the park. Once, I was looking at a pretty girl and went down some steps. Good thing I didn't get hurt seriously. (laughs) I couldn't explain the scrapes I got. I knew I was still normal but I wasn't a peaceful guy any more, you know.

When I saw what the Germans did, I would never buy a Volkswagen or even a Mercedes. Same with the Japs and I was never there. It's what they did to our American prisoners. I wouldn't buy a Japanese radio, car or anything, even today. When I went to buy my first movie camera in Plattsburgh I told the girl I wanted an American-made one and she told me I'd have to make one myself. There was so much damage done to the people and the countryside. They even did it to their *own* countries and to themselves. We would never do that to our country, especially here in this reserve. In Kahnawake we have economic development which is very strict. You can't even cut down a tree unless it deserves to be cut down. God gave the land to us and we should take care of it.

After the war, I was a happy-go-lucky guy. They gave us after-service pay for one year. It was like a subsistence allowance so we could get re-acquainted with the civilian world. For one year I didn't want to work and kept drinking and just having fun until, all of a sudden, I came to my senses and said, "What am I doing to myself? Is this what I fought for?" This happened to a lot of guys who went through bad things but I caught myself. I had no coaching but I caught myself. Indians have a lot of pride, you know, and no one wants to end up in a gutter somewhere. Nobody in my family was happy with what I was doing and I took a different track. I got a job and life went on. I got married and had two daughters and a son I had to support. I put it all behind me. I moved back to Kahnawake in the fifties because our neighbourhood in New York was getting full of drug addicts and stuff like that and it was safer back here. I think I made the right move because none of my children married outside the community and today they're all within my reach which makes me just about the happiest guy in the world.

The worst memory of the war is seeing women, children and old people suffer. That you never forget. That's why, today, I love children so much. The other day, I was invited to my granddaughter's pool party. She lives on a property which I call Sugar Bush because my grandfather used to make maple syrup there. I looked around and saw all these children having fun and thought that my grandfather must be looking down because it was the best afternoon of my life. I guess that's the reward I get that I'm still here

When I look at my children and grandchildren and all their friends I think, "How come those other people didn't have the same chance?" I am against war because I know what it means. I'm talking to you to give my version of war so it can be avoided. I can't give you all the details because it's impossible. Problems should be dealt with in a different manner, not by killing innocent people. I still feel guilty for what I did. I'm a Catholic and you know the fifth commandment, Thou shalt not kill. How do you expect me to feel?

We formed our Legion Hall, Number 219 Mohawk Branch, in the fifties. Now, let me give you an example of what happens at our Legion. An old friend of mine was a navy vet and he had passed away. His son came to see me and wanted to know where his father had served and what he did in the war. I said, "I have no idea. In that hall we never talk about war. Never! Not where we were or what we did because we don't want to bring it back up. Nobody wanted to talk about the war. I never knew where any of my buddies were." He couldn't believe me but I told him it was a fact. We never wanted to talk about it.

Frank Monroe

If anyone needed cheering up during the war, it was the troops serving overseas. Ready and willing to try to put a smile on weary faces were the entertainment groups of the three services. The army, navy and air force all had shows which entertained both in Canada and overseas. The entertainers, with very few exceptions, were made up of men and women in uniform—unlike the American USO and the British ENSA. Frank Monroe was born on Sebastopol Street in Point St. Charles. As leader of the popular "Bunkhouse Boys", a country-and-western group, he headed a group of elfin-faced youngsters who, by 1937, were drawing thousands of people to their variety shows at Marguerite Bourgeois Park, the N.D.G. Bonfire Theatre and the Kiwanis Club bandstand at Fletcher's Field. Frank Monroe entertained the veterans at St. Anne's Military Hospital for the first time when he was fourteen years old and, except for the years he served overseas, has not stopped since.

WHEN WAR BROKE OUT, the Bunkhouse Boys were well known. We were in the newspapers all the time and winning every prize going even though we were only youngsters. Frank Wilson, chairman of entertainment for the troops, contacted us and sent us to a couple of local barracks. He would pick us up at the door and bring us home safely. First thing you know, we were doing shows two or three times a week. The troop show grew to about ten acts, including Terry Bittle, the Rowley family, the Burtons, Jack Steka, Dorothy Carlin, Lillian Abrams, Tony Fitzanno, the Brown family and Ron Smith, a cartoonist from *The Gazette*. We appeared at camps all over the place—Farnham, St. Jerome, St. Hubert, Joliette, Sorel. We went wherever there were troops. In 1942, my youngest brother joined the navy even though he was underage. That broke the gang up. One of my other brothers also joined the navy and another went in the army. Of course, I followed and joined on April 1, 1942. Military District 4 was going to make me exempt from going if I stayed and entertained the troops but when I saw all my friends leave, I enlisted in the 79th Battery of Artillery in Point St. Charles. Major Tom Molson was my commanding officer at the time.

I trained as a gun layer. I was the guy who, when they called out the deflections, I beamed in on the aircraft. You'd better not miss either! (laughs) I wore earplugs and was sitting on the gun. It was only a 40mm Bofors and I don't know whether you could really hit it high enough to get the planes. There was a second ack-ack with the heavies that *could* hit the planes but we kept them high anyway. I went out to Vancouver and was posted on the coast for a while because they thought the Japanese planes would come over. Then we got leave. If you weren't due for leave, you knew there was something cooking. My parents knew I was going and didn't like it, but they felt it was important and it had to be, to defend the country.

Then it was down to the docks and onto the ship. There were 10,000 troops on board and we landed on Greenock, Scotland. Soon after we arrived, we were on parade square when we had visitors. A German Messerschmitt came down to greet us and riddled the parade square. We parted just like a cornfield and nobody got hit, thank God. We were happy when we found out that one of our own Spitfires was right on the tail of the Messerschmitt and got it. We were stationed mostly along the coast and I was in a holding unit where they dispatched reinforcements when the regiments were short of men and they *were* short of men, believe me. We needed all the reinforcements we could get. I was run over and hurt by a Bofors gun on a training accident and was re-categorized L5. I couldn't move my feet and there were open wounds which meant that I couldn't walk or march.

They were going to send me home but then Captain Dixon, the Recreation Service officer and Colonel Purdy, who was a CBC producer, approached me. They said, "You have a choice. If you want to go and entertain your own guys, you can join the Army Show or you can go home and miss all the fun." (laughs) Of course, I signed up right away and went into the Army Show. I loved entertaining and entertained all the time I was in England but not with the Army Show. The people in England didn't have very much entertainment and I put on shows in various little towns. I could smell out entertainers and anybody who came through, I'd speak to the colonel to hold them back a bit if they qualified as entertainers. We had a fellow by the name of Curly McGowan who was a top yodeler and country-and-western singer. Doug Romaine was a very famous comedian from Toronto. He was a pantomime artist like Red Skelton. We managed to put a good show together and we entertained wherever we could. The colonel also sent me on a bond-selling mission. I went with a captain and we went around to the different regiments and got the guys to save their pay and put the money into bonds so when they came back, they had those bonds instead of blowing all their pay in the pubs. The guys that I met later were very happy because that was all they saved, in many cases.

The Army Show was well organized. They had their headquarters in Guildford which was a holding unit for all the entertainers. They also supplied everything you needed. If they didn't have it, they'd get it for you. Sometimes I was a loner, going out to field hospitals with a piano player who sometimes couldn't even read music. We'd put on two, sometimes three shows a day and they'd send somebody out to check you too, to make sure you did, but they didn't have to check me. Then they'd send me out with the units and I'd fit in and take parts in various spots, any place where comedy was needed. I used to do impersonations, tell jokes, sing and dance and play all the different-size harmonicas. You had to be careful not to tell jokes to sick people that reminded them too much of home, you see. You had to make it funny and it was good to see them laugh and forget their problems for a little while.

The last few months of the war, I went over to Italy, Belgium, Holland and Germany. The Army Service Corps would transport us in trucks to various locations where the regiments were. We took a CWAC show right up to the front lines in Italy. We were safer there than in the back because the artillery were firing over our heads. They sent chaperons along with these women because the fellows over there hadn't seen Canadian girls for four or five years. We went to all the big, abandoned opera houses but, one time, we played in a bombed-out theater. It was so cold that the harmonica I was playing froze up. That's right. Froze up! In Holland and Belgium, we used the theaters when we could get them, but in Germany the shows were outdoors in a field. They'd try to find the best spot they could for us which wasn't too far behind the lines and they'd bring the troops out of the lines for a rest. The Army Service Corps would set up a stage for us right in the field. We had our own generators and lights and everything right there.

One of the best army show units I was with, called "About Turns" had a fabulous orchestra. Madeleine Léger was the singer and the musicians were Bob Crignan, Bob Redmond, Bob Swetland, Gus de Gagné, Nick Korn, Bill Johnston and Eddie Bergeron—some of these men are still entertaining veterans and shut-ins. The bandleader, Barry Townley, went to Los Angeles after the war and got into the big time there. We opened the show with a singing chorus line. We always opened with "There's No Business Like Show Business" which was a standard thing at the time. We wouldn't sing a song like "We'll Meet Again" in the front lines. That's a tearjerker. We had a few skits about the stuff that was happening. You'd go running out and say, "The war must be over. All the officers are up in the front." (But our officers went up to the front. They were good guys.) We did current hit songs and we'd joke about the food. I stuck to comedy. In one skit I was the stand-in. There were three shows a day and three times in each show I used to take a pie in the face. We were using real pies for a while until the cook figured out a better way to do it. The cook would decorate cold cream to look like a real pie and we tried to save the cold cream and re-use it. I also did my own musical novelty act. I played the harmonica from the inch-size up to the three-footers. I had them all strapped around me and I'd use every one.

One of our acts was done with a big, fake radio which was made up by our prop department. I was behind the radio with Jack Kelly, a broadcaster from Toronto. Different people would be sitting on the stage saying, "Let's see if we can get Roosevelt." We'd look at each other and one of us had to do Roosevelt behind the radio. Then it was, "Let's see if we can get Jack Benny." And one of us would do Benny. They would also ask for Sinatra, Churchill and Hitler. I used to do Hitler with a comb in front of my mouth and with my hair down in front. Lucky I didn't get shot! Some of these guys were just out of the lines. (laughs) Everything was just a mockery. I'd yell, "OCH GESHEESNICK SHTRING BEANS UND SOURKRAUT STRUNTEL. MICH HIECHICKUEKEN YOUP. UND SHNEAKEN DIE RUFFENSTINKING HITLER."

There were many close calls. Lots of times, if I had been there two minutes sooner, I wouldn't be here today. We had good guides with the Army Service Corps who were well trained in booby traps and so forth. The fields would all be checked out before we got there. There were no chairs. The men just sat down on the field and watched the show. One time I was on stage doing a comedy act that was going over big and then the bombs came down, BOOM, BOOM, BOOM. I said, "I don't think they like my act." I had to get that shot in. (laughs) Nobody was hit and we got out of there. They riddled our stage and everything but after they were gone, we fixed it right away. The army shows only came over late in the war and I had already been there for three years. I had experience with different things and was able to help some of the people who had just landed. Some of them were after souvenirs and I used to tell them that they were booby-trapped. One chap who was with us was going to take a Luger from a dead soldier on the side of the road. I told him not to move but he wouldn't listen to me. I carried a gun all the time so I shot the Luger and it blew up.

The Army Shows were all good, you know. They broke the big Army Show down to small groups and they must have had about a dozen units. Wayne and Shuster were in one of the groups. We used to run across them and I worked with them. I did some shows for the British troops with ENSA. They had George Formby who was a great comedy singer in England at that time. I remember he sang, "My Aunt Maggie's Homemade Remedy." This guy was fabulous, a big liner, you know. And Tommy Trinder who was like the Bob Hope of Great Britain—I put on a show with him too. I did some shows for the Americans too and they loved them.

After about a couple of months doing shows, our costumes started to get raggedy and we needed new ones. We needed new skits and songs too, so we'd go and spend about two weeks in the holding unit in Guildford in England to get re-tooled and then it was back to the front again. You could get everything there and then they'd send you God knows where. You didn't know where you were going until you got there. All the units had writers but I did quite a lot of comedy writing for the different units. I'm not a writer and I'm not a well-educated person but when it comes to the comedy stuff, I know a little bit about it. A lot of stuff was brought over that would make the guys cry out there and they didn't want that so I used to listen to the comedians' routines and write material for them. Sometimes I'd write five, six, even seven scripts and take them to the colonel for approval. He'd look them over and throw most of them in the wastebasket and just keep the odd one. When he was gone, I'd take the scripts out of the basket and go up to London and sell them to ENSA. They wanted some of our Canadian stuff and I'd get £5 for every script. (laughs)

I never did stop entertaining. My time came up to come back home and I was anxious to see my family. I had already been over there for nearly four years. I came back in the fall of 1945 and did my first New Year's Show in December 1945 at St. Anne's and Senneville which were two separate hospitals at that time. Senneville had more psychiatric cases. There were also two other hospitals, Queen Mary Veterans' Hospital and St. Hyacinthe which was the navy hospital. All the hospitals were packed and we did all four the same day starting in the morning. We had a bus and sometimes we were able to get a military escort because we had a lot of area to cover. (One time we even did St. Patrick's Orphanage in between!) It was a private show but some of the people from the Army Show and I put together some professional entertainment. Going back, we've had a lot of celebrities on the show. We had Percy Rodriguez, Dean Martin, Sinatra, Bob Hope, Tony Bennett. If they were in Montreal doing a show, they'd come and do one for us. Wayne and Shuster—I brought them in from Toronto. I met Roger Doucet at Army Show headquarters and then bumped into him in Italy. We worked together on the shows and Geraldine still comes.

If you ask entertainers to volunteer, you have to get them the expenses. They'll do it but in most cases they can't afford to. You take a magician. Sometimes they used $15-$20 worth of equipment in one performance—it's a lot more today—which is destroyed and can't be used again. The dancers have glittering costumes with sequins that have to be cleaned. It costs money to do this so I got Major General Walford, who was the comptroller of Morgan's and the aide-de-camp to the governor general at the time, to help me get started. Ernie Walls, the general manager of the T. Eaton Company, Wing Commander Victor Birks and Senator Molson all helped. I also talked to all the Legion people and got them to adopt a ward at the hospital and take out their own show. It doesn't matter what it is—could be a dance, a boxing show or a Bingo game. A lot of people take shows throughout the summer and winter but I was the one who started it.

It takes about three months to put on the New Year's Show. You've got to get clearance from all the unions to start off with and then you've got to line up the gifts. Do you know what you can buy for $20 today! We used to have 1,200 patients at Ste. Anne's and now we're down to 650. We give each one of them a gift and the doctors look the other way when we give them cigarettes. You've got to let the guys smoke if they get their kicks out of it and that's what they want to do. You're going to tell an old vet who's ninety-four years old that he can't smoke anymore! So we've got to find cigarettes, food, gifts, and take care of the entertainers. We need two buses and one bus now costs more than $600 to go out and back with the insurance on it and everything. You need a good safe bus because we're responsible for all those entertainers. We feed the volunteers who come and we have to pay for the stage props that we use. Many companies like the Royal Bank, Sun Life and Clarica give us donations. The Erin Sports Association and the Legions—R.M.R (Sports Association), Number 6, the Korea War Veterans, Point St. Charles, LaSalle, Verdun and St. Laurent have been generous to us. I have good friends who help me; Jimmy Barriere, Joe Mell, Pat Conroy, Red Storey, Jim Stevens and many others. Jerry Shears helped for more than fifty years before he himself became a patient at St. Anne's. My son Mark has worked with me since he was a youngster, too.

I love putting the shows on, you know. When am I going to stop? When they carry me out. (laughs)

Frank Monroe off to training camp, 1942.

War correspondent Gerald Clark in Holland.
"The war taught me to appreciate the fact that we live, not only in a civilized country, but also in a basically civilized world."
Montreal Star.

Gerald Clark

The war correspondents had the important duty of recording its victories and defeats for a pre-TV audience back home who were hungry for news about their loved ones and the progress of the war. Gerald Clark was one of those journalists. Soon after graduating from McGill University, he was sent to cover the Normandy invasion for *The Standard*, a sister newspaper of *The Montreal Star*, and stayed in Europe until a year after hostilities ended. Author of several books and winner of an Emmy for a CBS documentary on Red China, he was also the recipient of the National Newspaper Award for a series on Russia. He has been called a national treasure and few journalists can match the scope of world events and famous people he covered in a career spanning more than sixty years. Here he describes some of the dramatic events which heralded the end of the most destructive war in history.

MY MILITARY CAREER consisted of my attempt to enlist. I had a commission lined up in artillery and quit my job with great drama. I was all of twenty-three and working at the old *Montreal Standard* when I reported for my medical and was turned down because of high blood pressure. That high blood pressure saved my life because I would have been absolutely terrible as a soldier but it allowed me to continue in my civilian job which led to my being appointed a war correspondent for *The Standard*. I was able to go overseas and see everything that a soldier didn't see without getting into risky situations. I had the best of both worlds. I wore a uniform when it was necessary in a military zone but say, in London, if I needed to get a hotel room and knew that a soldier didn't have a chance, I wore civvies, so I took advantage of both.

There was some risk but it was always calculated. For instance, the liberation of Paris was worth any risk because nothing was more dramatic at that stage of the war than to hear the stories of Parisians who had gone through four years of occupation. The biggest risk was having to fight your way through crowds of embracing women who wanted to show their love for your great heroism. The city itself was liberated by the French and there were only a few token Americans and Canadians there but anybody in uniform was a hero. Militarily, it might not have made a prime objective; emotionally, it was matchless. Hundreds of people, a million people, pressed forward from the sidewalk and closed in on the jeep I shared with Maurice "Moe" Desjardins, correspondent for the French-language service of The Canadian Press. *"Merci,*

merci," they shouted, and I looked as quickly as my head could turn, from one face to another. I saw young women in front, laughing joyously and old women in the back, waving weakly, the tears flowing. "We will never forget you, we have waited so long," sobbed an old man, the medals dangling from his chest. This progressed for blocks, and always the buildings grew more magnificent and the crowd more thunderous. Then we heard the sound of rifle and machine gun fire—and the dull *broomph* of tank cannon. There was a tank battle just ahead, in the Jardin du Luxembourg and the Germans held the top of the street we were on. An FFI (French Forces of the Interior) car guided us across the Seine to the Scribe Hotel which had been requisitioned for Canadian war correspondents.

The Scribe was owned by the Canadian National Railways and had been taken over by the Gestapo in 1940. They had moved out hours before we checked in and the last registration card was signed by Joachim Hugo Klapper, Obersturmbannführer (lieutenant colonel) of the Gestapo. The Scribe became the official billet for all Allied reporters and soon the lobby was filled with men and women waiting for rooms. But meantime, they propped their typewriters on any available surface where they could work. The clicking of keyboards was rivalled by the hissing and popping of champagne corks. An Australian colleague weaved his shaky way toward me, and mumbled, "What a piece I wrote, mate, what a piece. Wanna hear it?" Before I could answer, he read it aloud: "Begin story. The story of Paris' liberation cannot be told in words. End story." It was probably the most intelligible account to come out of Paris that momentous day.

Working for a weekly which only came out on Saturday, I didn't have to do "spot news" as most of my colleagues did. I could go to the Canadian, British and American sectors—anywhere where the most interesting story was. We knew there were concentration camps but we weren't too sure what they consisted of. I was with the Americans when they liberated Buchenwald. I had no idea of the dimensions of it or what I'd see but I went there deliberately. It was a story you couldn't avoid. You *had* to do it because it was an aspect of the war that we knew little about. No part of the war could have been as horrifying as the entry into the death camps. I do not think I was alone among the correspondents to come across Buchenwald in utter shock and disbelief. The image of crawling skeletons, covered only with loose skin, registers forever in the mind's eye, along with the sight of similar but dead humans stacked in grotesque heaps. Seeing and smelling the corpses and the survivors who huddled there, I think, was one of the few times during the war I felt physically sick. I don't remember anybody coming up to me and saying *"Danke schön"* or throwing their arms around me. They were so numb and enfeebled that there wasn't too much they could do. Allied medical officers had to warn the American troops not to give them too much food because they couldn't handle it and it would kill them. Some had been overfed and had died as a result. It was an enormous sight and it doesn't leave you. It's there forever. Local Germans from nearby Weimar were brought in and made to go through the camp. I remember the look of absolute shock and disbelief on their faces. They pretended they knew nothing about the place but they *had* to know. They had to smell it and see the smoke rising from the chimneys. These were older people; the young ones had all been killed or were in the army.

As a Jew, many times since that day, I have thought that if my parents had not migrated to Canada (my mother from Galicia and my father from Austria) I would have wound up in the same situation. I must have had *countless* relatives who perished this way. This is the irony of life. Who determines what form your life is going to take?

Now witnessing the signing of peace was the most dramatic event because it was the end of the war which had gone on for six years. I had met a very nice girl named Jacqueline in Paris soon after the liberation, and I used to go down occasionally to meet her. On this particular day, I was playing hooky actually, because I should have been at the front where all the other Canadian correspondents were. Instead of that, here I was in the Scribe Hotel on a Sunday afternoon waiting for my date to arrive. As usual, she was late but while I was sitting there somebody from Supreme Headquarters rushed in, looked around the room and said, "Thank God I found a Canadian. Come!" I didn't know quite what it was all about but I had a great suspicion because the war was winding down.

The next thing I knew, I was on a bus with a dozen other correspondents being rushed out to the airport. We were loaded onto an airplane and then informed by Brig.-Gen. Frank Allen, chief of public relations at Supreme Headquarters, that we were flying to Reims to witness the German surrender. Now that was a pretty nice thing to hear. At five-thirty, the C-47 landed at Reims' airport. We drove to Eisenhower's headquarters in the *École Professionelle*, a modern technical school and, for the next several hours, we had to be isolated because of the nature of the transactions that were going on. While we were waiting for the German envoys to arrive, I remember looking out the window and seeing a flock of other correspondents who had heard of this development. Matthew Halton, who was the chief CBC correspondent, just glared at me because I was there. All I remember doing is shrugging as if to say, "Too bad." Only seventeen of us were privileged to share this first-hand writing of history and my commitment included doing a broadcast for the CBC.

At two in the morning, Monday, May 7, 1945, after waiting more than eight hours, we went upstairs and were ushered into the "War Room" and seated. It was not a large room—about forty feet long and thirty feet wide. Spotlights shone from the ceiling onto the maps that covered the walls. There were now about forty people in the room—army personnel, reporters, photographers and newsreel men. At 2:30 a.m. Allied officers began to enter the room. At a table in front of us were the representatives of Britain, the United States, France and Russia. (The Germans signed another surrender to the Russians the next day.) Then, clear and sharp, I heard the quick military steps outside. A SHAEF officer appeared. The Germans, General Jodl, Admiral von Friedeburg and their translator, then marched in briskly, with their hats off. Jodl looked haggard, his face heavily lined. Von Friedeburg was taller and more distinguished in appearance. They reached their chairs and bowed slightly. The Allied representatives sat down and then the Germans sat down, opposite them. They were read the terms of the surrender—unconditional, which was the key to the whole thing—they signed it at 2:41 a.m. It was over in five minutes. Then Jodl made a speech expressing the hope that the victors would treat the German people with generosity. General Smith, Eisenhower's Chief of Staff, just looked at him coldly and dispassionately. Then Jodl and von Friedeburg were led to Eisenhower's office. It was just a small cubicle—nothing more than a large dressing room with his desk occupying practically the whole thing. Jodl couldn't even get into it and had to stand in the entrance. I remember the cold look on Eisenhower's face when he demanded whether they understood and agreed to carry out the terms of surrender. Jodl said, "Yes."

I don't remember having any feelings of personal animosity or vindictiveness looking at these men. I don't think anybody did at that point. I saw all these people again when I covered the first four or five weeks of the Nuremberg trials. Again, I don't remember feeling terribly triumphant seeing these people as soldiers in uniform. I certainly didn't have any personal hatred for them. I was a reporter and not a fighting soldier. Maybe there's a difference but I doubt it. The overriding feeling I had, after knowing about the atrocities, was thinking, "It's not possible. They look like human beings."

I don't think my daughter's generation realizes that World War II was a Just War. It was not like any other war and it's important to remember that, because it puts it into a special context. Just imagine what would have happened if we had been defeated. I've asked myself this question many times, "Would I, as a Jew, have survived if the Germans had come here?" The war taught me to appreciate the fact that we live, not only in a civilized country, but also in a basically civilized world. Even after seeing the horrors of war, there is still more goodness than badness in the world. If you didn't believe that, what would be the point of functioning? I don't know if it took a war to make me realize that, but it certainly brought it into focus.

Families

Pierre Vennat

Journalist, writer, historian, former army reservist and war orphan, Pierre Vennat comes from a family with deep roots in Quebec's long military tradition. In 1994 the French government awarded him the Médaille du rayonnement culturel in recognition of the many books he has written documenting the contribution of French Canadians in the wars of the twentieth century. He is a member of the Officers' Club of the Fusiliers Mont-Royal, his father's regiment, and his brother, Michel, is its honorary lieutenant colonel. He was a child of two when his father, André, went overseas in February 1941 and his mother was two months pregnant with his brother.

ON MY MOTHER'S SIDE, I am a *"québecois de souche."* The Brisebois family arrived in Quebec in the seventeenth century and one of my mother's great-grand-fathers, Gauthier *dit* Larouche, was killed with *les Patriotes* in St.Eustache. Henri Thibault, my mother's uncle, went overseas as a sergeant in the First World War and came back with a British wife. My paternal grandfather was born in France and came to Canada at the end of the nineteenth century. One of his brothers (who had a lot of money) also came to Canada and that's probably how my grandfather was able to found a company which had, at various times, from fifty to 200 employees, 95 percent of whom were women at a time when French-speaking women were supposed to stay home and make babies.

When war began in 1914, my grandfather decided to volunteer in the French army. He was forty-five years old, had nine children and a business and certainly did not have to go. He was injured by gas, decorated and sent home in 1916. My grandmother ran the business while he was gone and became one of the founders of L'Association des femmes d'affaires de Québec. His son, my Uncle Jean, had belonged to the army cadet corps at Collège Mont St-Louis. He decided to follow his father and enlisted in the French army. He was killed at the battle of Chemin des Dames in 1917 and awarded the Croix de Guerre and the Médaille Militaire. Before the war, my grandfather had bought an estate of one square mile on Lac Labelle. He almost never spoke to me about war or about my uncle, but when he went to mass on Sunday he always wore his uniform with his Légion d'Honneur and his Croix de Guerre. Nobody made jokes about my grandfather. The neighbours were all proud of him and thought he was a general (he was not), and a count (he was not). Naturally, having one square mile made him a kind of *seigneur* and he had a maid and hired a farmer to cut the grass.

My father, who was the youngest in the family, was a professional musician with the Montreal Symphony Orchestra. He couldn't earn a living at that so he also played in nightclubs and on the radio as well as making records for RCA Victor. He was not a military man. He enlisted because his father told him that it was his duty to go and save his three sisters who had emigrated back to France in the thirties with their French husbands. (We learned only after the war that my father was killed to deliver France, thinking that his sisters were for De Gaulle but two of them were for Pétain and his Vichy government!) Then he came home and told my mother what he had done. He arrived in England in February 1941 and spent eighteen months there before going to Dieppe.

Survivors were so few that I don't really know how my father died. What I heard is that he was popular with his men. When the door of the landing craft opened, he shook hands with all the men and wished them good luck. He did not leave the landing craft but was probably wounded and died on the way back between Dieppe and England. I will never know. He was thirty-two years old and is buried in Brockwood Cemetery in Brighton, England. The inscription on his grave reads: *Mort si jeune pour que nous vivions libres*. The graves are arranged in twos and the one next to my father's belongs to a soldier named Beauséjour and I am married to a Beauséjour which I find an odd coincidence.

I have heard that many French-speaking families got bad news during the war in English because Canada was not bilingual then. Brigadier Marcel Noël was the deputy adjutant general in London with McNaughton. His wife, Madeleine, was a friend of my mother and gave her the news that my father had been at Dieppe. We were spending the summer in Repentigny when we got the news of his death. My mother was standing with her father when a car arrived with a letter written in French by a major general, even though my father was just a lieutenant. I think that the fact that my grandfather was still active in military circles and was an important businessman was the reason that we were notified this way. I was three-and-a-half and my brother was eleven months old. I remember my father's funeral. Military bands played and I saluted like John-John Kennedy on the steps of the St-Louis de France Church.

Captain Aimé Lefebvre, one of my cousins on my mother's side, went to Africa as a staff officer of Mountbatten. Another cousin was a major in the

Royal 22nd, another a squadron leader in the air force, another a sergeant in the air force who took part in the bombing of Holland. One of my American cousins served in the Pacific. It's important to understand that, growing up, I never heard about French Canadians who were against conscription. Never.

My mother was not the typical military widow. She was president of the French chapter (Montreal) of the Soldiers' Wives League, a prominent member of the French chapter of the Red Cross and the president of the Women's Auxiliary of the Régiment de Châteauguay which my father had joined in 1939 to do his officer's training before joining Les Fusiliers Mont-Royal. She was a popular young widow and maintained her social links with the military and went to all their balls and social events. I am proud of my father but his war was twelve minutes. What about my mother? She raised my brother and me and sent us to university when there was no free education in Quebec. My mother is as much a hero as my father but she was invited to a commemoration only once in 1952. Other widows, without my mother's political contacts, were never invited. My grandmother, who had two sons who died in two different wars, was never invited. What does the Canadian Legion do for the widows? Almost nothing! And I wonder why, when they invite a mother to Ottawa on Remembrance Day, it is almost always an English-speaking one?

Military historians are now beginning to say that Dieppe was a disaster instead of presenting it as almost a necessity for the D-Day landing of 1944. It had nothing to do with D-Day—absolutely nothing. The lessons for D-Day were taken from North Africa and Italy. It was useful but not for the reasons they say. We would not have won the war if the Russians had lost and, after Dieppe, the Germans were afraid of a Western offensive and began to send troops to Normandy which relieved the Russians in the East. To be frank, it is the only consolation we have. How did the British Secret Service not know about the rocky beaches and the cliffs of Dieppe when in the thirties Dieppe was where they spent their vacations? And they speak about censorship. There was no secret about Dieppe. After the men came back after the first attempt a few weeks before, they were not confined and went to bars and spoke to girls. I'm sure there were spies. My father, although a musician, was a bit of a writer and wrote a letter every day which was passed. They *did* want to fight, though. My father wrote that he had had enough waiting. He had left his wife and family and had been in England since February 1941. They were like boxers in a gym who were tired of fighting a punching bag and wanted a real fight. There might even have been a mutiny if they didn't send them into action.

Mostly, I blame Mountbatten for the Dieppe disaster. He was a "soldat de salon" and a member of the royal family who never fought anywhere. It might be just a symbol but when the men came back from Dieppe, he should have worn battledress instead of a beautiful uniform. Montgomery was always in battledress.

I have friends who are of German descent and I don't want to start the war again, but I've been to Germany three times and found the people as arrogant as ever even if they are less fascist. There is also a minority of neo-nazis which they tolerate. In 1992 when I was in France to celebrate the fiftieth anniversary of Dieppe, there were German veterans there who wanted to shake hands with the Canadian veterans but they almost all refused. A German woman of my age approached me and asked me if my father had been killed at Dieppe. She said that her father had also been killed and we shook hands. I mean, you can't go on hating for fifteen generations so it has to end with the children of the veterans.

I am a man of the media and almost the only one who writes books about French-Canadian veterans. I don't want them to be forgotten but it is sometimes a burden. I have been to Normandy three times, to Dieppe twice (on my first visit, I was shocked to realize that my son, who is a child to me, was almost, even then, older than my father was when he died). I have also been to Holland once, to Vimy three times and to Asia, and am invited to every commemoration there is. I am captivated by war. There is no war film that I can't see and no war film where I don't cry. Sometimes I have to escape and that's why I will go with my wife to Dieppe for the sixtieth anniversary (August 2002) but not on the day itself because I want to cry alone. I sometimes wonder, too, if I had not been at *La Presse,* who would have written about those French-speaking veterans and who will continue after I retire? Do I have more of a duty than others?

Elizabeth O'Reilly Devin

Elizabeth O'Reilly's two brothers, John and James excelled in sports at St. Leo's School in Westmount. Later, at Loyola College, Jimmy lost a split decision to Johnny Greco in the Loyola Golden Gloves and also set a Canadian indoor record in track. Today the two brothers lie in Holland, Lieutenant John O'Reilly in Holten and Flight Sergeant James O'Reilly in Flushing (Vlissingen).

I'm the youngest of seven children. We grew up at 356 Elm Avenue in West-mount. I had three sisters, Peggy, Sheila and Rita. My brother Peter died when he was a little boy and then I had two brothers; both were killed overseas in the war. One brother was James—he went to St. Leo's and then to Loyola. John did the same thing. They used to call them the O'Reilly brothers.

I'm not quite sure when they joined up but they thought they'd do something for their country. John was with the Victoria Rifles in Montreal and then joined the Lincoln and Welland Regiment. Jimmy joined the air force. I remember when John used to come home and I would shine the buttons on his uniform. He used to give me a quarter and I thought it was a big thing. (laughs) When you look back today, I can't believe it. James was very good too. He never had a girl and Mom was hoping he'd be a priest when he came back, but John was going around with a French girl who lived on St. Denis Street.

Mom was very upset when they joined and so was my grandma. Mom didn't like the fact that the people from England were coming here to train and we were going over there to fight. A French neighbour who lived across the street asked my mother why she let both her boys go. She had two boys but they went in to be priests and came out when the war was over. Did you know that some people did that?

My mom got a telegram at Christmastime saying James was missing in action and she never told us so we wouldn't spoil our Christmas. She gathered us all in the living room in the New Year—Grandma was there too—and told us. We just couldn't believe it. My mom always kept his room the same and wouldn't let anyone sleep in his bed. He was shot down near the Dutch coast and we never gave up hope until they found his body and two others in a dinghy. They were buried in Holland.

John was killed by a sniper in Germany on April 23, 1945 and is also buried in Holland. It just tore the inside out of my dad. I remember that so well. He couldn't believe he had lost two boys. On VE-Day, we went downtown to St. Catherine Street and saw everybody celebrating but we didn't stay very long. Some neighbours stayed with Mom. The doctor advised my parents to get out of the family residence so we moved to N.D.G. There were too many sad memories.

Bob Rainsforth

Maurice Rainsforth, Bob's father, came to Canada as an orphaned "home boy" from England at age sixteen and worked on a farm in Campbellford, Ontario for a few years before moving to Montreal. Bob's mother came from Glen Robertson, Ontario.

I WAS BORN on August 17, 1939 and the war started shortly thereafter, as you know. My father didn't go overseas right away because he was with the Royal Canadian Army Service Corps, a transport group. They were in charge of the trucks and tanks going overseas. As a result he didn't get over until June of 1942. I don't remember his leaving. My sister, Doris, was only a year old.

We lived on Jean Talon in Park Extension on what they called "Millionaires' Row". They called it that because everyone was so poor. My father's brother and his family lived three doors down from us. Every summer my sister and I would go up to my grandfather's farm in Glen Robertson, Ontario, and spend time with my uncle's children. There were many uncles on the farm so unfortunately my poor father didn't get missed very much. Life went on.

When my dad came back, I was six and had just started school. I recall everybody getting a day off school so it was a great day whether my father was coming home or not. I don't recall why we had a day off, maybe because all the soldiers were coming home. All the kids, probably about fifteen of them, were around the area and it was almost like a block party. My mother and aunt were getting dressed up. In those days we didn't even have a phone in the house so they were probably yelling across the back fence—"What are you wearing?" and this and that. I remember Mom taking a taxi to the station and we had to stay with Mrs. Towes. All I knew was that my father was coming home and it was okay with me. My sister was absolutely petrified. Who was this guy coming home? She didn't remember who he was.

My sister hid behind me when my father came in. I wasn't afraid of him but I don't remember any big gush of emotion or anything like that. I remember the big, heavy winter uniform he had on and I remember him hugging and kissing me. My sister went to hide behind my mother at that point because she was very much afraid of him and didn't know who he was.

Things got a lot better. Dad got a lump sum of money and we bought a refrigerator. We were the only people on the block who had one and everybody would put stuff in our refrigerator because they had iceboxes. My dad bought a motorcycle and I remember having to edge by it when I walked down the

(Above)
Lt. André Vennat, FMR, RCIC, killed at Dieppe,
August 19, 1942, at thirty-two years of age.

(Below)
Flt. Sgt. James O'Reilly, 429 Sqdn. RCAF (left)
Lt. John O'Reilly, Lincoln and Welland Regiment (right)
"It just tore the inside out of my dad. He couldn't believe
he had lost two boys."

Bob Rainsforth with his father Maurice standing behind
their home on Jean Talon street—"Millionaires' Row"—1941.
"Dad got a lump sum of money and we bought a refrigerator."

hallway. He didn't have it long because my mother insisted he get rid of it because there was no room in the home for it. We got a new car and had holidays. My two brothers came along in 1949 and 1951 so we are actually two families.

He was in France, Belgium, Holland and Germany, but talked very little about the war. Sometimes when he used to have old army buddies come in I'd hear war stories but we found out very little from him directly. He retired from the military when he was fifty and then worked in the civil service at what he loved doing—making films.

Remembrance Day was very important to him. He was a very emotional man and would cry and the whole day would be rather sombre. You'd have to be careful what you said to him that day. He was always like that his whole life. He was the head of the house and was an army sergeant. Need I tell you more? But he used to cry at movies and was very sentimental about the national anthem and I'm the same way. He thought Canada was a marvellous country and where else could he have been given such opportunities? He had a good life. He lived to a ripe old age and had a fair amount of money so he was able to enjoy a lot of comforts.

I certainly admire all those people who went over and fought for us and I just thank the Lord that I was born later and didn't have to get involved. Thank God that there were people who went over and gave their lives, many of them, to make a better life for everybody else. Unfortunately, many people today don't realize it and it needs to be knocked into their heads a little bit more than it is.

Jean Morrison McBride

While Canadian servicemen were off fighting, their wives had to bide their time and hope that a telegram would not arrive that would shatter their dreams of a happy future. Jean McBride was one of those who did receive a telegram. Her husband Bob had been shot down and was a prisoner of war at Stalag Luft III, a German POW camp for Commonwealth and American air force officers in Sagan (now Zagan, Poland), where seventy-six men crawled through a narrow tunnel in a doomed escape bid. Only three made it to freedom and fifty (including six Canadians) were recaptured and murdered by the Gestapo on Hitler's orders. The rest were returned to prison. Flt. Lt. Bob McBride never did make it out of the tunnel. As he lifted himself out of the ground on the night of March 24/25, 1944, he was met by the sight of a pair of German army boots and a glistening bayonet. Paul Brickhill's book about the event was made into the movie, *The Great Escape,* in 1963. The prisoners at Stalag Luft III underwent one final ordeal when they were made to march ahead of the advancing Allies during the final months of the war.

MY FUTURE HUSBAND BOB and I both went to boarding school in Ontario. I went to Hatfield Hall in Cobourg and he was at Trinity College School in Port Hope. Our school was often invited to watch basketball games or gymnastics exhibitions at Trinity and, every year, they were invited to watch our school play. One year we were doing *Romeo and Juliet.* I was no actress so they gave me the part of a page and all I had to do was go on stage, whistle and say, "My master cometh." I couldn't whistle, even though one of the teachers took me in hand and tried to teach me how. I was so nervous on that stage with all the boys in the audience (the play was so bad that the headmaster had to sit in the doorway to keep them in!) that I went, "Whooo, my master cometh," and brought the house down.

The next summer, Bob asked his sister if she would invite me for a swim. They had a beautiful home in Baie d'Urfé called Gay Cedars which became a gathering place for all the young people. The next year, he invited me to a tea dance at the school and, when I arrived, I found that he was in the band and I was forced to sit on the sidelines. I was smitten anyway. As time went by we fell in love and were planning to be married. He was working for his father who was an importer but when the war came along, all ships became troop ships and the import business failed. Bob then joined the air force and we went ahead with our plans to be married.

We were both twenty-two years old when we were married on May 31, 1941. It was a small wedding—neither of us wanted a big one—and the reception was held in my parents' home. We were fortunate to have three months together that summer. He was sent to Prince Edward Island to take a night navigation course and then he was gone. We went down to Halifax by train and I waved to the ships as they sailed out of the harbour. I felt absolutely miserable but fortunately, Bob had a sister and brother-in-law living in Halifax and I stayed with them for a little while before coming back to live with my mother and father in Westmount, not knowing what I'd do with myself.

I took a nursing course and a Red Cross transportation course where I learned to drive a truck. At that time, you could go overseas if you had $1,000 in the bank and these two courses. Bob was with Coastal Command based in England. I wrote and told him I was coming over and he wrote back telling me not to come. My parents never interfered but this time they *did* advise me. They told me that he had enough to worry about and not to go.

On November 27, 1942, I was out with my friends and got off the streetcar on Westmount Boulevard. It was quite a long walk up to my house on Upper Lansdowne and my parents were waiting for me at the door with the bad news that Bob was missing in action and presumed dead. Bob seemed to send me a message and I said, "It's not true." I don't know if anyone would believe this but I just knew he wasn't dead. He had been shot down over France in September while torpedoing a convoy in the Bay of Biscay. He was captured and sent first to Dulag Luft and then moved to Stalag Luft III. I received a postcard which said, "Wait for me a little longer," even before the Red Cross phoned me and told me that he was a prisoner.

Bob was good about writing and the mails were quite good actually. I think they were allowed to send one or two cards and one letter every month. Sometimes I would get a letter and his parents would get a card and we would share our news. I worked packing parcels for the Red Cross. This was arranged by an organization called the Prisoner of War Relatives' Association. We were taken by school bus to the Lowney's Factory where we would stand in front of a conveyer belt filling boxes. (I was actually on that school bus when they blew the whistles that the war was over, which was exciting.) There was a place for everything in the boxes and, as the belt went through, we'd put in our one item. Into the box would go tea, coffee, chocolate (a lot of chocolate) and cigarettes that they used to barter.

Morgan's store would ship "sports" parcels to POWs through the Red Cross and they made an arrangement that if you bought a tennis racket you could also send the shoes, socks, shorts—everything that goes with tennis. Sometimes the prisoners would take the racket apart, burn it to keep warm and use the gut for other things. Once I bought a pair of skates and was able to send the Canadians' hockey set—the sweater, socks and mitts—anything that would keep him warm. What they would do with skates was to wear the boots after removing the blades. The blades were then used to make tools. We were allowed to send as many as we wanted of these sports parcels. I also sent him a bowling set. Somebody said I was absolutely crazy but I envisioned a long hall in the camp and thought they could amuse themselves bowling because I felt they needed exercise and diversion. I got a letter from Bob saying, "The bowling set was marvellous. It burned forever." You see, it was hard wood and kept the fire burning for a long time. They didn't have any bed boards to burn because they were keeping them for supporting the mud in the tunnel they were building.

In his letters, Bob kept saying that he would be home soon and that things were looking up. I thought that he knew something about the war that I didn't, but it was the escape attempt that he was talking about. After that failed Bob was given two months in solitary confinement and I didn't hear from him. Towards the end of the war, they were told to take whatever they had and they were just shuttled out to go on that long march with the clothes that they had on their backs. It was wintertime and they were frozen. It was a tough time and I guess that's where he lost a lot of weight. When he was liberated, Bob was able to commandeer a Mercedes and he and his crew drove to Brussels where the Americans put them on a plane and he was in Trafalgar Square on VE Day. He had been shot down in his battledress and his uniform was still in England waiting for him.

When Bob came back, his parents and I were told to go to an air force hangar in Lachine. The men were put in formation and marched in. They were told not to break ranks until they were dismissed but that was absolutely impossible. We saw them and they saw us and it was bedlam. There was a ribbon in front of us but a little bit of ribbon wasn't going to keep us apart. When he was shot down, I think he weighed about 200 pounds but after that long forced march, he weighed only 145 pounds. Of course, there were two factions that wanted him desperately to themselves; one was his family and the other was me. We drove home. His parents were in the front seat of the car and we were in the back. It was very difficult; nobody knew what to say. I felt like a shy teenager on my first date except that you wouldn't go on a first date with your mother-in-law. That night at his parents' house, I told him I thought that we should get away for a little while by ourselves. It was difficult for him to tell his parents that we were going off on our own. They didn't understand at first and we were completely dependent on them. They lent us a car and we went away to the Seigneury Club for a few days. It's not easy when you haven't seen a person for four years. We were strangers, absolute strangers. He came back on May 30 and the next day was our fourth wedding anniversary. I don't remember how we celebrated it. It wasn't important, I guess.

A man who's been through a war is changed and Bob was very secretive. You don't tell any stories when you're in a prison camp. And for a long time, he wouldn't even go near an airplane. These things eventually melted away but he was the type to keep things inside. After the war, he worked for the White Motor Company. I don't know where they got his name but two of the German guards who had worked at the camp came to Canada and phoned him and he gave them both jobs as mechanics at the company. That's pretty forgiving. He was incapable of feeling resentment. It was wonderful to see because there's no point in carrying a grudge all your life.

We had two girls and then two boys. When Peter, our third child was a baby in my arms, Bob had a stroke and was sent to St. Anne's Hospital. He was in his early thirties and they never did find out what caused it. He was such an interesting case that Dr. William Cone, Dr. Wilder Penfield's partner, came every day to see him until he was out of the woods. His right side was paralysed and he couldn't speak. They thought he would never walk or talk again but he recovered completely. It was some sort of miracle. I guess you'd find his case in the medical journals. They came to the conclusion that it was a virus of some kind. It was rough going because he couldn't work for a long while and for him the days were long.

Bob devoted much of his life to helping young people with sailing in summer and skiing in winter and he made sure that our children took part in sports. He left all the nitty-gritty to me and I was the one who had to make sure that they did their homework. (laughs) He loved the TV program *Hogan's Heroes* but he would never put a foot in Europe. The forced march was all he ever wanted to see of Europe. We went over many times but only to the British Isles. He loved the British Isles, especially Ireland. It's the most gorgeous place. The people are darling and have a wonderful sense of humour. We were married for forty-seven years when he passed away in 1989.

Graeme Decarie

Graeme Decarie is a popular history professor at Concordia University. He is also a broadcaster who is a regular contributor to radio station CJAD's *Free-For-All* and a writer whose columns appear in the newspaper *The Chronicle*. His father served in the navy from 1943 to 1945.

MY FATHER worked for his father for extremely low pay and we were very, very poor. There was my mother, my father, my sister and me and we lived in a two-room, second-storey flat at 8159 St. Gerard Street in the north end. My father had a fight with his father, quit, and went down the same day and joined the navy. It was devastating news for us because, well gosh, you just did not quit a job for one thing and we had no money, though the navy paid more than my grandfather ever had. My father was away for two weeks, home for a short leave, and then he was gone. He didn't have to go. He was in his thirties, well beyond the draft age and married with two children. He became chief petty officer, RCNVR and I still remember the number I had to write on all the mail to him because we wrote back and forth daily. His number was V 76041. He spent most of the war stationed in Nova Scotia and St. John's, Newfoundland. He repaired ships which was just as well because he turned out to be dreadfully and chronically seasick.

What that meant was—and I didn't really fully appreciate it at the time—that for two years of my life I had no father. I was nine going on ten when he left and that had a permanent effect on me. My father would come home for leave once every six months and, although we had somewhat more money coming in, life was very hard. It was an end of town in which you were constantly caught up in fights with neighbours, people doing really unpleasant things to each other and squabbling in the church. My mother was left to cope with all of this alone. Why did they do it? Well, they did it to get away from their families. That's why. In effect they were abandoning their families. That's what my uncle did. He joined in 1939 and went over with the first contingent. I wonder about my father. Is that why he did it? Why the hell would he suddenly leave over this fight with his father which was almost a daily thing? Why would he leave us like that? When the war was over in Europe, why did he volunteer for the Pacific? That came as a bit of a thunderblow to my mother that he was going off again. As it happened, of course, he didn't have to go because the war ended but why did he do it?

It's rather important, I think, to note this—he volunteered for Pacific service. He didn't have to go. In 1945, even if you were *already* in the Pacific, you had to volunteer to stay there. There was one Canadian ship, the *HMCS Uganda*, in which the sailors had a vote and they said, "The hell with this. We're going home." They left the battle of Okinawa and sailed back to British Columbia. (One of the more embarrassing moments that most Canadian war histories don't mention.)

I don't think for a minute that my father was living the wild life or anything like that. He was a very straight-laced man who didn't smoke, drink or gamble. I don't think he wanted to escape the family to be a bachelor again or that he hated us. Not that. I think he wanted adventure. He wanted excitement. He wanted to wear a uniform. He wanted to wear a HAT. The closest he came to any enthusiasm was a yearning for the adventure of the sea which, I think, is why he chose the navy. We had a big picture of the *Bluenose* in the living room when he went away which we had cut out of a book somewhere. The first thing he did when he came home was to take down that picture and I never saw it again. As I said, when he got into the navy he discovered he was chronically seasick and could not stand it. I became an enthusiastic sailor later but my father would never get in a sailboat.

He wrote to me every day and I still remember the letters. He was a very good sketcher and in every letter there would be a sketch. He knew I liked cowboy stories so he always signed his letter, Adios. I can almost see the letters. He also sent back a trunkload of gifts for Christmas. At the time, I suppose, one thought: "What an affectionate father." Since then, I've sometimes thought, and maybe unfairly: "What a guilty father." My mother received $109 per month which would almost get us through. Our rent was $15 a month. We did most of our shopping at the corner store where we kept a running bill. The man had little books for all the people on the block. All purchases were made not by sizes or amounts but by price so my mother would give me money and say, "Graeme, get 25 cents' worth of pork chops." What we had for supper was whatever 25 cents would buy—25 cents-worth of sausage or 10 cents-worth of chocolate biscuits which was three chocolate biscuits. The last week or so we'd run out of money and that's when we'd start running up the bill.

There were no relatives to be of any help. In fact, they were a hindrance. There was a very bad relationship between my father and his parents which was probably why he was so badly paid for so long. They hated my mother and she hated them back cordially. So their major contribution in my father's absence was to spread malicious gossip which made the situation very tense. I recall that my mother was going to sue them. I hadn't been allowed to go to their house for months and when my grandfather came to the house I had no idea who he was. I had forgotten what he looked like. My mother had a twin sister who lived in Rosemount in an upper-storey place which had a balcony so she was far above us socially. Her only contribution was the occasional sneer. Her husband had a car and, very occasionally, perhaps once a year, they'd stop the car on the road downstairs and would honk the horn. That was the signal for us to come down.

When my dad came back from the navy, he scooped me up and I became a son again. He took me on hikes and used to walk my legs off. He took me to Scout camp up at Tamaracouta. I was also in the day camp at the YMCA. Fairly or unfairly, whatever he did after that, the old contact between father and son was never, ever, re-established. Over the years, I've wondered why not, but I suspect that, as a child, I had that sort of instinct of abandonment. The contact with my sister, I guess, was never really there very much anyway. But with me, it was almost as if I felt a reserve and a distrust. I often wonder, too, whether his going away and leaving my mother like that did not have a permanent effect on her. Here she was, unilingually English, left alone with the children in a hostile area which was 99 percent French speaking. She had very little education, having left school in grade seven to become a domestic servant and there was a fierceness, a combativeness about her. I can remember her scrubbing the floor down on her hands and knees and carrying on furious arguments with herself out loud.

I cannot recall ever having a discussion with my father about any part of the war. Now his war was not a fighting war. It was a war of fixing broken ships but he never spoke about it. He couldn't even identify the different kinds of ships. (laughs.) I later went to live in Nova Scotia so I was not far from the base where he had been. He never expressed any interest in seeing it or visiting it or hearing about it. Years later I went to St. John's, Newfoundland where he had been stationed for a year and I took pictures which he had not the slightest desire to see. For the rest of his life, he had no desire in any way to discuss or to remember anything about those war years.

In May of 1945, I was in grade six at Peace Centennial School. It was early in the month but I was suspended for the day because I had been late three times. I went home in fear and trembling, thinking I was going to get a spanking for sure. My mother didn't say a word. When I came in the door she just grabbed me and took me downtown. It was while she was taking me downtown that I realized that the war was over. So we got to St. Catherine Street and, oh, the crowds were enormous. Stores like Eaton's had their windows all boarded up. I remember one guy—I guess he was eighteen or twenty—leading a parade down the street. He was marching along with a big wire rubbish basket over his head which reached down to his waist. We went up to the McGill campus where I saw some soldiers parading for some reason or other and then we went back to St. Catherine Street and there I saw something that I remember most vividly. It was the corner of Drummond and St. Catherine. I saw two soldiers standing by the bank and I could tell by their kilts that they were Black Watch. One of them had just one leg and above them was a sign I had never seen before. You see so many posters during a war, you know—THE CANADIAN ARMY IS A DAGGER AIMED AT THE HEART OF GERMANY, and the V for Victory stuff. This poster said—WE WON THE WAR. NOW WE'VE GOT TO WIN THE PEACE. I looked at it and it's taken me all these years to understand what it meant and to realize that we didn't win the peace and we're not even trying to.

Rita Earle Savoie

Rita Savoie grew up in Griffintown with her twin sister, Alice, and nine other siblings. She is the widow of the famous Montreal boxer, Armand Savoie. Her father was from Newfoundland and her mother from Cape Breton. Wanting to enlist, her father reversed the usual trend and made himself younger in order to be accepted by the RCASC.

MY DAD WAS WORKING for Dow Brewery and he had eleven kids. We were all "steps and stairs"; the oldest was about fourteen. This Irish fellow who worked there had six kids. One day he said to my dad, "Mike, I'm getting laid off as of tonight." You know what my father did? He went to the boss and told him to let this man keep his job, that he would leave and get another job. So now he's got no job. Eleven kids! (laughs) So one day he went to join the navy with a couple of friends but he didn't have the education and he had too many kids. Dad couldn't read or write but he was very knowledgeable. He got a friend to help him with the papers and he joined the army early in 1940. You needed a job but there were no jobs to be had. He was born in 1899 but he told them he was born in 1905 and had six kids instead of eleven. That was the only way he could get in the army. So the army paid Mom for six children, not eleven. They gave my mother $69.40 a month. Okay, the rent was seven dollars but there were eleven kids to feed. He never said a word to us but, about a week later, he came with his uniform all wrapped up. He was so proud of that uniform. We used to shine his buttons and his boots. He had the best boots, let me tell you, one pair under the bed and the other on his feet. And the crease in the pants could cut you like a razor. He was proud, believe me. They sent him to Camp Borden and then he went off to England in September.

Mamie Clarke was our landlady. We used to go to the store for her and she'd always give us a nickel. I'll never forget the day we went to her house and saw a big Black Maria pull up and take Mr. "Schmidt" out of his house. He was German but had come before the war and was a fireman. It was heartbreaking to see that as a child. I was upset because I didn't know why they were taking him out. His wife was screaming and crying. They put him on St. Helen's Island for the duration of the war even though he had a job. They put a lot of people on that island—Mayor Houde and Dr. Decarie. They put them all there. Another time I was with my mother on St. Catherine Street and we saw vans pulling up to every club and tavern and they were taking out zoot-suiters. They wore baggy pants, and they were taking them out by the twenties and thirties. This was a shock. I didn't know what was going on. I was just nine years old and I cried. I was upset to see all these people being taken away.

When Dad was overseas, we'd be ironing and listening to all the war songs and start crying. We'd listen to Churchill and King George and heard about the bombings and thought that Dad would be killed and not come back. My mother would say, "What are you crying about?" I think with 11 kids she was glad to get rid of him for a while. (laughs) Since my Dad couldn't read, we had to write to the Red Cross and they'd read the letters to him. It was scary because soldiers were coming home wounded and crippled for life. You could see them coming in by train. They'd be blind in one eye or shell-shocked. There were quite a few who were put into the Verdun Protestant Hospital instead of the army hospitals.

About once a month, we'd have total blackouts. You couldn't have a curtain open or even a candle burning and it was total black inside. There were no lights on in the street. If you had a light that showed, they'd knock on your door and you'd have a fine. We were eleven kids in four rooms and couldn't go out. All we could do was sit on the beds in darkness. One lady in Griffintown had a store in the front of her house and her kitchen was in the back. She lit a candle because she liked to have a smoke and a little nip. (laughs) They knocked on her door and she got a heavy fine. The blackouts were important because you never knew what could happen and we used to hear the planes coming over Griffintown.

I think it was in 1943. We were all in bed. It was about one o'clock in the morning and the knock came on the door, BANG, BANG, BANG and from the back door too. Anyway, they came in the house. There must have been about 20 military police. My father was missing and they thought he had come home. They were all over, on the roof of the shed, the back gallery and the front door. We had a piece of wood like a door on the wall which you took off to clean the soot from the chimney. They took that off and there was black soot all over the place. We all helped clean that up. My mother said, "I don't know what you're talking about. How would he be here? Do you think he swam from England to Montreal?" Anyway, they didn't find Dad for three weeks. A bomb had hit and he was found unconscious with pneumonia. I don't know exactly where it happened but he was in a hospital. They wouldn't pay my mother while he was missing and the Red Cross helped us until things got established with my father.

He came back in June of 1944. One day, after lunch I was on my way to school at St. Gabriel's. My friend, Mary Hutchison told me that she had seen my father on the train and that he had waved to her. We all had to go through the tunnel and the train went near it over the bridge. I said, "My father's in England." I thought she was nuts. Anyway, when we came home from school, who's sitting in the chair as large as life, wearing his uniform—Father. We all sat there looking at him but we didn't say anything. We knew that life would be stricter now. While Dad was away, we had a little break. My little brother Mikey was born on July 23, 1940 and my dad left in September. He didn't go to my father because he didn't know him. He sat under the table and was looking at his boots and touching them. My father said, "What are you doing and he said, "Nothing Mike." My father said, "He called me Mike and I'm his father!" Until the day my father died, they never did get close. Then my dad gave us all ten cents each to go to the candy store. I guess he wanted to hug and kiss Mom. (laughs)

Joanne Schoeler Fitzpatrick

Born in Toronto, Joanne Fitzpatrick moved with her family to Westmount in 1938 to a street she laughingly describes as being, "on the right side of the railroad tracks but the wrong side of the streetcar tracks." A Montreal artist, she describes her life as the sister of two enlisted men and the wife of a veteran.

BOTH MY PARENTS were born in France and so was my elder brother, Gabriel (we called him Bob). My brother Paul and I were born in Toronto where my father had an import business. During the Depression, my father lost his business and we all went back to France to see if he could get started again. He couldn't so he returned to Toronto where Bob joined him. Again, they couldn't get the business started. In France, as early as 1937, there were many signs that war was coming and Mother, Paul and I were trying to get back to Canada. We eventually did and the family moved to Westmount, which my father knew was a nice district. We lived on St. Catherine Street and funds were very, very limited. Don't forget, it was the end of the Depression and we were not in a comfortable financial situation. I found school quite difficult. We wore a uniform at St. Paul's Academy and, since we couldn't afford to have it ready-made, my mother made mine out of my brother's old suit and that made me feel terrible. (laughs.)

My brother Bob (who incidentally was a terrific artist, rode horses beautifully, and spoke Spanish) wanted to join the Free French Forces when war broke out. Mother knew that we were going to remain in Canada and she feared what would happen to France so Bob joined the Canadian air force. He was killed accidentally in 1942 while training in Moose Jaw, Saskatchewan and we got the news about seven or eight o'clock at night. As soon as you saw the telegram boy—that's what we used to call them, telegram boys—coming up, you knew. Now, I have no recollection of whether I opened the telegram or not. All I can remember is my mother putting her arms around me and sobbing her heart out. Sobbing and sobbing. (she pauses) Now *I'm* going to cry, not so much for my brother but because of my mother. Anyway, life goes on. Bob, who was only twenty-three when he died, was brought back to Montreal and had a military funeral at the Ascension Church. I was there although I can't remember too much about it. St. Paul's Academy was right in front of the church and when, a little later, there was another military funeral, everyone in the class went to the window to watch. I couldn't bring myself to do it and stayed at my desk. It was dreadful at that time; every Sunday at mass, you held your breath hoping that no one else you knew would be named when the priest made his announcements from the pulpit.

My father had been gassed and then taken prisoner while fighting in the French army in World War I. Bob's death affected him and my mother greatly. My mother was never the same. She became very subdued and depressed. Within a year, my brother Paul had joined the army and was fighting in Italy. Again, we received a telegram. This time I opened it and yelled with joy, "HE'S ONLY WOUNDED! HE'S ONLY WOUNDED!" It was almost a moment of rejoicing so no one could cry. He had received shrapnel wounds in his abdomen and was shipped home. He spent some time at St. Anne's and then he was sent to the Queen Mary Vetran's Hospital and eventually recovered. I was, of course, well cared for but as a young girl with two brothers in the service, I felt almost invisible. As a mother now I can understand it. If I had two sons in the war and a daughter who was doing everything right, I would be more concerned about my sons. I studied hard, came third, and won a scholarship to Marianopolis College but always felt a certain void that has stayed with me.

I met my future husband, Ken, shortly after the war at a friend's wedding. He was a very good-looking man and had been discharged from the air force. During the war he had been a navigator in Transport Command (one of my young grandsons told his teacher that his grandfather had been an "alligator" in the war!) (laughs) He was studying engineering at McGill on the veterans' program when we met. In the summer of 1949 while working on construction at the Jewish General Hospital, he had an accident. For the rest of his life, he had to wear leg braces and use a cane. We married a year later in spite of Mother's warning of adding difficulties to the marriage. It was a good marriage and Mother came to love Ken and used to say, "You know, you don't appreciate that man." (laughs)

John Williams

John Williams is a general landscape contractor now living in Ladner, British Columbia. He grew up in Montreal and left Quebec with his family in 1972. His father, David Arvon Williams, enlisted in the Royal Montreal Regiment and left for England with the first Canadian deployment of troops in December of 1939.

MY FATHER JOINED THE RMR in 1939 and was stationed in England until D-Day. We have many letters that he wrote to my mother explaining how good the life was in England at all the places where they were billeted. From his letters, everything seemed to be rosy over there. The people were suffering but they went out of their way to help the Canadians. We were living on Jeanne Mance and I can say that we had a difficult time. My father was the only one on the street who signed up. Occasionally I would ask my mother why my daddy was gone and all the other daddies were here. She explained, in the best possible way, that he was serving his country and that these men couldn't for health or other reasons. The laws then didn't allow a married woman to work so we took in boarders who would help out by contributing about $5 a month which, back then, was a reasonable sum. The amount of help from family was limited. Occasionally we had help from my mother's parents who lived in Newfoundland and from time to time, my grandmother in Montreal would lend what assistance she could. I remember vividly my mother and I going down to the grocery store with the ration books and standing in line for sugar, meat, butter and other things. I can also recall the butcher telling my mother that she could take meat home and pay when her money arrived from the war department.

My mother's family was scattered throughout Canada and the States so she was totally alone here and there was no male influence in my life. I do recall a couple of happy incidences during the war when my father's brother, Uncle Malcolm, and his best friend Uncle Tom, who were both in the Royal Canadian Navy, would show up in port in Montreal. This happened two or three times and they did their best to provide some sort of male bonding. I always looked forward to them coming back but, of course, being wartime, they never knew if they ever would get back so it was always a great pleasure to see these two men come in with gifts and hugs and conversation. They would take me for walks and do whatever they could in the short time they were here.

I remember the telegram that came in September 1944. There was a knock on the door and my mother was scared to answer it. We were peeking through the curtains and my mother finally got me to open the door. There was a telegraph man and, on seeing him, my mother screamed holy blue murder and started to cry. She refused to take the telegram and he kept pleading with her, "Lady, I've *got* to deliver it." She wanted to know what was in it but he told her that the law forbade him from reading it. He asked me if I could read it but, of course, at six years of age, I wasn't into reading nor being able to digest the import of the telegram. He convinced my mother that it wasn't a notice of death so she read it. My father had been shot and wounded in Europe. Several days later we received a second telegram describing his injuries which were not serious.

On reflection, the only reason it was so rosy over in England for my father was because he was thoroughly involved with the local ladies in spite of having left a wife and one-and-a-half children behind in Canada. My sister was born in August of 1940. We found out later he promised to marry his local girlfriend in England. I don't know anything about the details other than rumours and stories from other people but I do know that my mother received mail from a

STANDARD TIME SEP 19 AM 1 14

SA24 67 NL GB 2 EXTRA=OTTAWA ONT 18

MRS DOROTHY I WILLIAMS, REPORT DELIVERY=(

5586 JEANNE MANCE ST MTL= 2065

6420 MINISTER OF NATIONAL DEFENCE SINCERELY REGRETS TO
INFORM YOU D76606 CORPORAL DAVID ARVON WILLIAMS HAS BEEN
OFFICIALLY REPORTED WOUNDED IN ACTION SEVENTH SEPTEMBER
1944 NATURE AND EXTENT OF WOUNDS NOT YET AVAILABLE STOP
WHEN ADDRESSING MAIL ADD WORDS IN HOSPITAL IN BOLD LETTERS
AFTER NAME OF UNIT FOR QUICK DELIVERY STOP WHEN FURTHER
INFORMATION BECOMES AVAILABLE IT WILL BE FORWARDED AS SOON
AS RECEIVED=

DIRECTOR OF RECORDS.

(Above)
Jean and Bob McBride on the train to Halifax before his
departure for England, 1941.

(Below)
Telegram to Mrs. Dorothy Williams from the Minister of National Defence.
"Lady, I've got to deliver it!"

(Above)
Sgt. Gabriel Schoeler, RCAF, a few months before his
accidental death on July 19, 1942, at the age of twenty-three.

(Below)
Gabriel Schoeler's funeral in Moose Jaw, 1942.

certain lady in England who was writing to her beloved husband-to-be and now that the war was over was looking forward to joining him here. My mother was really upset by this and I remember about twenty or thirty years later going through some of her belongings and finding a bill from a private detective agency. They said that there was nothing untoward happening here but that if she wished to pursue it in England, they would do it for a fee. Another thing comes to mind. I remember that my mother sent parcels over to England, supposedly to help some cute little girls whose father had been killed in the war. Now it turns out that these little girls maybe weren't so little after all! Clothing, food and money were sent and all, obviously, to support his second family over there. I can still hear the words to that song, "Whatever Lola Wants, Lola Gets." Lola was her name and Lola, baby, whoever and wherever you are; you sure screwed things up!

My father was due to be shipped home in August of 1945. I had been quarantined with scarlet fever at the Alexandra Hospital in Point St. Charles. He arrived the day before I was due to be discharged. I recall the nurse bringing me to the head of the stairs and saying, "Go on. That's your daddy down there." I said, "I don't have a daddy." She said, "Oh yes, you do. He's back from the war." I said, "What do I do? I don't know if that's my daddy." She said, "Run down and jump up in his arms." I was extremely reluctant to walk down and throw myself on this man. Here was a strange man looking up at me and saying, "Come on down, Son." So the nurse walked down with me and made me climb up into his arms. He said, "Get your jacket and your bags. We're going to Uncle Bob's." So I got on the streetcar with my bags and my new father and tried to talk to him. He told me to be quiet, that we would have time to talk later. We got to my uncle's house; I was thrown into bed and told to shut up. My father and uncle sat in the kitchen playing cards and drinking beer all afternoon. That evening, I was told it was okay to get up. They gave me some soup and then we went down to the station to get the train for Farran's Point which was a few miles west of Cornwall, Ontario. We had a summer place and the rest of the family was already there.

I recall my father staying there for two weeks. Then he had to come back to Montreal to be discharged or something and, from that point on, I saw him maybe two or three times over the next year. My mother was finding out about his escapades in England and jointly, they had agreed that it was time to move on. On one of his visits I got trounced by this man who claimed he was my father because I had lost my coat. There was never any discussion or fighting between my mother and father on these visits. Whatever transpired was always away from us and I guess I have to be grateful for that.

From that time on, I saw little of my father. He never was around for Christmas, birthdays or anything of that nature although he spent a lot of time with my cousins which used to bother me. It also used to bother me tremendously that they would get presents and there was nothing for my sister and me. He would never have anything to do with my sister and, as far as I was concerned, he tolerated me. It was a very troubled period for me. I was confused by his not being there and hurt by the fact that he spent time with the rest of the family and yet chose not to bother with us. As a result, during my pre-teen years, I had problems at school and was involved with family counselling. They tried to encourage some involvement on my father's part. My mother had to go to work and neighbours complained that I was being left alone. I appeared before a family court judge and was told that the best thing to give me some discipline in my life would be to send me to Shawbridge, the boys' farm and training center. It seemed like a great idea to me. The counsellors there ascertained quite quickly that here was a young boy who never had a male figure in his life and was in need of stability. The Reverend Stanley Smith, who was the rector of the school, became a very significant man in my life for the next two years. That was the most stable period for me because I had some sort of direction from the many good people up there.

I heard through relatives of my father's involvement with another lady that he met in Montreal. Yes, folks, this is number three! I felt very sorry for my mother because she was a class person who had nothing but love for everyone on earth. She was a registered nurse who cared deeply about people and through all her eighty-seven years I never heard her once complain about my father or what he did. I really don't know how she handled all those years of wondering what was going on overseas and never being able to have a decent life later. It must have been terrible. He was twenty-nine, beyond the age of conscription, when he signed up and I later thought he did it to escape from family obligations. My mother never said that the family situation was bad before he left. My parents never were divorced and I can recall being sent down to Henry Morgan's where my father worked as a retail clerk, to collect the maintenance money which was minimal. As a youngster I used to open the package and find $20 which might have to last for two or three months. Life was hard. Life was difficult.

I have to be honest. Remembrance Day is a painful day for me. I have taken my situation and feel that war was hell for everyone and I want no part of it and choose not to remember it. I realize that many people did a lot of good for us here but I choose not to remember my father that way. I see him as a lost cause who came from a dysfunctional family. The war took all these young men from Canada and put them in England where they had nothing to do for three or four years but have a good time at their families' expense back home and boy, it was a disaster! Did I ever hold it against my father? Yes, I did. There was a lot of bitterness and contempt for him. At his death, I felt the yoke was removed. I was a free person from then on. My wife Joyce and I have always been there for our three children. Now that they are grown up and married with their own children, we remain a close-knit family—a real difference from the way I grew up.

Victor Yelverton Haines

VICTOR HAINES teaches English at Dawson College and publishes essays on aesthetics. He also writes poetry. He describes himself, according to the bureaucratic term, as a "child of the war dead." His father and namesake, Victor Y. Haines (1918-1943), was a flight lieutenant in the RCAF who was killed when his bomber crashed near Trier, Germany, on November 26, 1943. In one respect "Tor" is luckier than most men who lost a father in the war. While his father attended Rothesay Collegiate, a boys' preparatory school in New Brunswick, he sent letters home on a regular basis. These became his legacy, indicating to his family the character and personality of the person whose life tragically ended at the age of twenty-five. In these letters one is struck by the endearing tone of a schoolboy's concerns. In one letter, he asks, "How's Aunty? Is she still tatting on the sofa?" (Nov. 12, 1934) Ominously, in a letter dated March 15, 1936: "It looks as if the warlords are just waiting for my birthday (his eighteenth) so they can have me go to war for them." At Rothesay, he excelled at sports and later attended Dalhousie University. He had everything to live for: an arresting beauty that made people stop and look at him on the street, talent, background and a young family. When he went overseas in May 1943, he left behind a beautiful wife who was pregnant with their second child. His son "Tor" was not quite two-and-a-half.

MY UNCLE KENNETH gave me a bundle of letters and mementos at the funeral of my grandmother, Emma Turnbull Haines in 1963, when I was twenty-two years old. I have opened it up again every November. So young was my father, the bomber pilot, that I am old enough to be his father. My father is like a son to me. In this bundle of keepsakes and letters, I can share a parent's grief. The child I was could not grieve his death; I could only be affected by it. But opening this bundle over the years has brought the power of grief into its own. His absence has become an exemplary power in this collection—in a lock of blond, baby hair stitched to a Borden's Eagle Brand Condensed Milk booklet, "My Biography"; a silvery baby picture in a long baptismal dress; a sterling Memorial Cross forwarded by the Ministry of National Defence; envelopes with stamps of King George VI; letterheads from Rothesay Collegiate School, *Virtus, Vigor, Veritas* (letters written at first in a boyish handwriting and later in a controlled hand with a good fountain pen); letterheads from the Royal Canadian Air Force, *Per Ardua Ad Astra*, with its eagle image; another eagle image on the Borden booklet and another on the family crest, *Vincit Veritas*. When I look at this bundle, I grieve for the absence left behind by all those who have lost their lives in violent conflict.

My mother, Margaret Dimond, was born in Montreal and lived in various foster homes until she was nine years old. I did not meet *her* mother until I was thirty. The Saunders, a wealthy family from Halifax, adopted her and so she had a life in the upper reaches of Halifax society. She was sent to the Halifax Ladies' College where she did very well, showing up all the other girls who didn't like this newcomer. She fell in love with my father who was the son of a Cambridge MA who taught and was the principal of a big high school but of course, not wealthy. My father got a job doing odd jobs for my grandfather, Bernard Saunders. Mother, who was a beauty herself, said that people would stop in the street to look at him. They were a good-looking couple. Both their parents said that they should wait until after the war to get married. His parents, especially, didn't want them to marry and, who knows, maybe it was because she was adopted. The Saunders had much more money but my father's family had an imperial background. They were from Ireland and my great-grandfather Henry Aylmer studied at Trinity in Dublin; became a doctor and went to India so there was that imperial glory that I smelled a little bit with my grandfather. My parents loved each other so much, and, finally her mother said to his parents, "They're going to get married with or without us so it might as well be with us." They were married the day after Christmas in 1939 and moved to Montreal where my father began training at the Montreal Light Aeroplane Club. My mother had friends in Montreal because, after going to Dalhousie, she trained as a nurse at the Royal Victoria Hospital. When they arrived in

Victor Yelverton Haines and Peggy Saunders on their wedding day,
December 26, 1939. As a flight lieutenant in the RCAF, he was
killed when his bomber crashed in Germany, November 26, 1943.

Montreal, these friends met them at the station and threw confetti.

When my father was killed, the telegram was first sent to his parents who held back the news from my mother for a few days. (Note: In the telegram his parents were told: "Please advise your son's wife at your discretion ... ") She was always irritated by that and felt a little bit dishonoured. My father might have arranged it that way because he didn't want the bad news to go to her first because she was pregnant. Overwhelmed with grief, she always had this question, "Why didn't they tell me first?" She remembers sitting in her parents' home and her father saying, "Poor Peggy. Poor Peggy." She saw my father's wraith just before she got the news. She had a dream that soldiers were coming back on ships and she was waiting with the crowd at the quay. Some of them had a white bandage around their head and they went off, not down the quay, but sideways. My father was one of them and a man standing beside her said, "Oh, those are the ones who are not coming back."

When I was young, I remember that after our bath, our mother would get my brother Peter and me to call out, "Daddy, come home. Daaaddy." We'd sing it out like a prayer or a chant, our mother joining in with us. A mystic coincidence happened one summer at a farm where my mother had taken us for a holiday. There was a lane down to the main road with a telephone pole and transformer. It was raining and we were swinging on the porch. My mother told me that my father had died in the war. (This would have been, I guess, in 1945.) The news made me cry although I was only four years old and completely unaware of the significance of it but I could feel the sadness in her. The tears welled up in her eyes and she started crying. Just then a huge bolt of lightning hit the telephone pole at the end of the lane with a huge crash.

In some family photos, you can see or you import into the picture my mother's disorientation at that time. Of course, I was in a lovely situation compared to children who lose all their family, like the Bosnian children. I was well protected from the horrible things that happen to children in war. I never was short of food or clothing and was protected in my powerful families. My grandfather, Bernard Saunders, was a wonderful gentleman and a big influence on me when I was growing up in Halifax. I always kept in touch with my father's family, and his aunt, who died only last summer (2000) became my fast friend; we travelled to India together when she was eighty-two. I'm kind of an Edwardian (laughs) and have an affinity with that age. My mother would sometimes say that I was the spitting image of my father to pump me up, I guess. I was her first child and had a special place in her heart. When she was close to death, she said to me, "I love you, dear. *I always have.*" Just the perfect words which I'll never forget.

My mother remarried in 1947, I think it was. I was six and my brother was three at the time. My stepfather was Major John Ralph Cameron who had been in the Italian Campaign. He and my mother had known each other in Halifax. He was trained in the law and stayed in the army after the war. When he retired, he became one of the back-room boys for the Trudeau administration. Whenever he came to visit us in Westmount, my wife was always surprised at how many people knew him and would speak to him deferentially. Peter was born after my father died and so John Cameron was the only father he knew and he worked very hard to bring us up. It is a pretty hard thing for a man to have somebody else's children. There was a question of whether we'd change our names from Haines to Cameron. We thought that was a good idea, you know, loyalty to the new man in the house, but we didn't. Maybe my stepfather decided that to honour my father.

They had a good marriage in many ways and had four children. I have four stepbrothers and so am the oldest of six boys. My mother protected me fiercely and my stepfather was very just. Whenever we misbehaved, there would be a trial. He cross-examined us like a French investigating judge and then if he and we (grudgingly) were convinced of our guilt he would spank us. He would hit us about ten times with his officer's stick which would leave bruises and welts. I never felt when I got a spanking from him that it was unjust. There was the natural competition between two males. I feel that my stepfather sometimes thought, "Why should I put up with this behaviour from an adolescent who isn't even my own kid?"

I had never visited Rothesay Collegiate until a couple of years ago. One tends, through laziness and perhaps a little bit of fear, not to investigate the past too much when it is so heavy and terrible for you. It is the school I probably would have gone to. There, on one of the windows in the memorial chapel, is the name, VICTOR YELVERTON HAINES, along with the names of other graduates who died in that war fought by rich and poor alike. The processional cross, which is used for every service, was a gift from his parents. It also has his name on it and is meaningful evidence of his time there.

My father's death is a part of history that isn't forgotten. Being a "child of the war dead" has been a huge influence on me. My relationship with my stepfather was a bit distant although he was formal with his own sons, too. I had divided loyalties and have a profound sense of melancholy about the

Second World War and sometimes feel close to tears about it. It's also a source of wisdom. I am strong enough now, to take this melancholy which, when I was young, would make me sick. Maybe yoga helps me to be strong enough physically to bear that intimation of mortality and cosmic sadness. And Christian theodicy of the Fortunate Fall gives me a balanced mind to rejoice in this grief.

Mary Armstrong Mérette

Intelligent enough to be accepted at the medical school of Leeds University in England in January 1943, and pretty and charming enough to have won the "Leeds Cover Girl" contest (after a friend sent in her picture) which included, among the many prizes, a screen test for the J. Arthur Rank Studios, Mary Armstrong was almost guaranteed a good life had she stayed in England. But then, one evening, she went to a dance with a girlfriend.

My father was a typical Irishman—a complete extrovert and everybody's friend. He was a big man, 6'4", and, oh, he was super. He was well read and could play the piano beautifully. He loved music and fine things and was generous to a fault. He taught me every song I know and told the most wonderful stories. I loved to be with him. He was so happy and always had time for me. My mother was a very practical Yorkshire girl who just seemed to want me to be clean, quiet and obedient. My father managed textile mills and was very good at his job. He used to take these mills that were going down and build them up and then move on. Finally, he bought this mill in Wakefield and one night, while he was working late on the books, the mill took a direct hit during a bombing raid and he was trapped under a beam all night. When the rescue team got him out, he said he was all right and refused to go to the hospital but he died a month later as a result of this attack. I had just turned eighteen and the bottom fell out of my little world. I still think that the most terrible sound in the world is that first spadeful of earth falling onto the coffin of someone you love. I wanted to die too, but knew I had to pull myself together. There was no question of me continuing my medical studies because the mill had to be sold and there was no money for university, so I joined the NFS (National Fire Service).

I was very depressed so the doctor told my mother to make me go out with young people and forget the past. I used to go to the movies and sometimes my girlfriends would ask me to go to dances with them. I wasn't crazy about going but at least I could see people. So I went to the Scala Ballroom on April 6, 1943 with my friend Joan. At one point, she said to me, "Oh Mary, look at the gorgeous Canadian who just came in." So I looked over and he really was gorgeous. (laughs) He had a handsome face and hair so black that it had blue lights in it. Joan was very pretty and could make "goo-goo" eyes (which I thought was stupid) and she said, "He's coming over. He's going to ask me to dance!" But he didn't. He walked around to me and said, "May I have this dance?" We started dancing and he told me his name was Jules Mérette. I said, "Oh, that's French, isn't it?" He wanted to know how I knew and I told him that I had just read *Around the World in Eighty Days* by Jules Verne. I must tell you that when we started dancing and I looked up into those brown eyes—THAT WAS IT! Really, that was it. Love at first sight absolutely and it never changed. We talked and we danced and then we sat on a sofa near the entrance and he got me tea and rock buns. He told me that he lived in Montreal (never heard of it) and showed me photos of all his sisters. Sisters, my eye, these were his girlfriends.

He wanted to take me home by taxi but I had heard about Canadians and taxis and it wasn't going to happen to me! Anyway, there were no taxis or trams and he asked how far it was to my house. I told him that it was five miles and he thought I was saying it to put him off but it really was five miles. (laughs) We got to my house, went through the front gate and sat down on the steps and talked for ages. By this time, I was really in love and when we said goodnight, he gave me one of the nicest kisses I had ever received. Then he left to walk the five miles back to town. On "cloud nine", I floated into the house to find my mother, angry as can be, waiting for me. "Where had I been? What had I been doing until such an indecent hour? What kind of girl was I turning into?" When I told her I had just met the most wonderful man and he was Canadian, I got another lecture.

Jules had just arrived from Canada the week before I met him and was in Leeds on a two-day pass. He was an airframe mechanic with the 431 (Iroquois) Squadron of the RCAF and was studying to be a navigator so they used to let him go up with different "ops." He was based in Burn, Selby when we met. He had promised his father before he left home that he wouldn't marry an English girl. That just wasn't done! He had many girlfriends in Canada who all thought he was coming back to them once the war was over. They would knit him scarves and gloves and send him Laura Secord chocolates which he would give to me. For my part, English girls had to endure rotten remarks from all sides: "How can you go out with a foreigner? Aren't English boys good enough for you?"

The Canadians were nice, not like the Americans—or Yanks as they were called—who were loud and bold and showed off their money. And certainly not like the English who just seemed interested in sitting in pubs and took years to tell a girl they liked her. When my mother met Jules, she really liked him and that lasted through the years. When he would visit with a couple of friends, they would cook and do the dishes, tease my mother, torment the girl next door, take the dog for walks; they were fun to be with. Sometimes, before he would come to see me, Jules would visit all the farmers around Topcliff. They'd invite him in for a meal and give him eggs, butter and sometimes even a chicken. He sometimes brought tea he had sweet-talked from the NAAFI girls. He shared all his parcels from home with my mother and me and, as food and candy were severely rationed, we really appreciated all this.

Jules had his twenty-first birthday in England and we became engaged in May 1944. He didn't have a ring so he gave me his signet ring He told me that he couldn't live in England after the war but would let me come back as much as he could. He wanted a big family and so did I. He said, "It might be hard for a while. I can't promise you a house like your father's but I'll take care of you and you'll always be happy." My mother had to sign the consent form because I was only twenty years old. I was an only child and my Uncle Arthur told me that I should find a nice English boy and settle down near my mother and take care of her. I told them that if they didn't let me marry Jules, I'd go live with him until I was old enough to marry him. My mother really loved Jules and was happy about it, and when Uncle Arthur got to know him he changed his mind.

There was a lot of paperwork to do. Jules did his part on the base and his parents sent a letter from the parish priest saying he came from an excellent family and was of sterling character. I had to fill in endless forms and my mother signed the consent form. Religion was not a problem. My mother was Christian Scientist but my father was Catholic and I had been baptized Catholic. Jules and I arranged to meet Monsignor Dinn (who was the Bishop of Leeds and had been a friend of my father) at St. Ann's Cathedral and we arranged for the banns to be published. We set a date—September 20, 1945. The weeks passed and we were finally winning the war, so we advanced the date to the 11 of June. Jules got me a lovely diamond solitaire and my future father-in-law sent a wedding ring from Birks in Montreal along with my wedding present from Jules, a lovely silver powder compact. I bought him a silver cigarette case which I had engraved with our wedding date. I scrounged and bought enough black market clothing coupons to get material for my wedding dress. We invited friends and relatives for June 11 and Jules managed to get enough flour, fruit, eggs and sugar for a small wedding cake to be made at the local bakery.

Then Germany surrendered and Jules phoned me at the weekend and told me that there was a rumour that they were returning to Canada the first week in June and all leaves had been cancelled. I asked him if he could get to Leeds with his best man, Bill Gallant. When he said he would do it somehow, I asked him if he would like to marry me on Monday, so he was always able to tell the children that I'd proposed to him! My dress was not ready so a friend lent me hers. I went down to the cathedral and arranged for the ceremony at 10 o'clock on May 29. Monsignor Dinn arranged for a dispensation so that Uncle Arthur, a non-Catholic, could give me away.

It was the most beautiful wedding ever, but maybe I'm prejudiced. My girlfriend Kitty Costigan was my only bridesmaid. I could hear Aunt Dolly crying, but Mother and Aunt Madge were smiling happily. Poor Uncle Arthur, I could feel him shaking as he walked me down the aisle and, not being familiar with a Catholic ceremony, he said a very loud "Ahhmen" after each prayer. The high voices of the boys' choir filled the cathedral and then we said our vows and I was really Mrs. Jules Mérette. There were not many people who came to the house later but there was a lot of laughter and we had a happy little celebration with sandwiches and wine.

We had arranged to spend a few days on the Isle of Man but as things turned out we spent our wedding night in Northumberland and next morning, Jules was recalled to Middleton St. George. It was so hard to say good-bye— we both knew that he was to be sent to the Japanese theatre of war and who knew if we would ever see each other again. The wedding cake was ready for June 11 and all the guests had been invited so the big reception was held then and everybody came. I cried like a baby the whole time because my husband was on the high seas going home. He left on May 31 and it was eleven long months before I saw him again.

The next months passed so slowly. I went to work every day and joined the Canadian War Brides' Club. We met weekly and were given lectures and shown slides of all parts of Canada. First priority was given to girls with children and pregnant girls. The rest of us were last. Suddenly, towards the middle of February, I received a huge bundle of forms to fill out which took two nights. Finally, I was told to be at Leeds Central Station at eight a.m. on March 19. I was up very early and the taxi came at seven o'clock. My dog, Buddy, disappeared so I couldn't say good-bye to him. I kissed my mother but she wouldn't come to the station with me. We went by train to Liverpool and had to stay overnight in different billets. Then it was onto buses for the drive to the Liverpool docks. The ship was the *Letitia* and looked very small. On board we were 500 war brides and 300 children plus the crew and next morning, we heard marching feet and over a hundred Canadian Fusiliers marched on board. There were all these little babies crawling around with dirty diapers and toddlers with snotty noses and I wanted to throw up—being very precious in those days!

It was early morning as we sailed out of Liverpool into the mist and the Irish Sea. As we left the dock most of the girls were crying. The band played, "There'll Always be an England", "Wish Me Luck as You Wave Me Goodbye" and other songs but when they started the Highland lament, "Will Ye No Come Back Again", it was too much and I cried, too. When it was time to eat, we were shown into this huge dining room—mahogany, white linen, gorgeous smells and were served the most fantastic meal of soup, salad, roast beef, tiny carrots, baked potatoes and sponge cake with strawberries and cream. The service was impeccable and the waiters were all dressed in white. Imagine how we felt! We had been rationed for the past six years and had forgotten what roast beef tasted like. The food was always super on the *Letitia* but I was very seasick until I finally found my sea legs.

We travelled from Halifax to Montreal by train. It was April and all we saw were fields with snow and log cabin type of houses. We stopped in Quebec City in the early evening and we wanted to buy magazines and chocolate but there was no way the woman would serve English war brides. She pretended she didn't understand us and we felt awful. They brought us into Bonaventure Station through St. Henry and we saw all these tenements with lines of washing hanging out. They kept us on the siding for an hour. Some of the girls were crying and it was very dark with wet slush everywhere. Then they told us to go up the platform into a room with very bright lights. I gave my name and they yelled it over the loudspeaker. All of a sudden, this tall, thin man was jumping up and waving and I thought, "Oh, my God. That's not Jules." He grabbed me and was kissing and hugging me. The last time I had seen my Jules had been in England. I was used to seeing him in uniform or in casual pants and sweaters, laughing and joking. Now he was so thin, he had lost thirty pounds and was wearing a long overcoat and a felt hat, a fedora like the ones I had seen in Halifax, but he still had the same voice and eyes. He gave me a lovely bouquet of flowers and introduced me to his mother and father who were with him. My mother-in-law was a very tiny person. Oh, she was so sweet! Her name was Isabelle. My father-in-law was tall and had piercing blue eyes and he used to scare the bejeebers out of you until you got to know him. He was a nice man and, although he didn't want Jules to marry an English girl, he took to me and, when he died, he had my picture in his billfold and not his daughters' or his wife's and I got a bit of flak for that.

Then we were driven home in a Red Cross car to Drolet Street. Jules and I sat and held hands and I kept peeping at this stranger my Jules had become. We were both very nervous. We had not seen each other for eleven months and did not know if his family would like me or if I would like Canada. I sat on the couch in the living room and met Jules's four sisters and six brothers and just kept saying hello to everyone. I liked them very much. Me, who had never had a sister or a brother, had a family at last! His parents spoke English but the others—not a word. My mother-in-law had been cooking for days but I was too nervous to eat. After supper, Jules's aunts and uncles arrived, along with *Grandmère*. Listening to his Uncle Yvon, I thought I could never learn French but Jules said, "It'll come. You'll see." The next day I bought a French-English dictionary and used it when I went shopping with his sisters.

Not everybody welcomed me, though. In my first job working as a private secretary at Roland, Lyman and Burnett in Old Montreal, there was a girl called Gilberte and she hated me. If she could do *anything* to me, she would. She used to get cockroaches and put them in my files so that when I opened them up, there was a cockroach. She said, "You English girls have no right coming over here and taking our boys." Later on, there was a couple with three girls who lived across the street and, one day while I was out washing windows, one of the little girls came over and said in French, "Is it true you eat babies?" I said, "No, who told you that?" She said, "My mommy says all English girls eat babies." Mostly, though, I had wonderful neighbours and my husband's family were super to me.

We bought our first house in Canton Bélanger, now part of Laval. It had two rooms originally, but gradually we added extra rooms and a second floor. Jules was very clever with his hands and I sewed and we made ourselves a comfy home. Canton Bélanger was a French village and I knew that nobody was going to learn English so I must learn French to talk to them. I made many embarrassing mistakes, but one day I said to myself, "I'm going to speak French and if they don't understand, that's just too bad." After that, it was fine.

In the beginning, Jules worked as a customs officer and then he became an investigator. He used to work at Blue Bonnets at night and, in 1972, he went to work there full time as the director of night operations. He was very happy there until he retired in 1985. We had eight children: Lorraine, Richard, Julie, Lucie, Carole, Robert, Claire and Michael. I spoke English to them and Jules spoke French. They're perfectly bilingual today. We put Lorraine and Richard in French school but the children were so mean to them that we pulled them out and they all went to English schools. I went back to England four times, but it wasn't the same and every time I was glad to come back home—to Canada. My mother visited us in 1961 when Claire was two and again for Lorraine's wedding. We lost two children. Richard died in 1973 and Lorraine died in 1995.

It was a wonderful life. After Jules retired we spent the next eight years going down to Florida for the winter. He was a great golfer and we had very happy times there. Lorraine died in February and Jules died in March of the same year. Our fiftieth wedding anniversary would have been in May. What my children did was a beautiful gesture. They arranged for me to go back to Leeds and be in St. Ann's Cathedral on the morning of the 29 of May at ten o'clock. When I got there the doors were locked but the priest let me in and I sat in the cathedral and cried. It was too soon after losing them both, but it was a beautiful thought.

Mary Armstrong and LAC Jules Mérette, St. Ann's Cathedral, Leeds, England, May 29, 1945.